School Desegregation Research

New Directions in Situational Analysis

CRITICAL ISSUES IN SOCIAL JUSTICE

Series Editor: **MELVIN J. LERNER**
University of Waterloo
Waterloo, Ontario, Canada

A Continuation Order Plan is available for this series. A continuation order will bring delivery of each new volume immediately upon publication. Volumes are billed only upon actual shipment. For further information please contact the publisher.

School Desegregation Research

New Directions in Situational Analysis

Edited by

Jeffrey Prager

University of California at Los Angeles
Los Angeles, California

Douglas Longshore

U.S. General Accounting Office
Washington, D.C.

and

Melvin Seeman

University of California at Los Angeles
Los Angeles, California

PLENUM PRESS • NEW YORK AND LONDON

370.19342
S372

Library of Congress Cataloging in Publication Data

Main entry under title:

School desegregation research.

(Critical issues in social justice)
Bibliography: p.
Includes index.
1. School integration—Research—United States—Congresses. 2. Community and school—Research—United States—Congresses. I. Prager, Jeffrey, 1948–   . II. Longshore, Douglas. III. Seeman, Melvin. IV. Series.
LC214.2.S357   1986   370.19′342   85-28286
ISBN 0-306-42151-8

Material in this book copyrighted by System Development Corporation under the title *Advancing the Art of Inquiry in School Desegregation Research* (1983) is reprinted by permission.

© 1986 Plenum Press, New York
A Division of Plenum Publishing Corporation
233 Spring Street, New York, N.Y. 10013

Printed in the United States of America

To the memory of
Herbert H. Hyman

Foreword

The *desegregation situation* is the keynote theme of the following chapters.[1] Each of them touches on a different dimension of the situation: the historical, the temporal, the spatial. But the reader, perusing the essays with the situation in mind, should remember that *the* desegregation situation should not be interpreted literally. Authorities and adults certainly, school-age children probably, are influenced by their awareness of a sequence of past and future situations. Some may even operate with William James's (1890, p. 608) notion of "the specious present" that "has melted in our grasp, fled ere we could touch it, gone in the instant of becoming," thus reducing the potency of the present situation. Others may be dancing to a slower tempo of change, thus becoming more responsive to the present situation. Whatever the perceived tempo, many must share the view that the future may reverse the direction of the past. Some may see that new future direction as unswerving, unending, or long-lasting; others may see it as short-lived. And it is through attention to the phenomenological description of desegregation that these issues can be explored; a theme that is considered in several of the following chapters.

It is not only the differing perspectives of participants that militate against a literal rendering of the desegregation situation. Demographic and ecological statistics about the migration of racial groups in the country shed new light on the problem. Millions of children move from one school to another, perhaps through many different kinds of schools, and gain cumulative experience with various kinds of segregated and desegregated situations. Within a single year, 1968–69, for example, a million-and-a-half children (aged 5–17) moved to a different state; another million-and-a-half children moved to a different county within the same state (U.S. Bureau of the Census, 1970). Sum such figures over the 12-year school career, make some gross adjustments for duplication and the bedeviled children chronically on the move, and you still end up with many

---

[1]This is a brief extract from a larger review and synthesis of the papers presented at the symposium, many of which appear in this volume.

millions of children whose school situations were not static. Indeed, using refined techniques, census statisticians estimated that the average American moves *three times* in the course of childhood (Long and Noertlein, 1976).

Such evidence of geographical mobility during childhood is surely suggestive but does not establish exactly how much change in segregation children experience in the course of their mobile school careers. However, the National Longitudinal Survey of samples of black and white members of the high school class of 1972 asked the seniors to report the racial composition of their 12th-grade class, and (retrospectively) their 1st-, 6th-, and 9th-grade classes. Trent has provided me with special tabulations on the sequences of classroom situations that black cohort experienced at the four stages of the school career.[2] If one were guided only by their current (1972) situation (the product of institutional trends and geographical mobility), one would overrate their long-run experience with desegregation and underrate the variety of sequences among the cohort and the oddity of the patterns some had experienced.

We present only some of the patterns of experience, but enough to establish our major points. For these purposes, we have defined a desegregated-classroom situation for a black student as being a class that is 50% or more white. Using a different cutting point, of course, would change the magnitudes of those who had experienced desegregation at a particular stage but would not change the basic finding of complex sequences. Although 39% of the national sample of that black cohort were at that point in a desegregated 12th-grade class, only 6% of the sample had experienced desegregation at all four stages of their school career. For 17% of the sample, the 12th-grade current experience was but a brief and late encounter with desegregation in the classroom, their 1st-, 6th-, and 9th-grade schooling having taken place in a segregated class. Although 11% had substantial experience with desegregation while in high school, having been in a desegregated class in both the 9th and 12th grades, their earlier experiences had been in a segregated class in both the 1st and 6th grades. Only 3% had been in a desegregated class throughout the three grades—6th, 9th, and 12th—after starting out in a 1st-grade segregated class. A tiny number—about 1%—had oscillating, perhaps jarring, patterns of experience: for example, 1st grade desegregated, then segregated in the 6th and 9th grades, then returned to desegregation in the 12th grade; or 1st grade segregated, then desegregated in the 6th, then returned to segregation in the 9th, and finally to desegregation in the 12th grade. Although 61% were currently in a segregated 12th-grade class, that should not be taken to suggest that they had no previous experience with desegregated schooling. The group who had experienced segregation at all four stages of their career was 51% of the sample.

---

[2]These unpublished data, gratefully acknowledged, were generously provided by Dr. William T. Trent of the Center for the Social Organization of Schools, Johns Hopkins University.

For those students, black or white, who go on to college where once again they may experience segregation or desegregation, the extended sequences of situations may become even more variegated. Braddock (1980), by an ingenious design and analysis, has documented for blacks a "perpetuation of segregation across levels of education," according to which those blacks attending segregated colleges are more likely to have come from segregated high schools. However, the magnitude of the association implies that many experienced inconsistent situations at these two stages of their schooling. And Trent (1982) has shown that the effect of the current, collegiate situation on the political efficacy and political participation of young adult blacks is contingent on the desegregation experienced at an earlier stage in the sequence.

Such studies of young adults enter our research agenda only when we construe the term *school* broadly enough to include college. To be sure, it complicates inquiry into the situation. The more advanced the desegregation situation we study, the more historical depth and complexity to the sequence of situations that produced the effects. But by including the college level, we—automatically—come close to studying long-term effects among adults.

To create unity out of the multiplicity of ideas presented in these elaborate, richly detailed chapters is not possible—even when aided by the key concept, the situation. Readers are bound to sense new opportunities for many fruitful varieties of research and to learn ways to improve their current research, but some may become bewildered. For those swamped by the cascade of ideas, defeated by the thought that they must explore all of the wide domain that has been mapped, all at once in their inquiry, let them take comfort in a simple but sound principle. Investigators like explorers can find untapped wealth in a small part of a large realm. Still greater wealth from further explorations of the realm may require a long-term commitment. Given the good that may come from successful school desegregation, that long-term commitment is called for.

HERBERT H. HYMAN

REFERENCES

Braddock, J. H. The perpetuation of segregation across levels of education: A behavioral assessment of the contact hypothesis, *Sociology of Education*, 1980, *53*, 178–86.

James, W. *The Principles of Psychology* (Vol. 2). New York: Henry Holt, 1890.

Long, L. H., and Noertlein, C. G. Geographical Mobility as a Social Indicator. *Proceedings of the Social Statistics Section, Part II*. Washington, DC: American Statistical Association, 1976.

Trent, W. T. *The impact of college race on the sense of political efficacy and political participation of young adult blacks.* Paper presented at the Annual Meeting of the Association for the Study of Higher Education, 1982, Washington, D.C.

U.S. Bureau of the Census, *Statistical Abstract of the United States*. Washington, DC: U.S. Department of Commerce, 1970.

Preface

This volume is the product of a 2-year project, funded by the National Institute of Education and administered by the Studies and Evaluation Department at System Development Corporation. The project was entitled "Advancing the Art of Inquiry in School Desegregation Research." Its aims were to reinvigorate discussion among social scientists about school desegregation and to introduce new themes into the scholarly debate. Prominent social scientists who had not previously applied their expertise to school desegregation research were enlisted to discuss relevant theoretical and methodological issues—both on paper and in person—with scholars already knowledgeable and known in the field. The infusion of new ideas would, we hoped, give new life to a field riddled by intense controversy and polarization. Eleven original articles were commissioned, and authors were charged with applying their expertise to identify new directions in research. Each article was reviewed by two individuals who had already made important contributions to school desegregation research.

Two conferences were convened in Santa Monica, California, attended by the authors, many of the reviewers, and other interested scholars. Discussions during these conferences helped the authors crystallize their own views on the topic and enabled us, as organizers of the conference, to try to forge a shared orientation to the problem. Three of the articles were to be synthesis papers, drawing together common themes and issues from the other eight. Syntheses were completed after the two conferences were held, so that they might reflect the discussion as well as topics raised in the written papers.

"Advancing the Art of Inquiry" was a project lofty in ambition; it is not often that social scientific research steps back and evaluates its direction, attempting to discover, perhaps, new paths to its objectives. But we were extremely pleased by the willingness of some of our most important social scientists to address this question, one that is significant not only for social science but also for social policy. And we feel that the project, and this volume that is its result, indeed defines new, promising possibilities for further research. The project was a collective effort; its success was a result of the seriousness of purpose and personal commitment shared by all participants. Even though we are unable to include in this volume all the materials produced, the following essays reflect the combined efforts of all concerned in the original project. As editors of this volume and as organizers of the research project, we would like to thank those people who contributed to the research project and who had a hand in this book: Jomills Braddock, Kenneth Clark, Thomas D. Cook, Robert L. Crain, Halford Fairchild, Roderick Harrison, Stanley Lieberson, David Lopez, Norman Miller, George Noblit, Melvin Oliver, Thomas Pettigrew, Harold Rose, Julian Samora, and Janet Schofield. We would also like to thank Jeffrey Schneider, Project Officer for the National Institute of Education.

Thanks, in addition, to Karen Linden in Los Angeles and Lucille Allsen of the Institute for Advanced Study, Princeton, who expertly typed the manuscript. Eliot Werner, editor at Plenum, has been very supportive of this project and extremely helpful during its final preparation.

If this book serves, in some small way, to energize school desegregation research and to refocus attention on this critical issue, we believe that all those who so generously committed their expertise, their time, and their efforts will be amply rewarded.

This book is dedicated to the memory of Herbert H. Hyman. Herb participated in the project from its outset. All of us who came to know him were touched by Herb's commitment to scholarship, always guided by principles of compassion and social justice. It is fitting that this volume, intended to enhance the prospects for racial integration, should honor the memory of this humanitarian and scholar.

JEFFREY PRAGER
DOUGLAS LONGSHORE
MELVIN SEEMAN

Contents

PART III: NEW THEORETICAL DIRECTIONS

PART IV: A RECONSIDERATION OF METHODS

Part **I**

INTRODUCTION

The Desegregation Situation

JEFFREY PRAGER, DOUGLAS LONGSHORE, AND MELVIN SEEMAN

The publication of this volume may come as a surprise to those who have followed the career of school desegregation research. Beginning in 1954 with the landmark *Brown* decision, scholarly interest in the topic steadily escalated through the 1960s and 1970s. As one community after another formulated and implemented programs to desegregate their schools and as controversy swirled around those programs, the research pace quickened. In response to various "stakeholders," all of whom wanted to know more about the phenomenon—government policymakers, judges, lawyers, school administrators, teachers, and parents—social scientists attempted to assess, in particular, the outcomes of school desegregation. But as the interest in, and commitment to, school desegregation has waned in the late 1970s and 1980s—by the public at large and by federal, state, and local governments—the impulse to understand the phenomenon through scholarly investigation has similarly diminished. Thus, a new consideration of school desegregation research now seems, from this vantage point, strangly anachronistic to the spirit of the age.

Yet there are sound reasons why we can benefit today from a rethinking of what we know, with an eye toward defining what we still need to find out about school desegregation. First, although desegregation may no longer be a social desideratum uppermost in the minds of policymakers, educators, or the general public, there is no question that the problems of racially integrated schools

JEFFREY PRAGER • Department of Sociology, University of California, Los Angeles, California 90024.   DOUGLAS LONGSHORE • U.S. General Accounting Office, 441 G Street, NW, Room 5844, Washington, DC 20548.   MELVIN SEEMAN • Department of Sociology, University of California, Los Angeles, California 90024.

in America continue to be pressing (Hochschild, 1984; Wolters, 1984). Whether legally mandated or not, the fact is that American schools will be more racially heterogeneous than ever before. We are currently witnessing a migration to America, from Central America and the Far East, unprecedented since the turn of the century and, in addition, dramatic movements toward the suburbanization of racial minorities—both of these migrations producing a clear movement away from the racially homogeneous school. Or, more to the point, we are seeing the end of the all-white public school. School desegregation, in short, will be a feature of our lives whether or not the public or the courts express a concern for the problem. This volume recognizes the endurance of this issue in American society.

It is our view that desegregation research could well benefit from reconsideration precisely because the topic is increasingly removed from the public spotlight. Once the press of events no longer propels research willy-nilly in different directions (often with different conclusions), serving different purposes, and speaking to different masters, it now becomes possible to take stock more calmly of what we know and what we still need to find out. Such stocktaking is seldom possible when academic research is closely monitored by involved and competing publics. And as we have suggested, this quiescent period may be the lull before the next storm; if so, it is a lull that is useful in order to consolidate findings and crystallize understandings. It is our hope that this volume will promote this end.

There is a further reason for this volume at this time, perhaps the most important one. As we see it, the intense commitment in the past to studying desegregation has not produced a commensurate understanding of the problem. In fact, there is little consensus about what we have learned, 30 years after extensive research on the topic began. We are not the first to note this. Recent literature reviews (e.g., Crain and Mahard, 1978; Epps, 1981; Longshore and Prager, 1985; McConahay, 1981; Miller, 1983; Schofield, 1978; Stephan, 1978) have come to similar conclusions. The intense preoccupation with assessing the effects of desegregation has produced only mixed findings. Why have such dedicated efforts produced relatively few payoffs?

1. INADEQUACIES OF DESEGREGATION RESEARCH

In our view, desegregation research has suffered because it has come to stand as a kind of scholarship guided largely by public concerns and public issues, not by theoretically generated empirical questions. Much of the research has been carefully crafted, but the questions typically asked about desegregation have very often been in the service of problems posed by various interested parties. It is no wonder, then, that as those parties became less interested, desegregation studies lost their impetus and rationale.

Two examples can be offered of the inadequacies of scholarly research when it responds so closely to questions formulated by the public. First, as previously noted, the preponderant concern of scholars has been to assess the impact of desegregation. But without sound independent guidelines, there has emerged little scientific consensus concerning the basic meaning of "*effects*" (academic achievement, interracial cooperation, equal-status contact, "white flight") or whether effects should be assessed in the short term or long term. Different social groups have emphasized different effects as important, and the discrepancy within the research on outcomes reveals the extent to which researchers have been defining their questions in terms of the interested parties, not in terms of scientifically derived criteria for evaluation. Scientific inquiry, in short, has sacrificed its autonomy and lacks a distinctive agenda of its own.

There is a second consequence of research that becomes entangled in public concerns. School desegregation research has lost credibility. Where scientific studies have typically played a pivotal role in American society to forge consensus by transcending ideological divisions, here they entered into the political fray and lost their ability to arbitrate. Thus, we have witnessed in the course of the past several years scientific controversy transposed to public debate (e.g., Armor, 1978; Coleman *et al.*, 1975; Pettigrew and Green, 1976). When science is governed by policy questions, it becomes instrumental, serving those groups capable of employing findings on their own behalf. Research findings, rather than offering clarity and credibility, become instead part of the heat of controversy. For this reason, we believe that school desegregation requires reconsideration—not in the interest of either pro-integrationists or anti-integrationists, probusing or antibusing advocates, nor even for the edification of judges, politicians, school administrators, or parents. Rather, it is our intention to claim the study of school desegregation for social science, as a researchable domain of inquiry driven by independent social scientific concerns.

One remarkable feature of past studies on desegregation is that no consistent definition of desegregation has emerged. Studies have defined desegregation in highly divergent and sometimes contradictory ways. For that reason, many commentators have suggested that desegregation research should move away from its preoccupation with effects and concentrate instead on the desegregation process itself. There is a pressing need, they argue, to begin with the problem of conceptualizing desegregation (e.g., Cohen, 1975; Epps, 1981; Hawley and Rist, 1975; Longshore and Prager, 1985; St. John, 1975; Schofield, 1978; Stephan, 1978). That, too, has been the inspiration behind this volume.

We have chosen to organize these chapters around one central, overarching theme: the *desegregation situation*. In our view, if we could theoretically comprehend the parameters of the situation and the elements that comprise it, and if we could specify the methods capable of measuring and assessing the situation, we would be moving forward to understanding what school desegregation is all about. We would be closer to understanding what we mean when we say *desegregation* and why it has proven to be successful in one setting and not in another.

There are both practical and, more fundamentally, conceptual reasons for insisting that we do not currently understand the desegregation situation. In practical terms, the racial proportions that distinguish *segregated* from *desegregated* schools have varied widely across locales and over time. Immediately after *Brown*, Southern schools were considered desegregated even if only a handful of blacks were enrolled. More recently, some desegregation plans have set more stringent requirements. In 1977, for example, a Los Angeles school with roughly equal proportions of white, black, Hispanic, and Asian students was considered segregated under the school board's plan because the proportion of whites in the school was not between 30% and 70%. Sociologists have defined desegregation in such divergent ways that schools considered desegregated in some studies would have been considered segregated in others (Schofield, 1978). For example, in one study, a New York school that was 90% black was considered segregated (Singer, 1966), whereas in another study, a Boston school that was over 95% white was considered "token desegregated" (Useem, 1976). In short, our difficulty with understanding the desegregation situation is partly definitional: What range of racial proportions is adequate for defining desegregation?

More fundamentally, however, the difficulty is conceptual. For the most part, social scientists have looked for the effects of desegregation (however defined) without linking those effects to underlying processes and without bringing relevant theoretical work to bear on the findings. Consequently, even when desegregation has had some measurable effect, we have no clear sense of why or exactly how that effect occurred (see Cohen, 1975; Longshore, 1982; St. John, 1975; Schofield, 1978; Stephan, 1978). Research based on contact theory (Allport, 1954) has linked effects with situational conditions in desegregated schools (e.g., Cohen and Rober, 1985; McConanhay, 1981; Miller, 1984; Schofield, 1982). But the conceptualization of those conditions has been imprecise, and the research lacks a comprehensive theoretical range, focusing more on micro settings (schools and classrooms) than on wider structural and cultural conditions. For example, equal status is variously defined in terms of student or staff numerical ratios (equal or proportional), socioeconomic status, staff treatment, and small-group participation rates, though the theoretical significance of these variables may be quite different. These practical and conceptual difficulties in comprehending the desegregation situation signal the more general failure among social scientists to come to terms with the concept of the *situation* itself.

2. THE "SITUATION" IN SOCIAL SCIENCE

The *situation* as a social scientific concept has a long history in the fields of sociology, social psychology, and psychology, but only recently has it been the object of renewed interest in those fields. And yet no single conceptual mechanism seems better suited to provide clarity and insight to disparate approaches in the study of school desegregation. To speak of the situation is to acknowledge, first, as Lewin (1935) established in his field-theoretical approach, that behavior is a product of a particular field of action that possesses its own unique qualities. Lewin's field theory was heavily influenced by Gestalt psychologists, for example, Wertheimer, Koffka, and Kohler, who were principally concerned with the psychology of perception. The central principle of Gestalt psychology is that qualities exist in the whole that are absent in the constitutive parts; thus, the context through which behavior is produced cannot be deduced from the separate pieces.

Lewin expanded on this theory of perceptual organization by offering a broader social psychology of individual behavior. He viewed the person and the environment as parts of a single field. Rather than observing a person as a separate entity divorced from the field, Lewin argued that one should study individuals in their field of forces, in a group and in light of their positions and roles within the group. Lewin's concern was to ascertain the significance of the individual's behavior and thereby to enhance scientific predictability.

To understand or predict behavior, Lewin insisted, the person and the environment have to be considered as a single constellation of interdependent factors. The interaction between these two, person and environment, produces thinking, striving, and individual action, that is, outcomes. Behavior, in short, is a function of "life space"; thus, the dynamic analysis of behavior must begin with the situation as a whole. Rather than beginning with isolated elements of the situation and later attempting to organize them into an integrated system, field theory begins with a description of the situation as a whole. After an initial characterization of the whole situation, it is then possible to examine it for specific elements and relations among these elements.

With respect to the psychology of desegregation, the importance of this situational perspective will become evident in several of the essays that follow. However, field theory as proposed by Lewin cannot fully satisfy a sociological orientation—one concerned more with identifying the relevant structures of the situation than with understanding the cognitive and perceptual process of individuals. Despite its extension beyond a purely perceptual psychology, Lewin's perspective remains essentially an approach to understanding behavior through a personal frame of reference. Reflecting this psychological bias, behavior, in the end, is conceived as individual choice, constrained by forces impinging on that person's cognition and perception. Situational and personal variables are not, in fact, treated together as dependent and as independent variables determining behavior; rather, Lewin posits the outcome variable, personal behavior, as contingent upon situational factors.

This is no less true of more recent work in the psychology of situations. Responding to the strength of trait theory in explaining individual behavior, some psychologists have insisted on a situational antidote to a psychology that has tended to ignore the environment. Walter Mischel—an author in this volume— is widely credited with this situational critique of trait theory (1968, 1973), and it has been further developed and refined in subsequent work (Bem and Allen, 1977; Magnusson, 1981). Distinguishing between actual environments, perceived situations, and person–environment interactions, these psychologists have moved towards conceptualizing and measuring the independent contribution made by the environmental setting in understanding behavior.

J. Milton Yinger, a prominent sociologist who is sympathetic to field theory and who provided the afterword to this volume, has argued, in fact, that behavior must be conceived as simultaneously situational and personal. According to Yinger, a genuinely social psychological approach would focus on "individual behavior in the social context" and, therefore, would incorporate both psychological and sociological factors. To neglect either of these approaches, Yinger insists, results in less accurate predictions of individual behavior. To accomplish this, Yinger perceives the need to reformulate Lewin's field theory to incorporate a richer sensitivity to sociological, or situational, factors.

> In Lewin's work, field means "psychological field," that part of the total series of forces that is perceived by an individual. It seems reasonable to a psychologically trained person to say that an individual cannot be influenced by a force of which he is unaware. . . . What is missed by this kind of observation is recognition that a person's perceptions are a function not only of his sensitivities but also of the available stimuli, may of them derived from culture and social structure. Priority in determining behavior can be assigned neither to the sensitivities of the person nor to the facilitating forces in the environment, because both are involved in the equation. (Yinger, 1963, p. 583; see also Yinger, 1965)

Accordingly, Yinger argues for an interdisciplinary approach to the study of human behavior, one that aspires to identify the pertinent variables and to measure their interrelationships. In an important way, Yinger's argument for such an approach, which situates the individual in context, can be seen to prefigure what many of the following essays have tried to accomplish.

From a somewhat different angle, *symbolic interactionism*, deriving from the pragmatic tradition of Dewey, James, and Mead, also points to the significance of situational analysis. This approach lays heavy emphasis on individual autonomy and voluntarism. Herbert Blumer (1969), for example, is sharply critical of sociological analyses that treat social structure, cultural norms, and the like as determinants of social action. At the same time, the perspective remains adamantly sociological in insisting that those "exogenous" variables are not irrelevant to understanding social processes but are mediated through a collective definition within given settings or situations (see, for example, Becker, 1961, pp. 34–45). These larger structural variables are best treated, it is argued, as resources available to various actors for negotiation. The emphasis on negotiation points not only to the autonomy of the individual, but also to the permeability or fluidity of social structure (Strauss, 1978).

More specifically, symbolic interactionists, in their concern for the "definition of the situation," are typically concerned with the degree of shared orientations that participants bring to a situation. The implication is that cooperative interaction is more likely to occur if participants in a situation share compatible definitions or orientations. Conversely, dissensus inhibits the emergence of concerted action.

Ralph Turner's role theory, for example, argues that cooperative action is more likely when actors share a similar repertoire of roles and can define one another's behavior in terms of that shared repertoire. When repertoires differ, or when the same roles are understood to mean something very different and participants interpret the "same" piece of conduct as an expression of different roles, cooperative action is less likely (Turner, 1970). Glaser and Strauss' (1964) discussion of awareness contexts and Scheff's (1967, 1970) work on consensus, although not focusing on different role repertoires, examine how different distributions of information can generate situations characterized by varying levels of consensus. Erving Goffman, too, has been concerned with specifying relevant attributes of situations. He suggests, for example, that situations can vary along a continuum of tightness (or looseness), "depending on how disciplined the individual is obliged to be in connection with the several ways in which respect for the gathering and its social occasion can be expressed" (Goffman, 1963, p. 199).

There are further examples of the sociological interest in the situation. The work of Joseph Berger and others interested in "expectation states" (see Berger and Zelditch, 1977, 1980, 1985; Cohen, 1982) implicitly holds a situational theory, where status characteristics are seen to operate contextually through individuals in determining given outcomes. Similarly, the "new sociology of education" embodies a micro-version of situational analysis in its ethnomethodological focus on how people construct the reality of their daily interaction, for example, the everyday classroom interaction between teachers and students (Karabel and Halsey, 1977; Mehan, 1979; Young, 1973; for a treatment of this, see Jules Rosette and Mehan in this volume).

In short, this attention to the situation represents a general appreciation of the variability and significance of context. The degree of shared orientation, or shared meaning, that individuals bring to a setting has consequences for the kinds of behavior produced by that context. The applicability of such insights to the desegregation situation, where individuals of different backgrounds and experiences interact, is self-evident. In addition to sensitizing the researcher to this variable dimension, symbolic interactionism has further suggested several domains that, within the situation, may be especially consequential for desegregation outcomes.

But although field theory and symbolic interactionism have long argued for attention to the situation, they have certainly not been well heeded in much of the recent research. Certainly with respect to desegregation studies, the situation has not been accorded the theoretical centrality it ought to if we are to understand the process and to predict possible outcomes. At the same time, we are not suggesting that field theory or symbolic interactionism, as a social scientific orientation, necessarily represents the magic key to fully understanding desegregation. Although both have focused on the situation, each has been accused rightly of failing to move toward a trans-situational perspective on the situation. Although critical of global psychological or sociological theories that attempt to understand and/or predict outcomes because of their failure to consider micro-contexts, these approaches have failed to provide a systematic inductive theory of the situation. As a result, we are hardly closer to the objective of understanding social processes beyond any one given context.

The problem with these two traditions is still more profound. In both, there is an inherent impulse to reduce social or psychological forces to those elements that are directly observable within the setting itself. Each shares in a tendency toward empirical reductionism, as Yinger has noted with respect to field theory. Anything that cannot be observed at the level of the situation cannot be studied. Thus, both perspectives suffer from a difficulty in understanding how larger structural parameters—for example, authority, power, resources—can influence behavior. (For a rather different view, see Stryker, 1981, and for an acknowledgment of the problems, see Jessor, 1980.)

No one can hope to bring these diverse perspectives into a single interdisciplinary theory of the situation. That is not the purpose of this volume. Rather, we have attempted to consider the problem of school desegregation research with the situation as the focal point of inquiry. We see the situation as that arena where social and psychological forces converge and impinge on individual behavior. In our view, it is important to appreciate and make vivid the fact that, regardless of theoretical orientation, outcomes are the result of real, concrete processes that occur in the social world. To focus on the situation is to insist that one's theoretical or disciplinary predisposition not obscure this fundamental fact. Seen as the setting in which various processes operate, the situation is offered less as a theory of outcomes, and more as an insistence that causality cannot be established without an identification and specification of the local processes through which outcomes are forged.

The following chapters are intended to provide a more thematic coherence to a field deficient in theoretical orientation. By considering and promoting the situation as the theoretical lynchpin around which school desegregation research ought to turn, we hope that the academic and policy debates might be subsumed under this more inclusive, less divisive, effort to realize the significant features of the desegregation situation. Although all the research is intended to better understand and predict specific outcomes as a result of desegregation, there is little consensus among researchers concerning either the appropriate scale of social research, that is, level of analysis, or the perspective from which outcomes should be evaluated. Our aim is to sidestep these controversies, seemingly endemic to social science research, which turn on the relative significance of macro and micro forces on social outcomes, the consequentiality of proximal or distal features in determining behavior, and the role of objective or subjective processes in orienting action. (For an elaboration, with reference to the extant desegregation literature, see Longshore and Prager, 1985.) We suggest that the situation be perceived as a variable in its own right. Regardless of scale or perspective, social outcomes are forged through the crucible of the situation. The relative merits of different approaches to social scientific research cannot be established *a priori* as theoretical proclamation. Rather, we should recognize that their impact varies by setting.

In social science research, the chasm between a global orientation and a microscopic one remains wide, and there is little evidence of convergence. Large-scale studies, using aggregate data from metropolitan, state, or even national sources, have competed with micro, experimental, or ethnographic studies of single classrooms (or, perhaps, whole schools). A theoretical appreciation of the significance of situational factors in determining outcomes would enable researchers, at both the macro and the micro levels, to identify relevant contextual variables affecting outcomes. Situational analysis, in short, does not solve existing theoretical controversies, but it does possess the potential to subsume them under a more inclusive pattern of research inquiry, where both macro and micro studies clearly ought to play a key role.

Just as a theoretical appreciation of the situation requires recognition of the role that concrete mediation plays between exogenous variables—whether social, cultural, or personality traits—situational analysis might also provide a mechanism of reconciliation between those researchers committed to understanding the objective world of institutional constraints and those principally interested in the subjective world of "meaning making." The consequentiality of either cannot be understood as separate from the setting in which those forces become manifest. Mediation is required within a given situation. The relevant properties of the context by which objective constraint becomes implemented is no less significant a domain of inquiry than the mechanisms through which certain meanings of the situation are crafted.

Similarly, as Morris Rosenberg discusses in this volume, explanations that view social action distally remain sharply counterposed to the more phenomenological, proximal orientation of certain social researchers. Situational analysis, as the appropriate locus of inquiry, requires that desegregation researchers hold simultaneously for the influence of both proximal and distal perspectives of the part of situated individuals.

In short, the significance of the situation lies in recognizing that, to the extent that they are of consequence, macro and micro processes, objective and subjective forces, and proximal and distal influences become operationalized *in situ*. To seek to uncover the situation's properties and to appreciate its centrality is to provide a mechanism of reconciliation with respect to controversies which, in terms of understanding outcomes in society, serve no useful or practical purpose.

Similarly, and more concretely, what now stand as central debates within the school desegregation literature—the degree of white flight, achievement levels, interracial attitudes, etc.—could be deprived of their overly powerful political potency through an appreciation of situational variability. Precisely because the situation has not played a prominent theoretical role in desegregation studies, findings that school busing has produced substantial white flight in large cities have been elevated to a more general conclusion that busing *per se* produces substantial white flight. Yet such a conclusion should only have been a preliminary finding, requiring that the outcome be properly situated within specific context variables. What was the context in those cities—politically, socially, culturally, demographically, and so forth—that framed the decision to bus? What was the meaning of the decision as understood by the various publics affected? And so on. Such an investigation, where the context becomes the prominent object of inquiry, would prevent social-science research from simply being appropriated by the public realm for non-social-science purposes.

In summary, the situation offers a conceptual apparatus best designed to advance the art of inquiry in school desegregation research. In addition to providing some theoretical coherence to widely disparate research traditions, it also coordinates well with the social and legal pragmatics of school desegregation, as suggested in a review by Hawley and Rist, "On the Future Implementation of School Desegregation." Their reconstruction of the assumptions and findings in existing research leads them to the conclusion that desegregation remedies will have "to be strongly *situation-specific*" (Hawley and Rist, 1975, p. 424; emphasis added).

3. THE CURRENT PROJECT

This project was initiated in 1980 by the National Institute of Education, under whose auspices and support the project proceeded. As editors of this volume, we had the responsibility of selecting outstanding social scientists to reconsider school desegregation research. And in the interests of "advancing the art of inquiry," we purposely selected social scientists many of whom had not already become highly identified with that body of research and who were not well known for established positions concerning school desegregation. Our intention was to have these commissioned authors apply their already demonstrated theoretical and methodological talents to this particular substantive field, and thereby to breathe fresh life into a research tradition which, although relatively new, was already becoming fractionated by political and ideological squabbling.

At the same time, we did not believe it wise simply to ignore the substantial expertise of the established researchers in the field. We asked some to author articles and others to participate as reviewers to help ensure that the central issues or available literatures were not ignored. Several reviewers, in addition, participated in the two conferences that were convened for the authors in Santa Monica, California.

These two conferences were held in August 1981 and March 1982. There, the situation was the central focus of the discussion. Whereas we were intent on giving the authors freedom to consider the field of desegregation research from their own perspectives, we expected that they would incorporate a concern for the situation. Our aim was not to produce abstract, scholarly treatises on the situation; rather, by sensitizing the authors to these issues of context and the problems they pose in seeking understanding and prediction, we hoped to produce a consideration of desegregation research from many diverse angles, but with the situation clearly embedded within the several discussions. As the reader of this volume will no doubt observe, certain social scientific orientations and perspectives clearly lend themselves more readily to situational issues; and the following chapters incorporate these concerns to varying degrees. But we trust that the reader will find the cumulative result impressive, giving credence and sustenance to our guiding conviction that desegregation research could benefit from a more self-conscious theoretical orientation.

The first two chapters in the volume (Part II, "School Desegregation in Context") are written by John Ogbu and Gerald Suttles, respectively. These are the most general in approach and are intended to place the study of school desegregation in the larger context of American racial and ethnic stratification. In both of these essays, the intention is to specify the relation of school desegregation to larger social processes. Each is critical of micro studies that fail to appreciate how macro forces become operationalized in the school setting.

Gerald Suttles, known principally for his own ethnographic work, challenges the overwhelmingly micro bias held by ethnographic researchers of school desegregation. In "School Desegregation and 'The National Community,' " he suggests that the school desegregation process is strongly influenced by ethnic politics in the society at large; hence the study of what goes on in the classroom cannot ignore the influence of this force. Moreover, Suttles's paper is an argument for the importance of macro cultural variables in school settings, first, by examining how ethnic-mythic history becomes translated into a psychological set held by individuals and, second, by observing the strength of cosmopolitan civic culture—variable by communities—and its influence on the desegregation process.

John Ogbu's work, "Structural Constraints in School Desegregation," similarly identifies macro variables, though in this case principally economic ones, that are consequential for the desegregated setting. Suggesting that changing technology and economic needs impinge on the perception of school administrators and staff and, further, that patterns of discrimination influence the epistemology of minority groups, Ogbu argues that school outcomes cannot be understood independently of this larger socioeconomic order.

The articles in Part III, "New Theoretical Directions," represent the search, inspired by attention to context, for new theoretical directions in desegregation research. In contrast to the work by Suttles and Ogbu, these chapters point to the limitations of solely macroscopic explanations of desegregation, with an eye to more carefully specifying how microstructures influence given outcomes. In so doing, they contribute to the process of identifying relevant situational variables.

Mark Granovetter, in "The Micro Structure of School Desegregation," explores in detail one of the most crucial situational determinants of behavior in desegregated settings: the structure of social relations among participants. For Granovetter, failure to appreciate the complexity of issues related to the social structure of desegregation is a major cause of the confusion concerning the effects of desegregation. Thus, Granovetter moves beyond a simple notion of social structure composed only of friendship ties and argues for an examination of weak and strong ties, ties of friendship and enmity, as well as for the need to situate the findings within a temporal and historical framework.

Hubert Blalock is also concerned with "situating" macro variables that operate distally within a micro theory of the situation. His concern, in "A Model for Racial Contact in Schools," is to locate a reasonably small number of general variables that operate at a very proximate level for the actors concerned. Blalock suggests a number of different contact dimensions and links them to characteristics of settings that may influence the nature of cross-racial or cross-ethnic contacts, thereby promoting different desegregation outcomes by situation.

Walter Mischel, as a psychologist, differs in approach and argument from the sociology of Blalock and Granovetter. Nevertheless, his "Trait Theory Revisited: A Cognitive Social Learning View of School Desegregation" is also an effort to understand the mediation of macro orientations through situational variables. In a powerful statement against trait theory, Mischel insists that what is done, or thought, or felt in a given situation cannot be understood through a knowledge of individual dispositions, but "depends on the physical and psychological context in which the event was experienced, the knowledge and skills that the subject brings to the context, etc." Mischel, further, delineates several features of the psychological situation intended to explain given and variable outcomes.

The main focus of the essays in Part IV, "A Reconsideration of Methods," is an evaluation of two major methodological approaches to desegregation research: attitude research and small-group research. Once again, the task in each of these articles is to assess these approaches with respect to their ability to measure the import that situational features hold for desegregation outcomes. Through this critique, the authors suggest new directions for assessment and measurement.

Morris Rosenberg, in "Self-Esteem Research: A Phenomenological Corrective," is sharply critical of the prevailing self-esteem research because of its failure to mediate its findings through the individual's experience. "If we are to understand the psychological impact of social structure or social context," he writes, "we must understand how it structures and governs the individual's experience." In the interest of promoting an analysis that can account for situational variability, Rosenberg argues compellingly against research that attempts to explain outcomes distally, that is, from afar. He takes issue with those who attempt to impute meaning from objective features of the setting, for example, as functions of race, socioeconomic status, or ethnicity. Rather, Rosenberg insists that research must interpret the emergent, subjective meanings as they operate phenomenologically and proximally in individuals embedded in the given context.

A similar position is struck by Bennetta Jules-Rosette and Hugh Mehan, in "Schools and Social Structure: An Interactionist Perspective." Suggesting, like Granovetter, that social science researchers need to refine their understanding of social structure by attending to its more micro properties, they further argue that desegregation must be situated within the "daily lives of educators and students to determine how its consequences may be most effectively assessed." Their interest, in fact, is not the social structure *per se*, as it is for Granovetter, nor the psychological situation, as it is for Mischel, but instead the social interactional patterns and adjustments of the desegregated student. Identifying specific arenas for further study (for example, classroom, testing, and referral within the desegregated school), Jules-Rosette and Mehan insist that the social structure/social interaction dualism—so pervasive an assumption in desegregation research—itself must be collapsed.

Taken as a whole, these chapters identify the central difficulties faced by researchers concerned with understanding and evaluating school desegregation. This effort to balance micro/macro, distal/proximal, and objective/subjective distinctions through a keen sense of the concrete setting through which these forces operate promises to give greater coherence to work on school desegregation. We hope that readers will take from these papers ideas on how to proceed in developing more reliable and more complete knowledge of the desegregation process, and on the relation of these situational factors to specific outcomes. What this volume hopes to accomplish, in short, is a greater sensitivity to the range of significant independent variables that, we believe, are essential to explaining outcomes like self-esteem, achievement, and interracial attitudes.

The focus on situational variability alerts us, moreover, to the fact that desegregation, in all likelihood, has other potentially advantageous outcomes commonly ignored in the standard literature. As Herbert Hyman (1983), who contributed a foreword to this volume, has written,

> When we weigh the effects of desegregation, surely it is fair and wise to put more on the scales. Why are beliefs and attitudes of child and adult minority and majority members about each other—so obvious an effect, so often discussed in the literature on contact and desegregation—neglected? What about true *knowledge* of each other's group, for example, of the hardship and victimization minorities suffer or of their high achievements despite those handicaps? What about *sentiments*, for example, sympathy for the underdog or hatred of the overdog? What about potential effects in *adult* life, such as membership or support for various voluntary associations, political participation, and support for various candidates—black or white, integrationist or segregationist? And what about effects on *adult* self-esteem which, as Seeman (1981) has noted, may differ from the short-run effect of the child's self-esteem?

We believe that the following chapters, taken together, represent an exciting collection because they have the potential to reinvigorate and redirect school desegregation research. In placing desegregation studies within the social scientific problem of the situation, and in establishing the connection of this empirical problem to a long-standing theoretical tradition in the social sciences, one may well restore the credibility and vitality of school desegregation research. Only time will tell whether the result of this volume will promote better understanding and a greater capacity to predict desegregation outcomes. But it is certainly true that, as a result of the contributions of these prominent social scientists, there is the promise that desegregation research can now become more firmly situated within social science. As a result, school desegregation research will possess greater potential to inform and educate the public rather than remaining a prisoner of the public mood.

REFERENCES

Allport, G. W. *The Nature of Prejudice*. Cambridge, MA: Addison-Wesley, 1954.

Bem, D. J., & Allen, A. On predicting some of the people some of the time: The search for cross-situational consistencies in behavior. *Psychological Review*, 1977, *81*, 506–520.

Armor, D. *White Flight, Demographic Transition, and the Future of School Desegregation*. Paper presented at the Annual Meeting of the American Sociological Association, 1978, San Francisco.

Becker, H. *Boys in White, Student Culture in Medical School*. Chicago: University of Chicago Press, 1961.

Berger, J., Fisek, M., Norman, R., and Zelditch, M. *Status Characteristics and Social interaction*. New York: Elsevier Press, 1977.

Berger, J., Rosenholtz, S., and Zelditch, M. Status organizing processes. *Annual Review of Sociology*, 1980, *6*, 479–508.

Berger, J., and Zelditch, M. (Eds.). *Status, Rewards, and Influence: How Expectations Organize Behavior*. San Francisco: Jossey-Bass, 1985.

Blalock, H., and Wilken, P. *Intergroup Processes: A Micro-Macro Perspective*. New York: Free Press, 1979.

Blumer, H. *Symbolic Interaction*. Englewood Cliffs, NJ: Prentice-Hall, 1969.

Cohen, E. The effects of desegregation on race relations. *Law and Contemporary Problems*, 1975, *39*, 271–299.

Cohen, E. Expectation states and inter-racial interaction in school settings. *Annual Review of Sociology*, 1982, *8*, 209–235.

Cohen, E., and Rober, S. Modification of interracial interaction disability. In J. Berger and M. Zelditch (Eds.), *Status, Rewards and Influence: How Expectations Organize Behavior* San Francisco: Jossey-Bass, 1985.

Coleman, J. S., Kelly, S., and Moore, J. *Trends in School Desegregation 1968–1973*. Washington, DC: The Urban Institute, 1975.

Crain, R. L., and Mahard, R. The effect of research methodology on desegregation-achievement studies: A meta-analysis. *American Journal of Sociology*, 1983, *88*, 839–854.

Epps, E. Minority children: Desegregation, self-evaluation, and achievement orientation. In W. Hawley (Ed.), *Effective School Desegregation, Equity, Quality and Feasibility*. Beverly Hills, CA: Sage, 1981.

Glaser, B., and Strauss, A. Awareness contexts and social interaction. *American Sociological Review*, 1964, *29*, 669–679.

Goffman, E. *Behavior in Public Places*. New York: The Free Press, 1963.

Hawley, W., and Rist, R. On the Future Implementation of School Desegregation. *Law and Contemporary Problems*, 1975, *39*, 12–26.

Hochschild, J., *The New American Dilemma. Liberal Democracy and School Desegregation*. New Haven, CT: Yale University Press, 1985.

Hyman, H. Themes and problems in research on the desegregation situation. In J. Prager, D. Longshore, and M. Seeman (Eds.) *Advancing the Art of Inquiry in School Desegregation Research*, unpublished monograph. Santa Monica, CA: System Development Corporation, 1983.

Jessor, R. The perceived environment in psychological theory and research. In D. Magnusson (Ed.), *Towards a Psychology of Situations: An Interactional Perspective*. Hillsdale, NJ: Erlbaum, 1981.

Karabel, J., and Halsey, A. H. Educational research: A review and interpretation. In J. Karabel and A. H. Halsey (Eds.), *Power and Ideology in Education*. New York: Oxford University Press, 1977.

Lewin, K. *A Dynamic Theory of Personality*. New York: McGraw-Hill, 1935.

Longshore, D. Social psychological research on school desegregation: Toward a new agenda. In D. Monti (Ed.), *New Directions for Testing and Measurement: Impact of Desegregation*. San Francisco: Jossey-Bass, 1982.

Longshore, D., and Prager, J. The impact of school desegregation: A situational analysis. *Annual Review of Sociology*, 1985, *11*, 75–91.

McConahay, J. Reducing racial prejudice in desegregated schools. In W. D. Hawley (Ed.), *Effective School Desegregation: Equity, Quality, and Feasibility*. Beverly Hills, CA: Sage, 1981.

Magnusson, D. (Ed.). *Towards a Psychology of Situations: An Interactional Perspective*. Hillsdale, NJ: Lawrence Erlbaum, 1981.

Mehan, H. *Learning Lessons*. Cambridge, MA: Harvard University Press, 1979.

Miller, N. Peer relations in desegregated schools. In N. Karweit and J. Epstein (Eds.), *Friends in School*. New York: Academic Press, 1983.

Miller, N. (Ed.). *Groups in Contact: The Psychology of Desegregation*. New York: Academic Press, 1984.

Mischel, W. *Personality and Assessment*. New York: Wiley, 1968.

Mischel, W. Toward a cognitive social learning reconceptualization of personality. *Psychological Review*, 1973, *80*, 252–283.

Pettigrew, T. F., and Green, R. L. School desegregation in large cities: A critique of the Coleman "white flight" thesis. *Harvard Educational Review*, 1976, *40*, 1–53.

St. John, N. *School Desegregation: Outcomes for Children*. New York: Wiley, 1975.

Scheff, T. Toward a sociological model of consensus. *American Sociological Review*, 1967, *32*, 32–45.

Scheff, T. On the concepts of identity and social relationship. In T. Shibutani (Ed.), *Human Nature and Collective Behavior*. Englewood Cliffs, NJ: Prentice-Hall, 1970.

Schofield, J. School desegregation and intergroup relations. In D. Bar-Tal, and L. Saxe (Eds.), *Social Psychology of Education: Theory and Research*. New York: Wiley, 1978.

Schofield, J. *Black and White in School: Trust, Tension, or Tolerance?* New York: Praeger, 1982.

Seeman, M. Intergroup relations. In M. Rosenberg and R. Turner (Eds.), *Social Psychology: Sociological Perspectives*. New York: Basic Books, 1981.

Singer, D. *Interracial attitudes of negro and white fifth grade children in segregated and unsegregated schools*, unpublished doctoral dissertation, Columbia University, 1966.

Stephan, W. G. School desegregation: An evaluation of predictions made in Brown v. Board of Education. *Psychological Bulletin*, 1978, *85*, 217–238.

Strauss, A. *Negotiations*. San Francisco: Jossey-Bass, 1978.

Stryker, S. Symbolic interactionism: Themes and variations. In M. Rosenberg and R. Turner (Eds.), *Social Psychology*. New York: Basic Books, 1981.

Turner, R. *Family Interaction*. New York: Wiley, 1970.

Useem, E. Correlates of white students' attitudes toward a voluntary busing program," *Education and Urban Society*, 1976, *8*, 441–476.

Wolters, R. *The Burden of Brown: Thirty Years of School Desegregation*. Knoxville, TN: University of Tennessee Press, 1985.

Yinger, J. M. Research implications of a field view of personality. *American Journal of Sociology*, 1963, *68*, 580–592.

Yinger, J. M. *Toward a Field Theory of Behavior*. New York: McGraw-Hill, 1965.

Young, M. F. D. Curricula and the Social Organization of Knowledge. In R. Brown (Ed.), *Knowledge, Education and Cultural Change*. London: Tavistock, 1973.

Part **II**

SCHOOL DESEGREGATION IN CONTEXT

Chapter 1

Structural Constraints in School Desegregation

JOHN U. OGBU

1. INTRODUCTION

The main objective of this chapter is to explore the definition of the desegregation situation from the participants' point of view and to explore the historical and structural forces that shape them.

This chapter is about some historical and enduring structural forces that impact on participants' definitions of the desegregation situation. Specifically, we will focus on those historical and structural forces shaping the epistemology of black Americans and on how the latter affects their definition of the desegregation situation. For historical and structural reasons, desegregation has different meanings for different groups of participants. And my own research among blacks suggests that their continuing struggle for quality education and for equal educational opportunity affects how they define successful school desegregation.

As we use the term in this chapter, *epistemology* refers to a people's "folk system" (Bohannon, 1957) or "folk theory" or their model of "social reality" (Berger and Luckmann, 1966) that forms the basis of their participation in and interpretation of social events (Ogbu, 1974).

JOHN U. OGBU • Department of Anthropology, University of California, Berkeley, CA 94720. Research for this paper was supported by faculty research fund, University of California, Berkeley, and by NIE grant, G-80-0045. The writing of the paper was supported by the Wisconsin Center for Education Research (University of Wisconsin, Madison) which is supported in part by a grant from the National Institute of Education (Grant No. NIE-G-81-009). I am grateful for the support of these institutions. However, opinions expressed in the paper are solely mine.

The rest of the chapter is organized into the following sections. The first presents a conceptual framework, a cultural-ecological framework, for studying the desegregation situation from the participants' point of view and the historical and structural forces that shape them. The next section will describe those relevant historical and structural forces shaping the epistemology of black Americans; that is, their notion of how the world, including the school world, functions. The third section takes up briefly how blacks perceive and interpret school segregation and desegregation and how these perceptions and interpretations influence their behavioral responses. The chapter concludes with a brief consideration of some methodological implications for research on the school desegregation situation.

2. A CULTURAL-ECOLOGICAL PERSPECTIVE

To fully appreciate the historical and structural influences on the epistemology of participants in school desegregation and the significance of the latter on their definition of desegregation situation, we will first note the importance of formal education in the United States. We will use the framework of cultural ecology to do this because this framework allows us to explore not only how participants perceive and behave in the desegregated settings but more importantly to analyze the influences of other societal institutions connected with the educational system on people's perceptions and responses. The inclusion of the linkages with other institutions is particularly relevant because schools are an agency that prepares young people to become adult participants in those institutions. From our point of view, the nature of the connection between those institutions and the schools may affect the ability of the schools to prepare young people adequately for adult life.

We will be specifically concerned with the connection between education and the economic system. Although educational systems of advanced industrial societies like the United States are influenced by political systems and ideologies (Cohen, 1975) and by religious beliefs and traditions, the most important source of influence appears to be the industrial economy. The latter can be seen in the assumptions and behaviors of governments, groups, and individuals (Berg, 1969; Dore, 1976). It is, of course, true that as Prager (personal communication, 1982) noted, in the American context "education has been identified as a central mechanism for greater inclusion of divergent groups and has been, therefore, an agent in the democraticization of the American public." He goes on to add that certain (ethnic?) groups have employed education "as a mechanism of leverage—to overcome the prejudice and discrimination that operate in the economic sphere." It appears that from this point of view the economic function of education is subordinate. However, the intended message in Prager's statement cannot be generalized to all American groups. As we will show later, education did not necessarily eliminate prejudice and discrimination for black Americans before the civil rights legislations of the 1960s because of their caste-like status or race (see Kahn 1968; Katzman 1973; Ogbu 1978a; Thernstrom 1973, especially chapter 8). But the point we want to stress is that even though education serves political and other noteworthy functions, and even though some Americans idealize the pursuit of education for its own sake, in reality, schooling in the United States and in similar industrialized societies has usually been structured on the commonsense idea of training in marketable skills and credentialing for labor-market entry and remuneration.

We shall, therefore, argue in this section that in the United States and in similar societies (a) the structure and content of schooling are shaped by *perceived needs* of the economic system, especially the needs of the labor force; (b) schools, whether they acknowledge it or not, try to satisfy the needs of the industrial economy by teaching future workers and consumers the beliefs, values, and attitudes that support the economic system (as well as other institutions), by teaching them practical skills and personal habits that make the economic system work, and by credentialing employees for labor market entry and remuneration; (c) the success of the schools in training and credentialing members of a given client population depends partly on the niche occupied by the population in the labor force, their epistemology, and their responses to schooling. Schools succeed in educating children according to conventional measures of school success if the epistemology and economic realities of their community foster positive responses to schooling; (d) when an alternative economic niche exists for a population, its requirements may either discourage or enhance conventional school success, and (e) the inferior economic niche usually occupied by caste-like minorities fosters both school training and an epistemology not conducive to conventional school success. The problem of minority educability is intimately related to the issue of school desegregation and the definition of the desegregation situation.

We will represent schematically in Figure 1 our discussion of the previous points or some of them. Because of the limitation of space, we will not elaborate on each of the connections shown in Figure 1; and all the points we will discuss are not necessarily shown in the figure. We would like to point out that some parts of our discussion will lack adequate supporting research data because no such research has been done. Our statements in such cases should be taken as reasonable speculations or hypotheses and as a challenge to researchers to extend their investigation beyond the conventional scope.

2.1. Industrial Economy and Education

The relationship between industrial economy and education has long been a subject of intense debate between technological functionalists and human capital proponents, on the one hand, and on the other, conflict theorists and proponents

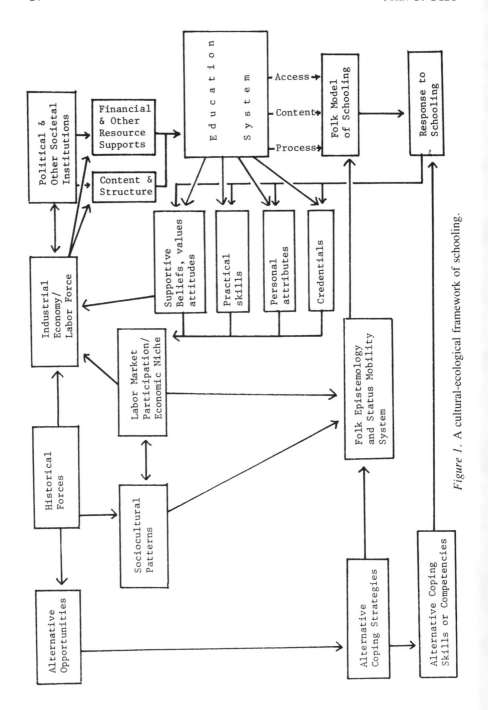

Figure 1. A cultural-ecological framework of schooling.

of a dual labor market. According to the former, there is more or less a direct relationship between cognitive and technical or practical skills acquired at school and the technical skills required at the work place for productivity and remuneration (see Blair, 1971; Dore, 1976; Harrison, 1972; especially Schultz, 1961; and Weisbrod, 1975). The opposing groups find no such relationship; rather, some contend schools teach children social control—how to conform to the authority relationship of the workplace (Bowles and Gintis, 1976; Hansell and Karweit, 1983 Spring, 1972). Moreover, they claim that because different segments of the workforce differ in authority relationship, schools socialize children from different social classes differently according to their respective destination in the labor force. In addition, because of racial and gender discrimination (Levin, 1979) or because of dual labor market (Doeringer and Piore, 1971; Gordon, 1971; Piore, 1975), minorities and women do not necessarily obtain jobs and remunerations commensurate with their education.

The issue of practical skills is important, but for our purposes what appears to be even more important is what the participants (employers, the powers-that-be, and school personnel) believe that future employees need and what they think schools can or should do. We will, therefore, first try to show how the economic system shapes schooling in the United States for training in marketable skills and for credentialing; then we will examine how schools try to accomplish the task of preparing children for recruitment into the labor force.

2.1.1. Industrial Economy's Influence on Structure and Content of Schooling

There are many episodes in the history of American education that show that the structure of schooling, content of curriculum, and financial and other supports for education are highly dependent on what Americans perceive as essential for the well-being of their economy, and what role schools should play through the preparation of future workers. Indeed, changes in present-day schooling under the impact of current technological and economic changes provide a good illustration of the mutual historical relationship between schooling and the economy. We appear to be witnessing a reordering of educational priorities and a reorganization of schooling to meet the needs of a new kind of labor force. The changes in schooling caused by technological and economic trends manifest themselves at precollege and at college levels.

The competition between the United States, Japan, and other industrialized countries for high-tech economy and the growing influence of the computer industry on American economy are at the heart of the new economic forces reshaping American education from kindergarten through graduate school. In the public schools the economic influences are mediated through pressures from the government and from industrial leaders. For example, in 1982 the State of

California provided extra funds in its educational budget for strengthening the math and science curriculum in the public schools. And Franklin (1982, p. 16) reports that the powerful

> 1900-member Industrial Education Council of California is seeking ways to attract more students to math and science, to provide training for teachers and ultimately to bring more qualified people into the state's rapidly expanding high-technology industry.

Gordon Weiss, the executive vice-president of the Council, emphasized that the Council wants to make parents aware of the fact that future graduates with strong backgrounds in math and science have good employment prospects. Industrial leaders are on the whole quite explicit about their objective, namely, to restructure public school and college education to serve industries more effectively. As Gordon Weiss puts it, it is

> *not just a question of having kids come out with math and science skills. It's a question of California's economy.* Will we have people who are functional and can produce? (*San Francisco Examiner and Chronicle*, February 14, 1982, cited in Franklin, 1982, p. 16; emphasis added)

For their part the public schools are responding quickly and positively. In some school districts there is now in place or a plan to introduce computers in almost every classroom from kindergarten through 12th grade (*Oakland Tribune*, October 25, 1982, p. 1). Despite its worries about the lack of students and funds, a school district in Minnesota reports that its "budget makers have put together a $150,000 arsenal of more than 200 Apple, Commodore and Atari microcomputers for the district's remaining 6,000 students; (and) 20 more computers arrive soon" (*Oakland Tribune*, February 2, 1983, p. C3). Just as more affluent families respond more quickly to pass on the advantage of the new education to their children, so also do more affluent schools. Those who do not change to the new order will be "training a whole generation of computer illiterates who are doomed to be a social underclass" (*Oakland Tribune*, February 2, 1983, p. C3).

The restructuring of precollege educational priorities by parents, local schools, and school districts, and by state authorities in response to current technological and economic changes is underscored by a national movement for a stronger science and mathematics education to prepare children better for the job market. This movement led to a convocation on science and mathematics in the schools sponsored by the National Academy of Sciences and the National Academy of Engineering in 1982. Both President Reagan's message to the convocation and the "Foreword" to the *Report* of the convocation by Frank Press, President of the National Academy of Sciences, and Courland Perkins, President of the National Academy of Engineering, noted that the objective of the convocation was not to seek out best ways to encourage the pursuit of science and mathematical knowledge for its own sake, but how to better prepare children for a changing labor force. President Reagan told the delegates:

> The problem today in elementary and secondary school science and mathematics education is serious—serious enough to compromise America's future ability to develop and advance our traditional industrial base to compete in international marketplaces. Failure to remain at the industrial forefront results in direct harm to our American economy standard of living. (NAS and NAE, 1982, p. 1)

And according to Press and Perkins,

> The convocation was not concerned primarily with preparing young people to be scientists and engineers. The more difficult and perhaps more serious problem, conferees agreed, is that we appear to be raising a generation of Americans who lack the education to participate in a world of technology—the world in which they will live and work. (NAS and NAE, 1982, p. 1)

The recommendations of the national convocation will eventually feed back into and reinforce the ongoing curriculum and other changes brought about by other movements with similar concerns. Among the latter are those advocating "back to basics," "competency-based education," and the like. It is reported that there are currently several curriculum reform groups around the nation (Sleeter, personal communication).

At the college level, student enrollment has fallen dramatically in the social sciences and humanities, fields where graduates face scarcity of jobs. Complementing students' responses, college authorities shift their resources away from the social sciences and humanities; and in some cases, like at California State University at Sonoma, authorities have gone as far as to dismiss 10% of their

> tenured faculty—due to steadily declining enrollment and a shift in student interests away from humanities and social sciences and toward more "applied" fields such as business and nursing. (*Los Angeles Times*, May 6, 1982, p. 1)

One university official summarized the situation at Sonoma by saying that

> not only are kids no longer interested in the humanities and social sciences, but with Hewlett-Packard Industries opening up their new building across the street, we'll need to train people for their jobs. (Franklin, 1982, p. 17)

Thus, student enrollments in "applied" fields, especially in those preparing students for employment in business and "high-tech industries" where jobs are plentiful and wages are good, have risen sharply. In consequence, college authorities are shifting their emphasis and resources to those fields. The University of California, for example, has introduced a different and higher salary scale for professors in business administration and engineering disciplines (University of California Bulletin, vol. 30, 20, February 22, 1982).

Corporations are actively encouraging these changes in the educational priorities of students and colleges and often they initiate them because of their changing manpower needs. For example, *Newsweek* (November 17, 1980, cited in Franklin, 1982), reports that in 1980 corporations like Bechtel were spending large sums of money for scholarships to train students to meet their manpower needs. Other corporations like General Electric, General Motors, and Boeing contributed about one million dollars toward building a "production center" at one university where students would study techniques and problems of American industries. And Wang Laboratories, among others, were setting up their own graduate schools.

In summary, as in the past new developments in American technology and in the economy are reshaping American education, especially in the direction of restructuring schooling to train and credential future employees according to perceived needs of the economy. Indeed, the influences of technological and economic trends on priorities and structuring of schooling in America has been subject of repeated editorials in *Science*, of feature articles and comments in national magazines, and of news reports in national and local newspapers (e.g., *The Daily Californian*, October 14, 1976, p. 1; *New York Times*, September 9, 1981, pp. 19, 29; November 11, 1979, p. 28; *Newsweek*, Jan. 9, 1978, pp. 65–66; May 14, 1979, pp. 110–112; *Oakland Tribune*, June 1, 1980, p. A9; and *Science*, August 16, 1974; February 14, 1975; December 1, 1978; October 1982).

2.1.2. How Schooling Prepares Children to Support the Economic System

The educational system implements the task of recruiting people into the labor force by teaching them (a) the beliefs, values, and attitudes that support the economic system; (b) some practical skills that make the economic system work; (c) by enhancing the development of some personal attributes compatible with the habits required at the industrial workplace; and (d) by credentialing them to enter the workforce.

Anthropologists and others studying nonindustrial societies have explored how children in those societies acquire the beliefs, values, and attitudes that support their economic systems (see Barry, Bacon, and Child, 1959; Murdock and Whiting, 1951; Ruddle and Chesterfield, 1977; Sutton-Smith and Roberts, 1970). we have no comparable research for children in the United States. However, content analysis of schoolbooks in the 19th century suggests that schooling plays an important part in teaching American children beliefs, values, and attitudes that support the American economic system (see Spindler, 1974).

One such study done by Elson (1964) shows that in the 19th century the schoolbooks taught children both the nature of American economy, its superiority over other economic systems, and how to succeed in it. Elson found repeated statements, emphases, and pictures portraying the nature of the economic system and suggesting that it was the best in the world because of "American liberty and industry" (p. 246). The overall picture of the economy is that

> the child reading [the] books would view the whole industrial revolution as the product of American talent. He would also be likely to anticipate a perpetual glorious future in which man's control over nature will be steadily extended. (p. 246–47)

The books also conveyed the idea that a person of any background could get ahead merely through personal hard work, rather than by joining labor unions or through collective bargaining. They identified labor unions with "irresponsible violence and probably with doctrines subversive of American institutions" (p. 251). On the whole the schoolbooks extolled the acceptance of American labor conditions and hardwork as the best way to get ahead and taught that poverty was the result of idleness, wealth the fruit of hard work, and that private property was a sacred right whose accumulation should be universally approved (p. 256). All the schoolbooks analyzed by Elson "accepted as axiom that the law of history," for the individual and for the nation, "is one of steady and inevitable progress toward greater material wealth and comfort as well as toward greater virtue and freedom" (p. 258).

Although we have no comparable study for the contemporary period, some analysis of contemporary schoolbooks by consumer advocates (e.g., Harty, 1979) and some feminists (e.g., Adams and Laurikietis, 1977; Frazier and Sadker, 1973) would suggest that the schoolbooks continue to play an important role in teaching children beliefs, values, and attitudes that support the economic system. The economic beliefs, values, and attitudes are also reinforced by "field trips" to industries sponsored by business establishments and by presentations in the public schools by representatives of corporations (Franklin, 1982).

Schools also teach some practical skills essential to make the industrial economy work. The most obvious are reading, writing, and computational skills. Consider for the moment how the American banking system would work if its employees and clients did not learn to read, write, and compute. But we know from ethnographic studies of interns, such as the study of interns in brokerage firms (Hagerty, n.d.) that important practical skills are acquired on the job regardless of the educational background of the intern. For example, Hagerty reports that one intern wrote in her journal that although a college degree helps, it is not necessary (p. 28). To be successful, the intern must learn the culture and language of the brokerage office. And learning that language involved learning to speak and "understand a rapid, highly-technical and often computational language composed of computerized abbreviations, symbols, and wealth of new terms" (p. 23). The intern must also learn to watch, listen, read, and ask questions; asking questions involves phrasing them in a way that would elicit the desired information in an appropriate manner, place, and time. Other skills acquired on the job by the interns are initiative appropriate to the job, ability to extract information from accountant executives, social skills, and successful identification with role models.

Ethnographers and other researchers have documented that schooling enhances the acquisition of other personal attributes. Among these are punctuality and competition. Waller (1932, 1967) argued long ago that schools teach children the competitive values of American economic and political life through intramural and extramural athletic games and similar activities. In our own research in Stockton, California (1968–70) we learned from interviewing employers that they expect schools to teach children punctuality through enforcement of school and class attendance rules. One employer told us that he usually examined the high school attendance records of local graduates before considering hiring them on the belief that if they had poor school attendance records or were tardy to classes they were likely to do the same on the job. LeCompte (1978) and Wilcox (1978) examined the structure and process of classroom tasks and concluded that they appear to teach children personal habits like conformity to a schedule, conformity to authority, keeping busy, maintaining order, and the like, paralleling the habits of punctuality, obedience, dependence, perseverance, deferring gratification, predictability, and others valued by employers.

Scrupski (1975) has argued that schools are better suited than the family to inculcate these and other qualities needed to participate in an industrial labor force. The reason, according to him, is that the organizations of social relationships and tasks of the school are closer to those of the workplace than are those of the family. The family, for example, is characterized by intimate and diffuse relationships, by particularistic and ascriptive standards, and by dependence on others. In contrast, the social organization of the schools encourages impersonality and specificity in relationships, universal criteria and achievement standards in rewards, as well as self-reliance in task structure and performance, features that are also characteristic of the corporate workplace.

Finally, Cohen (1972) speculates that the way American classrooms are organized influences children's styles of thought. For example, she says that conventional classroom organization, unlike "open" classrooms, encourages development of analytic cognitive performance. She further argues that classroom organization and the structure of their activities have changed with different phases of American economic development (e.g., period dominated by extraction of raw materials from nature; period of manufacturing tangible goods; and period of service provisions). Each period required a particular kind of organization. Whether or not by design, Cohen argues, there were modifications in classroom organization and in curriculum that tended to enhance the development of the functional personal qualities.

The schools, further, serve to credential people prior to entering the workforce (Jencks, 1972). The importance of this function came to our attention during our research in Stockton, particularly in my interviews with two groups of informants. One was made up of local United States citizens who told us that they knew how to do different kinds of work, such as boat repairing, carpentry, and the like, but they could not practice these trades because they did not have "papers to show for it." That is, they had not been credentialed by some educational agency and therefore did not have license to practice. The other group consisted of immigrant professionals, especially dentists from the Philippines.

Although the immigrants had trained as dentists in the best educational institutions of their homeland and had practiced dentistry in their homeland, they could not practice in Stockton without credentials from a Californian educational agency. Regardless of training, experience, and expertise, these immigrants had to be first examined and certified by Californian schools.

In summary, then, schools are structured to prepare workers for the industrial economy. For its part the schools try to accomplish this task in a number of ways, though they may not always recognize or acknowledge that they are doing so.

2.1.3. Epistemology and Educability

However, neither the political nor economic interests of society, nor the changing requirements of the economic system, nor the efforts of the schools themselves, can guarantee that schools will succeed in educating children of a client population. Schools' success depends in part on the folk epistemology of the people and their resulting model of and responses to schooling. The folk epistemology or people's perceptions and interpretations of how thinks work, especially how their society and its economic system work and how schooling fits into the scheme of things, is affected by several factors. Among them are the social organization of the society (e.g., the degree and nature of social stratification) and how groups are situated within it, their historical experiences, their religious and other values, etc. With respect to the epistemological aspect of schooling, the most important influence appears to be people's experiences with the labor market. In a population in which a significant number of people from varied backgrounds have become successful or have "made it" in the wage labor market, there will be a tendency to believe in the kinds of teachings portrayed in the 19th century American schoolbooks; namely, that "the laborer who accepted American labor conditions and worked hard would get ahead" (Elson, 1964, p. 251). Likewise, where people's access to better jobs, wages, chances for promotion on the job and the like are enhanced by schooling, people will not only want education but also will exert the necessary efforts to do well in school (Ogbu, 1983b). Favorable perceptions of linkages between schooling and opportunities in the labor market usually lead to favorable perceptions of schooling and to the emergence of a folk model of schooling that promotes a strong pursuit of educational credentials in terms of effort investment.

The specific factor that connects folk epistemology arising from cultural values, labor market experiences, and other forces, on the one hand, and schooling on the other, is a *status mobility system or a folk theory of getting ahead*. Every society or population has its own theory of getting ahead; and each theory tends to generate its own ideal behavior and its own ideal successful persons or role models—the kinds of people who are widely perceived by members of the society or population as people who are successful or who can get ahead because of their personal attributes and behaviors. Parents usually try to raise their children to be like such people (LeVine, 1967). If education or schooling is perceived over a reasonable period of time to explain why such people are successful, then the pursuit of education becomes incorporated into the status mobility system or the folk theory of success. In other words, where there is a strong connection between school success and later economic and societal success and later economic and societal success in adult life, people will develop a positive image of schooling; they will value going to school, and they will learn to persevere or work hard to do well in school; eventually it will become common knowledge as to what makes people succeed in school. Among such people there will likely emerge shared beliefs, values, and attitudes that support both the desire for and the perseverance and hardwork in the pursuit of school credentials. Eventually these become culturally sanctioned instrumental and categorical beliefs, attitudes, values, and behaviors enhancing school success, almost as if it were a cultural tradition or "natural endowment."

In that kind of a community, parents and other child-rearing agents would tend to teach their children consciously and unconsciously the categorical beliefs, values, attitudes, and behaviors promoting children's striving to do well in school; they will also tend to guide and supervise the children in a manner that ensures that the children actually conform to expectations of school success. For their part, children in such a community will likely respond positively to schooling. By positive response we mean that children accept and internalize the beliefs, values, and attitudes that support striving for school success, as well as those that support the economic system and other societal institutions with which schooling is connected; that children make concerted effort to learn what schools teach; and where there is positive response, they may even, as they get older, take the initiative to search out those qualities essential for future participation in the labor force and learn how to acquire them. Children respond positively because of what their parents and other child-rearing agents teach them. Moreover, they observe among older members of their community that there is a reasonable connection between schooling on the one hand and, on the other, jobs, wages, and other societal benefits. Furthermore, children's positive responses are reinforced by the shared cultural knowledge and folklore of their communities when these embody the beliefs that school success and success in adult life are related. From all these, children acquire the "facts" that enable them to form appropriate cognitive maps about their society's or community's status-mobility system and the place of schooling within it. They eventually develop a cultural conception of how to get ahead or how to "make it" and what role school plays in getting ahead. Where schooling facilitates getting ahead, children are taught, learn, and believe from the early period of their school careers that school success requires a reasonable degree of conformity to school rules or requirements and expectations. And in actuality they show a reasonable degree of conformity to those requirements and expectations.

2.2. Caste-like Minority Status and Schooling: The Missing Link

2.2.1. Job Ceiling and Minority Schooling

Under structured inequality, especially one involving *caste-like minorities*, the relationship between schooling and the economic system changes in some important respects. Caste-like minorities (e.g., black Americans) are minorities who have been incorporated into "their country" more or less involuntarily and permanently and then relegated to menial status. Membership in a caste-like minority group is usually acquired at birth and one does not escape from collective subordination except through "passing" or emigration, options not always available. The economic status of caste-like minorities is usually low because of economic subordination; their employment in wage labor depends on dominant-group members' beliefs about the minorities and their proper place in the labor force. Generally the minorities are excluded from the more desirable jobs through a *job ceiling*. A *job ceiling* serves to selectively assign the minorities to jobs at the lower level of status, power, dignity, and income while allowing members of the dominant group to compete more easily and freely on the basis of individual ability and training for more desirable jobs above that ceiling.

The level of the job ceiling and other forms of subordination, including unequal power relations, shape dominant-group members' ideas about the minorities' status, their role in the economy, and how the minorities get ahead or should get ahead. These dominant-group's beliefs, in turn, determine how the schooling of the minorities is designed, including how much and what kind of access to formal education the minorities have; whether the minorities attend segregated or integrated schools; what the schools should teach them; and how the schools should treat them. But regardless of differences in access, structure, and process, schooling among caste-like minorities, like schooling among dominant-group members, is also structured to prepare children for future employment. The main difference is that the minority employment is in the inferior sector of the economy; hence, the dominant group tends to design inferior and often segregated schooling for the minorities.

2.2.2. Minority Epistemology, Minority Educability, and the Desegregation Situation

The design and implementation of minority schooling do not, of course, fully account for the fact that, on the average, caste-like minorities do less well in school than members of other minorities or of the dominant group. The performance of caste-like minorities depends also on their own epistemology and coping responses, which are usually different from those of the dominant group. The epistemology of castelike minorities is often characterized by *a sense of enduring collective institutionalized discrimination*; (Lewis, 1979, 1981; Ogbu, 1974). Their perceptions and interpretations of how things work frequently lead them to conclude that they are given inferior and segregated education deliberately to prevent them from qualifying for the more desirable jobs open to members of the dominant group. They also are inclined to believe that they cannot easily improve their chances in the labor market merely through individual efforts to obtain school credentials. They believe that their school credentials do not translate into the same kinds of jobs and other economic and societal benefits that similar school credentials bring to whites. Consequently, caste-like minorities often resort to collective struggle to eliminate or raise the job ceiling against them and to abolish segregated education and achieve equal educational opportunity through equal access, curriculum content, and treatment. In addition, the minorities develop other coping responses, some of which are not necessarily conducive to conventional school success. The point to stress, however, is that castelike minorities' definition of the desegregation situation rests chiefly on their epistemology and their efforts to amelioriate and cope with their menial status.

3. THE CASE OF BLACK AMERICANS

3.1. The Significance of Racial Stratification

The issue of school desegregation has historically been associated with the education of racial minorities, especially black Americans. In most studies of the problem, however, race is treated as an important variable, but not racial stratification. Our cross-cultural studies suggest that it is not race *per se* but racial stratification that is the important variable (Ogbu, 1978a). *Race*, as the term is used in this chapter, is a folk category, a culturally defined concept. It is not a biological phenomenon in the sense of subspecies defined by gene frequencies (Loehlin, Lindzey, and Spuhler, 1975, p. 13; Ogbu, 1977).

Whether race is biologically or culturally defined, racial-group membership does not necessarily lead to differences in school performance; nor does it call for school desegregation. Children from different races (e.g., Caucasian Americans, Asian Americans, such as Chinese and Japanese) can equally do well in the same or separate schools (Coleman, 1966; Ogbu, 1983a). On the other hand, children from groups belonging to the same race may not do equally well in the same or separate schools. This can be seen by comparing Oriental Jews and Ashkenazi Jews in Israel (Ackerman, 1973; Ogbu, 1978a; Rosenfeld, 1973); and in Japan a similar disparity in school performance exists between the Burakumin and the non-Burakumin (DeVos and Wagatsuma, 1967; Ogbu, 1978a;

Shimahara, 1971). Significantly, the disparity between the Burakumin and the non-Burakumin disappears in the United States where the two groups are not stratified in dominant-minority relations (Ito, 1967). Thus, race is an important variable in educability and school desegregation only when racial groups are stratified so that the subordinate racial-group members, among other things, are denied equal educational opportunity (e.g., through segregated and inferior education) and equal rewards for educational efforts and accomplishments (e.g., through the job ceiling).

Yet, not all instances of racial stratification raise the issue of educability and school desegregation to the same magnitude as those in the black American situation. These problems are more pronounced when racial stratification approximates caste-like stratification, as in the case of black-white stratification in the United States. *Caste-like* is an analytic concept for describing stratification systems more rigid than class stratification but not necessarily a caste system in the classic Hindu sense (Ogbu, 1977, 1981a).

3.1.1. Social Change, Epistemology, and Desegregation

In order to understand current black epistemology and its relevance for blacks' definition of the desegregation situation, we need to take note of two features of the changes that have been taking place since the 1960s, especially with respect to the job ceiling: one is that increased black opportunities for employment above the job ceiling is not due to a change in the requirements of the industrial economy; rather, it is the result of social and political pressures from blacks and their supporters—the results of collective struggle; the second feature is that the changes in job opportunities have not evenly affected all segments of the black population.

The forces that have contributed to raise the job ceiling, that is, to increase black employment in professional, white-collar, and skilled jobs, have been almost all outside the economic system itself. They include executive action like the establishment of President Kennedy's Committee on Equal Employment Opportunities in 1961; legislative actions at state and federal levels, such as Title VII of the Civil Rights Act of 1964, and the Economic Opportunity Act of 1964; direct pressures on white business establishments, such as civil suits filed by NAACP, boycott, and similar protests by various civil rights groups; pressures from the U.S. Commission on Civil Rights on public and private institutions, including public schools and colleges and universities to hire blacks and other minorities at all levels of their job classification; and government encouragement of public and private institutions and businesses to adopt affirmative action policies and programs. These measures had some rippling effects on private industries and other business establishments, especially among those holding federal contracts. It has also become a good public relations strategy since the mid-1960s for white businesses to have some minority employees (Ogbu, 1978a; 1983a). These efforts were so successful that between 1960 and 1970 the number of blacks employed in two top-level categories—professional and technical workers—rose by 128%, although the increase for the general population was only 49%; and the number of black managers, officials, and proprietors increased by 100%, even though the general population experienced an increase of only 23% in the same job categories (Brimmer, 1974, p. 160; Ross, 1973). As reported by Freeman (1978), the average number of recruitment visits to predominantly black colleges by representatives of American corporations was only 4 in 1960. This rose to 50 in 1965 and then to 297 in 1970. To reiterate, these improved employment opportunities for blacks (unlike the course of change in white employment opportunities) were not the result of changes in the needs of the economic system or labor force requirements as perceived by the employers.

The other feature to be noted is that not all segments of the black population have experienced these improvements in employment opportunities. Deliberate government policies backed by legislation and other forces noted above have helped mainly middle-class blacks, especially young college-educated blacks. It is true that some legislations in the 1960s and 1970s (e.g., The Manpower Development and Training Act of 1962, The Economic Opportunity Act of 1964, The Emergency Employment Act of 1971, and The Comprehensive and Training Act of 1973) spawned a variety of job training programs for "the disadvantaged," among whom blacks are disproportionately represented (e.g., The Neighborhood Youth Corps, the Job Corps, Work Experience, Operation Mainstream, New Careers, the Concentrated Employment program; Work Incentive program, Job Opportunities In Business Sector or JOBS, etc.). The underlying assumptions of these programs attribute unemployment and menial employment of blacks and others similarly situated to their lack of education or skills and ability needed and rewarded, that is, human capital, in the labor force. Their effectiveness in improving the employment opportunities of "the disadvantaged" has long been questioned (Harrison, 1972; Levitan and Taggart, 1976). Moreover, these programs are favorite targets of criticisms by various politicians.

Few blacks attribute the higher unemployment rates of blacks to lack of education or to differential qualifications. Blacks ask why non-college-educated whites are more employable than non-college-educated blacks. They point out that exclusion of blacks with similar backgrounds to whites increases when the pool of jobs is small.

An adequate study of the desegregation situation will have to consider how such matters impact on the epistemologies of the major participants. In the next section we will explore briefly their possible impact on black epistemology, especially on how blacks define the desegregation situation and their subsequent responses.

3.2. Black Perspective on the Desegregation Situation

3.2.1. Segregation

We have suggested elsewhere, (Ogbu, 1974, 1978a, 1981b) on the basis of our ethnographic and cross-cultural studies of minority education, that blacks have developed an epistemology marked by what may be called a *collective institutional discrimination perspective*, because whites have long denied blacks equal educational opportunities and equal societal rewards (e.g., jobs and wages) commensurate with their educational accomplishments. We are not suggesting that a collective institutional discrimination perspective is the only feature of black epistemology. However, it is a dominant force that has made the question of access and quality education the overriding concern of blacks in school desegregation.

Nor are we suggesting that the concern for equality and social welfare is totally absent in the white population. In other words, there are overlapping interests between the black and white segments of American society. But these interests and epistemologies are not identical because of differences in actual experiences and in perceptions of the reasons for the differential experiences.

The discrepancy between societal beliefs or between white epistemology and white expectations and white treatment of blacks is illustrated by the exclusion of blacks from "industrial education" in the 1930s and from skilled jobs in war-related industries during World War II. That blacks are aware of and dislike the discrepancy is seen in their long-standing collective struggle to change the way whites treat them. The way blacks perceive and interpret the discrepancy is also evident in the way Benjamin Hooks, the director of the NAACP, recently explained the decrease in white participation in civil rights activities on the behalf of blacks. According to Hooks, white participation in civil rights activities was high in the 1960s because at that time blacks appeared to be demanding things that were not economically threatening to whites: the right to ride the bus, drink water from the fountain, and buy and eat hot dogs. "*Now*," however, he added,

> what we are after is different;: we want to reach an economic plateau. That is much different. People who supported us in our right to drink water from the fountain may not support us in our right to make the water fountain; those who supported us in our right to buy and eat hot dogs may not support us in our right to make hot dogs or be president of the hot dog company. There's a vast difference in our objectives. (Harris, 1983, p. 11A, emphasis added)

3.2.2. Education Desired, but Schools Distrusted

Blacks do not believe that their public school education is designed to educate their children as effectively as the schools educate white children. This perception and interpretation have resulted in a relationship between black people (not just individual blacks) and the public schools that is characterized by conflict and distrust. It is important in this analysis, however, not to confuse the attitudes of blacks toward education *per se* with their attitudes toward the public schools as a societal institution controlled by white people.

Historically, there have been many events in black–white relationships that have left blacks with the feeling that whites and the institutions they control, including the public schools, cannot be trusted. Blacks, for instance, view their initial exclusion from the public schools and subsequent segregation and inferior education as deliberately designed to prevent them from qualifying for more desirable jobs open to whites. Consequently, they have been fighting whites who control the schools and the schools themselves for better or "quality education." The impression we have gained from interviewing blacks of different social class backgrounds and from reading writings of blacks is that as a people, not just as individuals, blacks are more or less convinced that the public schools cannot be trusted to educate black children well.

An illustration of this distrust comes from our observation at a panel discussing the causes of overrepresentation of blacks in classes for the mentally retarded or special education classes. Blacks in the panel were more inclined to blame the schools, expressing dissatisfaction and frustration about the way schools treat black children, including the quality of instruction; they did not attribute the overrepresentation to biological characteristics of black children, to the home and family environments from which the children came, as white members of the panel were inclined to do.

Another illustration comes from our research in Stockton, California (1968–70). During this study we attended and tape-recorded all the public hearings on a local school desegregation plan. Black speakers were nearly unanimous in blaming the schools for the academic and behavioral problems of black students. In our interviews with local black leaders, including a local lawyer and a member of the schoolboard, and with parents and students, we found the same pervasive element of distrust and hostility. And case studies of school desegregation in other parts of the country suggest that the hostility and distrust is a nationwide phenomenon (see Clement and Livesay, 1980; Collins and Noblitt, 1979; Kirp, 1982; Kluger, 1977). That the distrust of the public schools is shared by middle-class blacks is evident in their writings about the school situation (see Bullock, 1970; Clark, 1965, 1971; *Freedomways*, 1968; Haskins, 1973; Wright, 1970). It is also shared by black school employees—teachers, counselors, and administrators—although the latter do not generally feel free to express their personal views openly; nevertheless, our ethnographic interviews reveal that they do not trust public school policies and practices toward black children.

We suggest that the nature of the black–school relationship may make it difficult for blacks to teach their children effectively and for the children to acquire the beliefs, values, and attitudes that support the educational system and its assumptions and practices. Specifically, it may make it difficult for the children to accept and internalize the schools' rules of behavior for achievement. Black children are also likely to be skeptical about what schools teach about American economic systems, especially the supporting beliefs, values, and attitudes. For these reasons, we think that in order to understand black children's school behavior in desegregated settings, we need to know more about what kinds of cultural knowledge, beliefs, and attitudes they bring with them to school, their origins and their relation to current behavior.

3.2.3. Collective Struggle

Hostility and distrust are not the only responses arising from black perceptions and interpretations of the public schools' treatment of blacks. Another is the more organized effort to change the way the schools treat blacks and their education; desegregation is one of these organized efforts. However, the school desegregation movement is also a part of a larger strategy used by blacks to attempt to break down the caste-like barriers against them. Blacks call these efforts "collective struggle," whereas whites call them "civil rights activities." Blacks have long used this strategy to force or convince whites to change some aspect of the racial stratification, such as to raise the job ceiling, to improve their schooling, and the like. The points to emphasize are (a) that blacks interpret segregated education as inferior education designed to prevent them from qualifying for the more desirable jobs and positions open to whites; and (b) that it is important to eliminate school segregation in order to achieve quality education for their children. That is, the primary objectives of school desegregation for blacks is to achieve quality education. Regardless of the beliefs or epistemology of social scientists and regardless of what their technically constructed instruments purport to measure, our understanding of the black perspective is that their primary interest in school desegregation is to achieve quality education that would enable their children to do better in school in the conventional sense: obtain higher school marks, better school credentials, and, eventually be able to get better jobs and wages. Their primary objective in demanding school desegregation is not to improve their self-concept or race relations, although they would welcome these additional benefits if they follow.

3.2.4. Desegregation

Prior to 1960 blacks wanted to desegregate the schools in the South primarily with three or four objectives in mind: to abolish the separate schools because these schools were unconstitutional and also symbolized inferior status of blacks; to enable black children to go to schools within a reasonable and convenient attendance area of distance like white children; to gain access to the same educational resources available to white children within the same community; and, ultimately, to improve their chances of school success. Under this circumstance, then, the school desegregation situation meant for blacks a situation or setting in which there were no separate schools designated by law specifically for blacks. Blacks and whites would attend the same schools within the attendance areas defined equally for convenience for both races. Furthermore, by attending the same schools as whites, desegregation would make black education more equal to white education by eliminating the differences in building and physical facilities, distance travelled by children to school, curriculum, and extracurricular activities, length of school year, teacher qualifications, and grading and promotion systems (Ashmore, 1954, pp. 109–110; Bell, 1972; Ogbu, 1978a, p. 70; Weinberg, 1977).

In the North, blacks also interpreted the desegregation situation more or less in the same manner. Although segregated urban schools were not established by law, blacks have generally presented evidence to show that the official role at one level or another was involved in the development of segregated schools or that the definition of attendance boundaries for the convenience of the child has been manipulated so as to segregate black and white children.

If one made a detailed and careful case study of desegregation—a study that would begin with blacks making a request to a school board to desegregate its schools or filing lawsuits to achieve the same goal, to actual reassignment of students—the researcher would find that the dominant concern of blacks is *equal education*. In our ethnographic research in Stockton, California, we were fortunate to study various phases of the school desegregation movement in that community, particularly between 1968 and 1977. The general impression emerging from a preliminary analysis of our data is that blacks and Mexican-Americans who supported desegregation did so primarily because they believed that desegregation would enable their children to receive the same kind of education as white children. The underlying black assumption in Stockton, San Francisco, and elsewhere is that the chances are greater that their children will receive equal or quality education if they attended the same classes with white children. Many parents said that in a desegregated school, classroom minority and white children would be exposed to the same curriculum materials and other resources and would most likely be treated alike by teachers and other school personnel.

Note, however, that the perspective on the desegregation situation given by these parents is not the same as that held by social scientists. For social scientists, black children attending integrated schools would be provided with an opportunity to interact in a mutually accepting manner with their white middle-class peers who would provide them with models of success in school and later life (Miller, 1983; Ogbu, 1978a, p. 71, 1978b, p. 10, 1979; see also U.S. Commission on Civil Rights, 1967, p. 106; U.S. Senate Commitee Report, 1972, p. 220).

In recent years some blacks appear to be changing their definition of the desegregation situation. This is because they have found that sending their children to attend schools with whites—to desegregated schools—has not led to quality education. Usually it has brought new problems or increased old ones. More black children are suspended; whites "flee" or leave the public schools; the schools respond, perhaps to prevent further white flight or to please the residual whites, by resegregating black and white children. The latter is done "legally" and "objectively" by increasing special education programs and classes for "the gifted" and "the retarded." White children dominate "the gifted," and blacks "the retarded." Kirp (1976, p. 602) sums up the situation in San Francisco as follows.

> Classes for the gifted, hastily expanded with the adoption of the Horseshoe Plan have a white enrollment proportion twice the district-wide average and a correspondingly small black enrollment. Blacks make up three-fifths, twice the district-wide average, of classes for the educable mentally retarded and educationally handicapped, traditional dumping grounds for difficult-to-manage or slow-learning pupils.

Because of such developments, some blacks no longer believe that quality education can be achieved merely by going to the same schools and the same classes with white children. Consequently, the desegregation situation now means not only going to the same schools and the same classes with whites but also not being resegregated.

REFERENCES

Ackerman, W. "Reforming" Israeli education. In M. Curtis and M. Chertoff (Eds.), *Israeli: Social Structure and Change*. New Brunswick, NJ: Dutton, 1973.

Adams, C., and Laurikietis, R. *The Gender Trap: A Closer Look at Sex Roles, Book 1: Education and Work*. New York: Academic Press, 1977.

Ashmore, H. S. *The Negro and The Schools*. Chapel Hill. The University of North Carolina Press, 1954.

Barry, H. A., Bacon, M. K., and Child, I. A cross-cultural survey of some sex differences in socialization. *Journal of Abnormal and Social Psychology*, 1959, 55, 327–332.

Bell, D. A. Integration: A no win policy for blacks? *Inequality in Education*, 1972, 11, 35–44.

Berg, I. *Education and Jobs: The Great Training Robbery*. Boston: Beacon Press, 1969.

Berger, P. L., and Luckmann, T. *The Social Construction of Reality: A Treatise in the Sociology of Knowledge*. Garden City, NY: Doubleday, 1966.

Blair, P. M. *Job Discrimination and Education: An Investment Analysis*. New York: Praeger, 1971.

Bohannon, P. *Justice and Judgment Among the Tiv*. London: Oxford University Press, 1957.

Bowles, S., and Gintis, H. *Schooling in Capitalist Society: Educational Reform and the Contradictions of Economic Life*. New York: Basic Books, 1976.

Brimmer, A. F. Economic development in the black community. In E. Ginzburg and R. M. Solow (Eds.), *The Great Society: Lessons for the Future* (pp. 146–163). New York: Basic Books, 1974.

Bullock, H. A. *A History of Negro Education in the South: From 1619 to the Present.* New York: Praeger, 1970.

Clark, K. B. *Dark Ghetto: Dilemmas of Social Power.* New York: Harper, 1965.

Clark, K. Education in the ghetto: A human concern. In A. H. Passow (Ed.), *Urban Education in the 1970s.* New York: Teachers College Press, 1971.

Clement, D. C., and Harding, J. R. Social distinctions and emergent student groups in a desegregated school. *Anthropology and Education Quarterly,* 1978, 9 (4), 272–282.

Clement, D. C., and Livesay, J. M. *The Development of Black Community Influence in a Southern School District.* Unpublished manuscript, Department of Anthropology, University of North Carolina at Chapel Hill, 1980.

Clement, D. C., Eisenhart, M., and Harding, J. R. *Moving Closer: An Ethnography of a Southern Desegregated School. Final Report, Field Studies in Urban Desegregated Schools.* The National Institute of Education Contract Grant #400-76, 1978.

Cohen, Y. A. The state systems, schooling, and cognitive and motivational patterns. In N. K. Shimahara and A. Scrupski (Eds.), *Social Forces and Schooling: Anthropological and Sociological Perspectives.* New York: David McKay, 1975.

Coleman, J. S. *Equality of Educational Opportunity.* Washington, DC: U.S. Government Printing Office, 1966.

Collins, T. W. and Noblitt, G. W. Stratification and Resegregation: The Case of Cross-Over High School, Memphis, Tenn. Final Report, The National Institute of Education Contract Grant #400-76-009. Washington, DC: The National Institute of Education, 1979.

The Daily California, 1976, vol. vii, no. 193, October 14. Students favoring job-oriented majors. p. 1.

Doeringer, P., and Piore, M. *Internal Labor Markets.* Lexington: D.C. Heath, 1971.

Dore, R. P. *The Diploma Disease.* Berkeley: The University of California Press, 1976.

DeVos, G. A., and Wagatsuma, H. (Eds.), *Japan's Invisible Race.* Berkeley: The University Press, 1967.

Elson, R. M. *Guardians of Tradition: American Schoolbooks of the Nineteenth Century.* Lincoln, NE: The University of Nebraska Press, 1964.

Franklin, R. *Corporations, Consumerism and Education: The Linkage of Schools and the Economic Structure of American Capitalism.* Unpublished manuscript, School of Education, University of California, Berkeley, 1982.

Frazier, N., and Sadker, M. *Sexism in School and Society.* New York: Harper, 1973.

Freedomways: A Quarterly Review of the Freedom Movement, 1968, 8(4), Fall. Special issue: The crisis in education and the changing Afro-American community.

Freeman, R. B. *Black Elite: The New Market for Highly Educated Black Americans.* New York: McGraw-Hill, 1978.

Gordon, D. M. *Theories of Poverty and Underemployment.* Lexington: D.C. Heath, 1972.

Hagerty, B. *An Ethnographic Study of an Experimental Learning Program—A Preliminary Approach to Evaluation.* Unpublished manuscript, School of Education, The University of California, Berkeley, no date.

Hansell, S., and Karweit, N. Curricular placement, friendship networks and status attainment, in J. Epstein and N. Karweit (Eds.), *Friends in School.* New York: Academic Press, 1983.

Harty, S. *Hucksters in the Classroom.* Washington, DC: Center for Study of Responsive Law, 1979.

Harris, J. Issue: Black America. *USA Today,* January 20, 1983, p. A11.

Harrison, B. *Education, Training and the Urban Ghetto.* Baltimore, MD: Johns Hopkins University Press, 1972.

Haskins, K., You have got no right to put a kid out of school. *The Urban Review, 8* (4):273–287, 1973.

Ito, H. Japan's outcastes in the United States. In G. A. DeVos and H. Wagatsuma (Eds.), *Japan's Invisible Race*. Berkeley: The University of California Press, 1967.

Jencks, C. *Inequality*. New York: Basic Books, 1972.

Kahn, T. The economics of inequality. In L. A. Ferman, J. L. Kornbluh, and J. A. Miller (Eds.), *Negroes and Jobs*. Ann Arbor, MI: The University of Michigan Press, 1968.

Katzman, D. M. *Before the Ghetto: Black Detroit in the Nineteenth Century*. Urbana, IL: University of Illinois Press, 1973.

Kirp, D. L. Race, politics, and the courts: School desegregation in San Francisco. *Harvard Educational Review*, 1976, *46* (4), 572–611.

Kirp, D. *Just Schools: The Idea of Racial Equality in American Education*. Berkeley, CA: University of California Press, 1982.

Kluger, R. *Simple Justice*. New York: Vintage Books, 1977.

LeCompte, M. Learning to Work: The Hidden Curriculum of the Classroom. *Anthropology and Education Quarterly*, 1978, *9* (1), 22–27.

Levin, H. M. Education and earnings of blacks and the Brown decision. In M. V. Namorato (Ed.), *Have We Overcome? Race Relations Since Brown*. Jackson, MI: University of Mississippi Press, 1978.

LeVine, R. A. *Dreams and Deeds: Achievement Motivation in Nigeria*. Chicago, IL: University of Chicago Press, 1967.

Levitan, S. A., and Taggart, R. *The Promise of Greatness*. Cambridge, MA: Harvard University Press, 1976.

Lewis, A. *Power, Poverty and Education: An Ethnography of Schooling in an Israeli Town*. Forest Grove, Oregon: Turtledove, 1979.

Lewis, A. Minority Education in Sharonia, Israel, and Stockton, California: Comparative Analysis. *Anthropology and Education Quarterly*, 1981, *12* (1), 30–50.

Lochlin, J. C., Lindzey, G., and Spuhler, J. N. *Race Differences in Intelligence* San Francisco: Freeman, 1975.

Miller, N. Peer relations in desegregated schools. In Epstein, J., and N. Karweit, (Eds.), *Friends in School*. New York: Academic Press, 1983.

Murdock, G. P., and Whiting, J. W. M. Cultural determinants of parental attitudes: The relationship between social structure, particularly the family, and parental behavior. In M. J. E. Sean (Ed.), *Problems of Infancy and Childhood*. New York: Josiah Macy, Jr., Foundation, 1951.

National Academy of Sciences & National Academy of Engineering, *Science and Mathematics in the Schools: Report of a Convocation*. Washington, DC: National Academy Press, 1982.

New York Times. Vocational schools are on the upswing. November 11, 1979, p. 28.

New York Times. Business schools fear shortage of teachers. September 9, 1981, pp. 19, 29.

Newsweek. What do diplomas mean? January 9, 1978, pp. 65–66.

Newsweek. The golden passport. May 14, 1979, pp. 110–112.

Newsweek. Education and the economy. November 17, 1980.

Newsweek. The Ph.D. meat market. February 4, 1980, p. 74.

Oakland Tribune. Schools Adjusting to Computer Use, October 25, 1982, p. A-9.

Oakland Tribune. U.S. Sues Cicero, Illinois, for Discriminating Against Blacks, January 22, 1983, p. C-1.

Oakland Tribune. Schools grapple with the issues of computers in the classrooms, February 2, 1983, p. C-3.

Ogbu, J. U. *The Next Generation: An Ethnography of Education in an Urban Neighborhood*. New York: Academic Press, 1974.

Ogbu, J. U. Racial Stratification and Education: The Case of Stockton, California. *ICRD Bulletin*, 1977, *12* (3), 1–26.

Ogbu, J. U. *Minority Education and Caste: The American System in Cross-Cultural Perspective.* New York: Academic Press, 1978a.

Ogbu, J. U. School desegregation in racially stratified communities—A problem of congruence. *Anthropology and Education Quarterly,* 1978b, *9* (4), 290–292.

Ogbu, J. U. Desegregation, integration and interaction theory: An appraisal. In M. L. Wax (Ed.), *Desegregated Schools: An Intimate Portrait Based on Five Ethnographic Studies.* Washington, DC: The National Institute of Education, 1979.

Ogbu, J. U. Education, clientage, and social mobility: Caste and social change in the United States and Nigeria. In G. D. Berreman (Ed.), *Social Inequality: Comparative and Developmental Approaches.* New York: Academic Press.

Ogbu, J. U. Black education: A cultural-ecological perspective. In H. P. McAdoo (Ed.), *Black Families.* Beverly Hills, CA: Sage, 1981b.

Ogbu, J. U. School Ethnography: A Multilevel Approach. *Anthropology and Education Quarterly,* 1981c, *12* (1), 1–20.

Ogbu, J. U. Minority status and schooling in plural societies. *Comparative Education Review, 27* (2), June 1983a.

Ogbu, J. U. Schooling in the inner city: A cultural-ecological perspective. *Society,* 1983b, *21* (1): 75–79.

Piore, M. J. Notes for a theory of labor market stratification. In R. C. Edwards, M. Reich, and D. M. Gordon (Eds.), *Labor Market Segmentation.* Lexington, MA: D. C. Heath, 1975.

Rosenfeld, E. *A Strategy for Prevention of Developmental Retardation Among Disadvantaged Israeli Preschoolers* (Research Report No. 175), Jerusalem: The Henrietta Szold Institute, 1973.

Ross, R. A. *Negro Employment in the South: Vol. 3. State and Local Employments.* Washington, DC: U.S. Department of Labor, 1973.

Ruddle, K., and Chesterfield, R. *Education for Traditional Food Procurement in the Orinoco Delta.* Berkeley: University of California Press, 1977.

San Francisco Sunday Examiner/Chronicle, Employers join educators to ugprade math, science, February 14, 1982.

Schultz, T. W. Investment in human capital, *American Economic Review,* 1961, *51,* 1–17.

Science (editorial). Engineering education and national policy. Oct. 8, 1982.

Scrupski, A. The Social system of the school. In N. K. Shimahara and A. Scrupski (Eds.), *Social Forces and Schooling, Anthropological and Sociological Perspectives.* New York: David McKay, 1975.

Shimahara, N. *Burakumin: A Japanese Minority and Education.* The Hague: N. Martinus Nijhoff, 1971.

Spindler, G. D. The transmission of culture. In G. D. Spindler, (Ed.), *Education and Culture.* New York: Holt, 1974.

Sutton-Smith, B., and Roberts, J. M. The cross-cultural and psychological study of games. In G. Luschen (Ed.), *The Cross-Cultural Analysis of Games.* Champaign, IL: Stipes, 1970.

Thernstrom, S. *The Other Bostonians: Poverty and Progress in the American Metropolis, 1880– 1970.* Cambridge, MA: Harvard University Press, 1973.

U.S. Commission on Civil Rights. *Racial Isolation in the Public Schools: A Report, Vol. 1.* Washington, DC: U.S. Government Printing Office, 1967.

U.S. District Court for Northern California. *Larry P. vs. Wilson Riles: Opinion.* San Francisco, CA: Mimeo, 1979.

U.S. Senate, Select Committee on Equal Educational Opportunity. *Toward Equal Educational Opportunity.* Washington, DC: U.S. Government Printing Office, 1972.

University of California Bulletin. U.C. sets different salary scales for business administration and engineering. Feb. 22, 1982.

Waller, W. *The Sociology of Teaching*. New York: Wiley, 1967 (original work published 1932).

Weinberg, M. *A Chance to Learn: A History of Race and Education in the United States*. New York: Cambridge University Press, 1977.

Weisbrod, B. A. Education and investment in human capital. In D. M. Levine and M. J. Bane (Eds.), *The "Inequality" Controversy: Schooling and Distributive Justice*. New York: Basic Books, 1975.

Wilcox, K. *Schooling and Socialization for Work Roles*. Unpublished doctoral dissertation, Department of Anthropology, Harvard University, 1978.

Wright, Nathan (Ed.), *What Black Educators Are Saying*. New York: Hawthorn, 1970.

Chapter 2

School Desegregation and the 'National Community'

Gerald D. Suttles

What can an ethnographer, usually in solo practice, tell us about such an open-ended, volatile, and prolonged process as school desegregation in America? Obviously some have already risen to the occasion, demonstrating the versatility of this approach. In what follows, I hope to build on that accomplishment. The aim, however, is not simply to summarize the findings and methods of these studies or to recommend specific procedures. Because ethnography is almost always a highly localized effort, the pressing need is for a broader macro-sociological framework that does three things for the ethnographer: (a) links findings to those of other studies, only some of which are ethnographic; (b) provides a mapping of relevant variables that places these studies in a comparative and cumulative research tradition; and (c) directs ethnographic studies to those strategic areas that have been neglected and are especially appropriate to its intensive, *in situ* approach.

My intention, then, is to provide such a general framework, but in doing so I will probably depart from precedent by emphasizing three assumptions about school desegregation. First, school desegregation is best viewed as the continuation of several social movements that seek to negotiate the status claims of primordial groups.[1] That is to say, it is not simply a movement to improve education in the narrow sense of increasing student abilities or the capacity of

---

[1] I use the term *primordial* to indicate groups who claim a common origin "in the past." Often, this claim is largely fictive and corroborated only by references to similarities of dialect, regional birth, or selected items of appearance or belief. The advantages of such a term is its comprehensiveness, including in one stroke what we often separately call ethnic, religious, regional, or descent groups.

Gerald D. Suttles • Department of Sociology, University of Chicago, Chicago, IL 60637.

students to compete in an open class system. It is as well a social debate of national dimensions in which various primordial groups seek to exercise their political will by redefining their relative status and their membership in the national community itself. This is one of the reasons that debates over school desegregation have a tendency to enlarge themselves to include a host of tangential issues, including access to jobs, community control, and what I will call the founding myths of national membership.

A second reason for this decision to generalize over a wide range of issues is the continuing imbalance between American judicial and political processes. Judicial initiative on school desegregation has persisted for over 25 years. Within the political party system, however, the debate remains unresolved. Indeed, political support for school desegregation is so soft that is practically invites opposition. The persistence of political irresolution has created a profound ambiguity that permits groups to open and reopen almost any issue that they think bears on school desegregation. This, I suppose, is one reason there are so many studies that seek to prove that desegregation is "good" for school children rather than simply an integral element of civic life in a democratic society. Supporters and opponents of school desegregation continue to grasp for evidence to support their claims because political leadership so frequently teeters on the edge of support or opposition.

Third, public schools in America are only weakly differentiated from the local community. This is so not only because of their accountability to client representatives and the interpenetration of youth and school cultures, but also because schools are susceptible to the episodic emergence of novel efforts to influence them from a host of directions: to include school prayer, to teach creation science, to expunge controversial literature, and to define the historic contributions of different primordial groups. Sometimes a school staff is able to neutralize the board by controlling appointments, co-opt parents through the PTA, and contain the student subculture with extracurricular activities (Bidwell, 1965). But the onset of school desegregation almost invariably tests the boundaries of school systems and shows them highly vulnerable. What happens, however, seems to be extremely variable and circumstantial. Sometimes it is the occasion for the emergence of new and demogogic leadership; a Louise Day Hicks, a William Poe, or a George Wallace. But it can also be the occasion for parental initiative motivated out of a simple concern that school desegregation be a relatively peaceful process.[2]

Taken together, these observations move me toward a macrosociological

---

[2]Crain (1968) told us that some Southern political leaders conceded to local school desegregation because they did not want the dispute over it to interfere with regional plans for economic development. The room for "seepage" between the local school and wider community may depend primarily on the degree to which local leaders can head off opportunities by finding something like local development that creates a unified front among them.

approach to school desegregation. By this I mean a perspective that assumes that the outer perimeter of influences is the dominant one, that social movements and primordial contests for status tend to set the agenda for judicial institutions and political parties, that the latter tend to define much of the situation for local communities, and that the schools are buffeted from every quarter and possess only a limited capacity for self-regulation. In approaching this topic I will follow the same general pattern, starting with the broader picture and working my way inward toward the local school and community. Implicitly, I am suggesting that ethnographers do the same in formulating their studies if they are to serve as more than case studies.

1. STUDIES OF THE GENERAL CHARACTER OF AMERICAN SCHOOLS

In reviewing the literature on school desegregation, I am persistently surprised at the positive expectations of researchers.[3] It is expected that minority performance will increase, that interracial relations will improve, and that local civic life will quicken. Actually, in most instances I would have expected the reverse. After decades of pervasive school segregation, there is little reason to expect agreeable interracial relations in the short term. A strong academic social climate is always difficult to achieve in our public schools, where problems of social control are intensified (Bidwell, 1965; Waller, 1932). Civic cooperation usually rests on durable relations and some form of local patriotism.

Accordingly, it is with some perplexity that I find that most studies of school desegregation show some modest positive effect on interracial relations and achievement if not on civic cooperation. Of course, there are some substantial differences, but the outstanding finding seems to be their unevenness with respect to desegregation itself (McConahay, 1981; St. John, 1981; Schofield, 1978). It is possible that one reason for this is that we—and I include myself here—have forgotten what our schools are like before or after desegregation, that we have assigned to the school too instrumental and pedagogic a role on the one hand, and overemphasized the unity of the social world of the student on the other hand. To get a handle on this, it is useful to go back and reexamine some of the charter studies of schools before desegregation became such an overwhelming issue. Waller's (1932) work is a good starting point not only because it is synthetic, but because it is informed by the kind of long-term personal experience

[3]Like St. John's (1981), my reading of the literature indicates that social scientists have been so pro-integrationist that they have persistently looked for positive findings. This is not at all inconsistent with the parallel tendency of social scientists to view any positive finding as suspect unless it survives persistent reanalysis and new controls. In a discipline without a strong theoretical paradigm, "debunking" has a strong appeal and causes persistent apprehension.

that ethnographers rely on. On inspection, Waller's work is permeated with observations on the weaknesses of the academic subculture in American schools. It competes effectively for the attention of only a minority of students, most of whom are more attracted by alternative avenues of popularity and associational choice. This sort of internal differentiation seems built into the American conception of a "common school." It was designed not just for the purpose of maximizing academic achievement but for providing a shared civic experience as well. In this respect, the common school was more nearly a form of a nation-building than academic preparation alone. What students got out of the school was a shared sense of membership, a familiarity with some elements of popular culture and bits and pieces of national myth and ceremony (Janowitz, 1980).[4] Some, of course, became well educated but the academic subculture always included only a portion of the student body. The social worlds of the school were intensely experienced, but most were only lightly shaped by the educational institution itself. In such an accommodating environment it is to be expected that students would carry along with them many of their initial differences while acquiring only a smattering of common knowledge and national culture.

Gordon's (1957) study on this topic remains one of the most persuasive. It is as if school staff found it necessary to leave unchallenged fundamental differences among students in order to accomplish a modest level of generalized cognitive and civic education. There are differences, of course, especially in the degree of staff professionalization and bureaucratization and their contributions to school autonomy (Bidwell, 1965). In some of our larger cities, schools became highly differentiated and more able to establish a stratification system emphasizing academic excellence (Street, 1969). Still, it was primarily a system that facilitated educational attainment; it did not concentrate its incentives so as to create an intensive and pervasive educational experience.

Despite its shortcomings, such a school system did function to reduce differences in educational attainment among ethnic and racial groups, at least up to a point. The most conclusive evidence on this is the recent work of Stanley Lieberson (1980), who shows that by the early 1930s differences in educational attainment among Northern-born whites, Northern-born blacks, and Northern-born descendents from Southern, Eastern, and Central Europe had practically disappeared except for somewhat higher levels of attainment among Jews. It was after this time that differences between Northern-born blacks and all the other groups began to widen.[5]

---

[4]Janowitz suggested that this effort at civic education may have been reasonably effective when it was aimed at immigrant populations who had effectively "burned their bridges" in coming to America. The situation is drastically changed for more recent immigrants who more nearly resemble commuters with continuing contact with their place of origin.

[5]It would appear from Lieberson's findings that white hostility toward blacks increased across the board as their numbers grew outside the South—in the home market before 1920, in educational opportunity and the job market by 1920.

The relative improvement of black school performance in the non-S
came to an end as their numbers outside the South markedly increased dur.ng
and after World War I. Lieberson's very reasonable explanation is that hostility
toward, and the segregation of, blacks was essentially a response to the growing
threat they posed in the competition for jobs, housing, and institutional dominance. Prejudice, then, is not simply a uniform and persistent feeling based on
racial distinctions and historic origins.

Lieberson's conception of latent prejudice aroused by increases in the black
population does not fit well in either our older conceptions of ethnic groups as
distinctive carriers of their own culture and self-image or more recent conceptions
of internal colonialism (Blauner, 1972; Ogbu, 1974, 1978). The first tends to
forecast a gradual waning of group differences over time, but what Lieberson's
findings show is an initial decline in educational differences followed by a sharp
reversal. The internal colonialism approach assumes that there is a real—not
socially constructed—difference in how minority groups are incorporated into
the national society. Such a view, however, would not lead us to expect either
a reversal or initial decline in educational differences between blacks and whites.
The possibility of a more socially constructed conception of group membership
and status has an obvious attraction in coming to grips with such a fluctuating
pattern of educational attainment. The internal colonialism argument provides a
useful way of opening up this topic.

2. THE FOUNDING MYTHS OF NATIONAL MEMBERSHIP

The most articulate and empirically grounded of the studies using the
internal colonialism approach to schooling and segregation is that of Ogbu (1974).
Distinguishing between immigrant and subordinate minorities, he states that the
"former are characterized by high success in school whereas the latter are marked
by failure" (Ogbu, 1974, p. 253). Subordinate groups—by which he means
blacks, Mexicans, and Indians—feel themselves defeated from the start. Immigrant groups share a self-fulfilling sense of self-determination. Essentially, the
distinction rests on the degree of voluntarism in the history of minority arrival
in the country. Certainly, Ogbu finds that blacks and Mexican Americans often
see themselves as people coerced by circumstances rather than willing members
of the national community.[6] If one takes this distinction literally, however, it
tends to break down on the basis of historical analysis. As Alexander (1980)
points out, nation-building practically everywhere has involved substantial coercion without necessarily being accompanied by persistent ethnic fragmentation.

[6]However, it should be noted that the self-classification Ogbu reported for Mexicans is somewhat
divergent on this point. Moreover, those whose presence in the country could be considered the
most involuntary—that is, those native born or the descendents of native born—seem the most
likely to classify themselves as members of the national community.

Indeed a literal reading of the distinction would lead to the classification of the Mormons or residents of the Confederate States as subordinate minorities, not to mention the Vietnamese or World War II refugees.[7]

What seems to make the difference, then, is not so much the actual history of minority groups as the founding myths of national membership. It is mythic history, selected, elaborated, and dramatized elements of history, that requires analysis here. The fact that it is taken as cognitive certainty is what makes this form of prejudice so slippery a phenomenon, as it loses its most direct forms of expression to reoccur in ones that seem downright humane, sympathetic, or scientific.

Ogbu's study of several different ethnic groups in Stockton is especially revealing on this point. Competing definitions of national membership are most immediately expressed in the taxonomy of racial and ethnic classification he reports (Ogbu, 1974, pp. 40–41). Diverse groups, presumably of European origin, present themselves as "American," "whites," "taxpayers," and "Anglos." The inclusiveness and interchangeability of these terms indicate their unity and their claim to full societal membership as a single race, as contributors to the corporate community and as members of the "core solidarity" (Alexander, 1980).[8] Among Ogbu's Bergersiders, terminological usage is more complex and less certain. The term *Mexican American* lays claim to membership in the national community whereas *Spanish American* seems to establish membership among *whites* and the founding community. *Chicano*, however, asserts separate membership both racially and nationally. Indeed, it seems to imply a pan-national membership defined by descent group alone. Ogbu does not report anyone's using the term *Afro-American*, a term that would seem to be comparable to

---

[7]Indeed, a host of U.S. groups could be conceived of as subordinate minorities: Tory Nationalists, indentured servants, Appalachians, etc. Incidentally, some relatively isolated and distinctive groups of whites do seem to show patterns of school behavior and achievement not that different from that of blacks and Indians (Ellis, 1980; Gazeway, 1974) whereas some blacks, like the West Indians, show high levels of entrepreneural success (Light, 1972). Ellis' study is particularly revealing because it compares two groups of whites with the same early history, of almost identical extraction, but with very different recent careers of economic and educational attainment.

Of course one can always adjust the internal colonialism argument so that educational and occupational failures become the defining characteristic of subordinate groups (i.e., their failure becomes an indication of their subordination), but then it becomes a circular argument.

[8]Alexander did not directly address the mythic dimensions of the core solidarity. However, it is clear that the central thrust of his paper was to emphasize the social construction of national solidarities in general. Undoubtedly, such myths are based on facts, which is one reason for their plausibility. But the facts are selective and incomplete. What stands out in the case of the early New Englanders and Virginians is the extent to which they have remained useful to us in footnoting and accounting for our differences from other societies—usually differences that have either been flattering or at least convenient. Baltzell (1980) explored some of these developments by showing how the traditions of Boston and Philadelphia still inform our political struggles.

Mexican-American. Instead the terms *colored, Negro,* and *black* are used alternatively, apparently indicating degrees of claimed parity with whites without seeming to assert a common membership in the founding community. Ogbu reports other elements of this taxonomy in some detail and clearly there are some local variants that differ from usage in other communities, say Chicago.

However, the overall pattern is very nearly what we would expect on the basis of the more obvious myths of national membership. These myths have always emphasized the Northern European flight from religious persecution, the establishment of the first effective communities in Virginia and Massachusetts,[9] the taming of the frontier, and the closure and defense of national boundaries. Elsewhere (Gronbjerg *et al.*, 1978) I have argued that dramatic military service, capped by World War I, was the basis for reinstating Southerners, at least white ones. The New Deal and World War II expanded these myths to include the new immigrants from Southern, Eastern, Central Europe, and paradoxically, the Japanese.[10] By no means does it appear easy to alter the boundaries of these incorporative myths, as will be evident to blacks who have made an extraordinary effort to accomplish mythic change by emphasizing Afro-American history as the basis of black pride. What seem to be required are selective and dramatic contributions to national solidarity during periods of crises: military service[11] (especially in wartime), unionization and worker mobilization during depression, heroic expansion of the frontier, or expansion of the national boundaries. It is possible that the Civil Rights Movement itself will provide some basis for similar heroic judgments in the future, although continued resistance to making Martin Luther King's birthday a national holiday indicates some of the obstacles. In any case, it would appear that some historic distance is essential to such a heroic enlargement of the past.[12]

I do not mean to suggest by this that there is some inevitable, linear trend toward an enlargement of American founding myths. The result may be otherwise, with retribalization, pan-racism, or some other form of separatism winning out. Ogbu's work and that of others (Isaacs, 1981) show nascent movements in this direction. Nor should one conclude that such an expansion of incorporative

[9]The emphasis given the Puritans in our rememberance of Thanksgiving is revealing because they were apparently outnumbered by the more fun-loving Anglicans in the Plymouth Colony.

[10]What is most paradoxical about the national inclusion of the Japanese is that it seems to have been extended to all Orientals. One way of thinking about this is to recognize that the previous exclusion of them had been based on their classification as *Oriental* rather than anything very specific about the Japanese as against, say, the Chinese.

[11]One of the tragedies of the unpopular Vietnam War was the inability of blacks to emerge from it as heroic defenders of the nation state. Indeed, the entire history of black military service seems to have been a repeated tragedy of being at the wrong place at the wrong time.

[12]In the future, it would seem likely that other ethnic groups will have to use the Civil Rights Movement as a way of "footnoting" their claims to status, just as diverse groups now use the statements of Jefferson, Madison, etc., to footnote their claims.

myths simply erases group boundaries and distinctive reputations. Some threshold of civic membership does seem to be essential; the Mormons as "latter day" pioneers, the Japanese as long suffering patriots, the Cubans as our "most recent economic miracle." These recent, celebrated instances of collective accomplishment seem to bring group consciousness into sharper relief, setting a higher standard than that expected of "ordinary Americans."[13] Such a fresh (and imperiled?) awareness of group gains seems to impart a sense of transcendence—the conviction that one is moving in union with others toward some "higher goal."[14] Schooling and mobility in general require considerable discipline and self-sacrifice. Only the most doctrinaire economist of human resources can believe that the individual profit motive will move people to make the effort. Something like group patriotism seems to be involved, but it is group patriotism that is informed by recent reassurance.[15]

Undoubtedly, the symbolism of these myths of national membership is infinitely complicated and compounded with racial and ethnic identities that extend beyond the American experience.[16] But basically one suspects that we have here another of those contrastive structures so common in the analysis of symbols. The native-born whites provide the benchmark against which others are compared. If and when other groups are incorporated in one of these myths, they may be seen as "better than," the "same as," or "less than" this benchmark.

[13]Interestingly, Ogbu's findings show that minorities expect no more than ordinary school achievement from native whites.

[14]John Dewey, of course, would argue that there must be some linkage between individual and collective aspirations for education to surpass brute memorization.

[15]I suppose that something like this is aimed at by those who emphasize "black pride" but this seems to mean singling out some long-standing element of group reputation (athletic achievement) rather than a distinctive and often exceptional element (litigiousness) that contributes to group mobility. Anderson (1979) observed that many young blacks have very high self-expectations but that these expectations are not based on any distinctive collective instrumentality. However, it should be noted that Gurin and Epps (1975) did find among college blacks clear evidence of field choices that are aimed to further the collective goals of blacks.

[16]In particular, it seems that the reputation of the Jews and overseas Chinese must be regarded as an international accomplishment. Partly, this must be due to the fact that they are an international people. But in the case of the Jews, there seems to be a special relationship to Christians; for Jews the prospect of assimilation has usually involved not simply the adoption of another culture, but the judgment of their own as inferior. Thus, their persistence as an ethnic group over such a vast time is more understandable as is certain elements of their identity that seem to be a kind of inversion of the reputation of Christians.

Practically all of the "middleman minorities" who have made exceptional educational or economic accomplishments seem to be (a) groups with a claim to a "high culture" and (b) groups with a written language that allows them some control over their history. As Goody (1968) pointed out, a written language "objectifies" group memory in a way that oral traditions do not. Bonacich (1973) attempted an alternative interpretation of these groups, but her model seems unable to explain their initial ambivalence to their host society. My argument is that this ambivalence stems from a "documented" sense of their superiority to the host society.

Recent and exceptional mythic accomplishments—especially those against the odds—may provide a strong sense of group transcendence. Long-term, more ordinary mythic accomplishment, for example, the steady labor of Eastern Europeans, seem to liken the group to native-born whites.[17] What stands out in the case of those groups Ogbu calls "subordinate minorities" is the lack of a clear incorporative myth shared both inside and outside the minority and the continuation of competing myths of exclusion. It is not to be expected that this situation will resolve itself gradually without some circumstantial "evidence" of mythic proportions.

At one level these myths of national membership are very general and change only crescively. Yet, they do change, and for studies of school desegregation they provide the most obvious source of the cultural set that gets translated into a psychological set where minority behavior is selectively singled out for mutual characterization. These same folk beliefs also figure into the selection and evaluation of what we mean by equal-status relations. Much of the research on equal-status relations is marred by the assumption that socioeconomic background is the perceived marker of status, rather than examining this problem from the vantage point of the cultural filters operating between minority groups.

This incorporative process bears some resemblance to what Glazer and Moynihan (1963) referred to as the "group process," that is, a queue of primordial groups whose movement toward fuller membership is largely incremental but occasionally punctuated with dramatic instances of recognized "national service." But it differs in the relative importance of the role played by the core solidarity in defining and recognizing "national service."

3. IMPLEMENTATION OF SCHOOL DESEGREGATION

Although these incorporative myths seldom change rapidly, it appears to me that in the United States they have been increasingly formulated within a more voluntaristic vocabulary. That is, group differences are discussed as the outcome of collective experiences rather than as ineffable essences or heritable genes. In some ways this may be a product of the enormous publicity given debates over school desegregation and the disadvantage this works against those who express their prejudgment in a brute and simplistic manner.

[17]Sowell's (1981, 1983) recent work on American ethnic groups is interesting, because it takes as literal history these mythic accounts. Certainly, there has to be some empirical evidence for this sort of mythic construction and, as with all myths, they survive best when they become self-fulfilling prophecies. But there is an interactive element here. Not only must there be some evidence of distinctive group ability, it has to be selected out and given credence by others. In this respect, Sowell's book is a compilation of those myths that have survived to become prophecies.

Debates over school desegregation in Charlotte, Boston, Los Angeles, or Chicago are national events that exercise all the manipulative powers of the mass media. The result is not only a highly politicized issue, but a decision-making process in which private deals are difficult. Indeed, any hint of such deals seems simply to increase the publicity. The frequent outcome then seems to be a rather legalistic and mechanical approach. In the South, such an approach might work because large consolidated districts reduced the threat to whites. For the same reason desegregation could be readily extended by state boards of education to many small towns where minorities constituted a low proportion of the population. In large cities or communities with an increasing minority population, there has been strong resistance and progressive reliance on court orders. The accomplishment in the South and smaller communities should not be belittled, but it would appear that further efforts at school desegregation will be tried where they are least likely to succeed:[18] in districts already heavily segregated, in districts with an increasing minority population, and in districts where invasion and succession have already stiffened racial attitudes. For court action to take place violations must precede it, and this calls for substantial backtracking rather than simply the avoidance of further segregation.

I know of no ethnographic effort directly aimed to link court action and its specific consequences.[19] Two outcomes, however, seem to be frequently reported. First, community leaders take no action lest their efforts be interpreted as an admission of past, intentional segregation. Second, because the courts (or state boards of education) are seen as external to the community, opposition to court-ordered desegregation is easy to arouse although not necessarily that easy to organize and control. Partly this seems to be due to the fragmentation (an invisibility) of local leaders. But it is also difficult to get someone to sponsor openly what is sure to be seen as the cause of bigotry. The dynamics of the situation, however, seem very difficult to anticipate. The Charlotte case is particularly interesting because it moved from organizations primarily opposed to integration to organizations aimed to mollify the consequences of desegregation (Barrows, 1973). Both causes were an occasion for the emergence of new leaders rather than the arousal of those already in office. One suspects that considerable difference may exist among communities in their civic culture and capacity to manage local conflict. The relative lack of initiative shown by small communities may arise because of a false sense of their own inadequacy or the hopelessness

---

[18] As Coleman (1981) pointed out, the legal approach outside the South is on such weak grounds that it not only invites opposition but cannot very easily draw to it public support of any breadth. Indeed it appears that support for school integration is not that overwhelming within the black community itself (Wilson *et al.*, 1973).

[19] Crain's early studies (1966) dealt only with communities undergoing court-ordered desegregation, whereas Orfield (1981) did not distinguish among Southern cities according to the degree of court initiative.

of avoiding court or state action. Bidwell (personal communication) tells me that two communities in Michigan completely preempted court action by initiating their own programs. Both were characterized by a unified leadership unlikely to be challenged in electoral politics.

Because the courts provide such a convenient external enemy, debate outside the South seems especially prolonged (Orfield, 1981) and generalizes to other issues: who will share the burdens of busing, the allocation of school jobs, the teaching of English as a second language, etc. Secondary gains or losses may come to overshadow the basic issue (Berry, 1979). Despite all these obstacles, however, there is some evidence that a special kind of civic culture—one composed of groups with national linkages and a commitment to cosmopolitan values—can intercede to reduce conflict (Damerell, 1968; Goodwin, 1979). Turf-bound communities, even when well organized, seem to have only a capacity for resistance (Suttles, 1972). It would appear that it is only in these more cosmopolitan civic cultures that minority and majority have some common history of cooperation and mutual trust. The more hierarchial churches play a role here, but often they are secondary to groups like the League of Women Voters or independent voter associations.

When such a well-publicized conflict precedes school desegregation, one cannot help believing that it penetrates into the school-age population, but we know very little about this. Ogbu's study reports that some of the young people he talked to were politicized, as does the study by Sullivan (1979). However, there is very little research on school-age populations that takes them as people who watch television or occasionally read the newspapers. Instead most researchers seem to assume that students are only carriers of parental beliefs.[20] This seems especially implausible in the case of some minority-group students who have ambivalent and difficult relations with their parents. I recall that in 1961 black students in a high school on Chicago's West Side took to the streets protesting the school administration, much to the surprise and alarm of their parents. Later—after Martin Luther King came to town—some of their parents joined them, but frequently the students referred to adults collectively as "handkerchief heads." Some blacks have pressed upon me the view that all this has changed and maybe it has to some extent. Still, I think that ethnographers must take the continuity between parent–child attitudes as problematic especially in those populations where parental emphasis on sex and age segregation competes with wider notions of early, more equalitarian and voluntaristic relations.

Even in the North there are exceptions to prolonged conflict and some communities do take the initiative without court prodding. Alongside a more

---

[20]Patchen et al. (1977) claimed to have found a close relationship between student and parental attitudes toward desegregation. But their findings are based on student reports of their parents' attitudes.

cosmopolitan civic culture, other community characteristics seem to contribute to this outcome: a liberal activist tradition often sponsored by a Jewish population or a local university, a relatively small black population, and considerable distance from the main wave of minority invasion. The sheer size and newsworthiness of large cities probably reduces the ability of local groups to take similar action. Nonetheless, Hyde Park, a local community in Chicago, was able to desegregate some of its schools in the late 1950s despite general inactivity elsewhere (Rossi and Dentler, 1961). The institutional strength of the University of Chicago and its community support were critical in maintaining white enrollment. Here, as in other instances, local initiative at school desegregation was aimed more at preserving a stable desegregated community than at simply complying with the law. Ironically, citywide desegregation plans may especially imperil these more desegregated communities by reducing their capacity to hold white residents. Goodwin's (1979) study suggests that despite its proximity to an expanding ghetto, Oak Park was able to desegregate its schools in a more general effort to maintain a balanced community. Once the alternative is between a balanced community and complete succession, white residents may yield rather easily to school desegregation. Within large cities, like Chicago, however, the general inability to control the pace of residential succession seems to undermine people's confidence in school desegregation (Molotch, 1972).

On the basis of Kornblum's (1974) study, it appears that a common pattern in heavily industrialized communities is the residential dispersion of black workers as compared to whites. Thus, even a relatively liberal union like the United Steel Workers is unable to help manage school desegregation. Something rather different is apparent in the industrial community of Gary, where a black mayor has been able to accomplish rather limited school desegregation while avoiding criticism from blacks or court action.

Whether locally managed or court-ordered, one is struck by the tenuousness of any particular pattern of school desegregation. Because of the ambiguity left by political inactivity, new inequalities will continue to be discovered and in fact develop, as in the South were considerable resegregation is taking place. Often changing circumstances will find leaders locked into publicly declared positions that now preclude compromise. The situation may be especially complicated where teacher unionization vastly expands the issues, as in the Oceanhill Brownsville community of New York (Cole, 1969). Activist leaders in favor of desegregation may feel caught between the belief that if they do nothing resegregation will take place, whereas activism itself may deprive them of control over the process of desegregation. Studies of resegregation promise to be especially revealing not only because they present interesting difficulties to the courts but also because they allow the ethnographer to make a comparative study out of what appears to be a case study.

Throughout local debates over school segregation, one is impressed with the extent to which the findings or at least the ideas of sociologists are used to establish the standards by which school desegregation is evaluated. As Crain (personal communication, 1982) points out, this may not extend to the courts. But educational achievement and attainment seem to remain the key measures for popular and political evaluation. As Coleman himself points out, this is perilous because his own findings document the very modest contributions to achievement made by schooling or desegregation. Wilson (1979) has shown that although desegregated schools may contribute little to educational achievement, they probably do contribute to black academic attainment, that is, blacks stay in desegregated schools longer (Regarding long-term effects on attainment, see Bradock *et al.*, 1984). More recently, Crain and Mahard (1983) have demonstrated a small but persistent gain in test achievement for minorities in desegregated schools. Still, one is impressed with the tenuousness of the equal protection argument, given the ongoing findings of sociologists.

4. THE RESPONSE OF SCHOOL STAFF

There has been a long-term trend toward administrative centralization and bureaucratization in American schools, especially those in big cities (Street, 1969). In part, this grows out of post-Sputnik, but it also grows out of earlier reforms aimed at reducing political patronage and a vague claim for the advantages of scale. The net result, however, seems to have been to insulate schools from community influence while at the same time reducing teacher autonomy and claims to professionalism (Cole, 1969; Street, 1969). Accordingly, school boards and administrators are often unprepared to respond to either the local community or the courts in desegregation cases. Often, they see their power directly challenged or become stalemated because they reflect irreconcilable groups in the community (Crain, 1966). Administrators may even fear a return to older patterns of patronage, especially when public debate extends to community control over such issues as teacher selection. Despite reforms aimed at decentralization, Street's (1969) view is that they usually suffer "death by incorporation," that is, they exist in memos and charts but practice remains the same. Mayer's (1969) personal account of his experiences in the effort to decentralize some of New York's school districts presented this kind of bureaucratic intractability in all its gory detail.

Actually, some of the most interesting experiments carried out in schools are ones that somehow get done without the school board or higher administrators knowing anything about it. Despite the formal authority of higher administrators, they are in a poor position to know what is going on in such a physically dispersed system. As a result, school principals often have a great deal of latitude in what they attempt and a number of studies have focused on their different styles of administration (McPherson, 1970; Noblit, 1979; Queeley, 1969; Schofield and Sagar, 1979). What seems to be present is an entrepreneurial style that allows principals to extend their power by enlisting the support of others, particularly parents and teachers. Clearly some element of leadership is involved, and it is the sort of thing that too narrow a focus on structural characteristics is apt to overlook.

The more pervasive administrative response seems to be a frantic search for new innovations. Especially attractive are new hardware, teacher specialization, and techniques said to increase student motivation (Hawley, 1977; Street, 1969). As Hill (1977) pointed out, this sort of piecemeal innovation actually reduces organizational adaptability, that is, the serial alteration of different innovations with the aim of finding something that will work with a few students but without the expectation that it will work with all of them. Hill argues that this commitment to perpetual innovation, aimed to work for everyone, is deeply rooted in federal funding agencies for American education, that is, innovators get the money.

Desegregation, of course, is only one of the conditions prompting this search for innovations (Bossert, 1978). The classroom, however, can be an almost impenetrable barrier, and persistent demands for innovation seem to be among the circumstances that are moving teachers to build a second wall around the classroom. A fascinating study by Lortie (1975) showed how both the gratifications of teaching and a sense of being embattled with parents and administrators encourage this search for classroom boundaries. His "craft model" of the school teacher role—conservatism, individualism, and attention to immediate pressing demands—deserves further research attention.

All this means that there are several junctures at which the substantive intent of desegregated schooling can be subverted. The most blatant example I know of was a West Side Chicago school where blacks and whites were housed on different floors and arrived and left at different times. This did not improve racial relations, as each day the blacks walked silently, in mass, to and from school in a largely white neighborhood. One assumes that large-scale quantitative studies of integrated schools make some effort to determine classroom composition,[21] but a special effort by ethnographers is needed to disclose the numerous evasions that crop up and give an inverted meaning to desegregation.

There is an abundance of classroom studies, most of them focusing on sociometric choice (Schofield, 1978, 1982), although St. John (1975) reported only one using observed choices rather than self-reports or questionnaires. The

---

[21] In fact, a recent quantitative study by Jackson (1982) indicated that blacks, whites, and Hispanics are heavily segregated by classroom in "desegregated schools."

general finding seems to be that students manage to replicate some of the segregation existing in the wider community (Clement *et al.* 1979; Patchen, 1982;
Schofield and Sagar, 1979). Specially contrived efforts to broaden interracial
contacts seem to have no effects or slightly negative ones. Schofield and Sagar
(1979) provided evidence that undirected classroom behavior tends to confirm
stereotypes and worsen interracial relations. In all these accounts one suspects
that an important ingredient is the extent to which desegregation is regarded as
an irreversible and accomplished fact. Once firmly in place, it is probably easier
for both minority and majority students to accommodate themselves to one
another. Indeed, over time, most do seem to adopt a pattern of mutual tolerance
and even find friends in the other group (Crain and Mahard, 1983). But it is
very difficult to evaluate this sort of classroom experience without some appeal
to social philosophy. That is, should the question be whether or not we expect
instant acceptance or go along to suffer through a difficult experience rather than
face something yet worse down the road? Irresolution itself on this point may
be one of the prime contributors to a reluctance all round to make the best of
desegregation.

5. THE WIDER COMMUNITY

The most obvious way in which the community imposes itself on schools
is simply by its composition and economic structure. Studies as separated in
time as those by Lewis (1964) and Ogbu (1974) show that smaller cities with a
limited range of economic activities tend to have an entrenched, conservative
elite that closely guards access to occupational mobility. Elites in these smaller
places seem to think of the job market as a fixed pool where every job going to
minorities is lost to the majority. Both unions and employers seem to gang up
to insure that groups stand in their accustomed queue leading from school to
place of work. A disproportionate increase in minority population probably
stiffens this kind of thinking even when it is expressed in the more tempered
vocabulary of well-educated people (Glazer and Moynihan, 1963). The situation
should be at least somewhat different in large metropolitan areas that have a
much more dynamic labor force and a more differentiated minority population.
In Atlanta, New York, Chicago, and Los Angeles, for instance, the labor force
is not so dominated by a single industry, and some members of minority groups
have been able to constitute elites of their own. Dual labor markets are probably
less sharply drawn, and one sees an increasing presence of minorities in local
political life. Frequently, there is a limited but cosmopolitan nexus within which
majority and minority experience equal-status relations, for example, universities, a few integrated communities, a few organizations like the Civil Liberties
Union, and an increasing number of politically appointed *ad hoc* study groups.

The dependency of minority elites may still be apparent, but the barriers to interracial relations are not so sharply drawn and some elites may even hope that the improvement in human capital will benefit everyone. These larger cities also have the basis for a much more differentiated school system. Most also have growing private school systems that are only beginning to be studied by quantitative researchers (Coleman, 1981).

Of course, the most obvious reason for focusing research on the larger cities is that this is where most of the minority population is. But there are even more compelling reasons in my view. First, major cities still seem to set the pattern for the rest of the country, despite the movement of population to the suburbs or exurbs. Second, our major cities are undergoing an in-movement of new immigrants that has not been matched since the 1870s. In most of these cities, there is no longer any identifiable white majority. The Hispanic population is extremely diverse (Mexican, Puerto Rican, Cuban, Salvadorian, Dominican), and the black population is becoming increasingly so with a variety of immigrants from the Caribbean. On the one hand, these populations present novel problems to school desegregation simply because the courts have nothing to work with but minorities. On the other hand, this wide mixture is especially interesting because it creates a sort of continuum of color and racial identity that in some ways resembles the one created earlier among Europeans. The racial identity of many of these people is problematic and one hears from one's students in the field references to all sorts of gradations that no longer seem to coincide with country of origin. Such a process of partial assimilation, however, depends on a core solidarity with sufficient numerical, political, and moral strength to set the standards by which incremental gains are made. Massive in-migration into our larger cities, like that occuring during the last decade, could mean that assimilation or acculturation loses its direction, leaving us without a dominant mainstream. Then the ethnographic task will invite comparisons as distant as the Romonov Empire and the Islamic Millet system.

6. THE LOCAL NEIGHBORHOOD

The local neighborhood and the school have usually been linked in two ways. First, the neighborhood has been closely identified with the school as a sort of primal basis for residential cohesion and separateness (Perry and Williams, 1931). Indeed, some researchers take the local attendance area as a surrogate measure of neighborhood, assuming that student contacts and parental loyalties converge to make it a little area of common use and patriotism. Second, the school is seen as linked to the local neighborhood by the competing demands that peer groups put on students. Where the school is thought to support scholastic performance, the neighborhood is usually thought to retard it.

The extend to which local communities form strong loyalties to their schools is far more problematic than this suggests. In large measure, it seems to depend on how nearly local community organization itself can establish more or less equalitarian relations with the education bureaucracy. Elsewhere, I have argued that one can view neighborhood organizations in the United States as the cumulative outcome of a series of national social movements, some of them dating back to the Colonial Period (Suttles, 1979). Many of our older, white, inner-city areas have layers of community organization that resemble strata in an archeological dig: the self-help organizations of the Reform Period, underlying ethnic associations formed between the two world wars, followed by the movement toward confederations after World War II, and succeeded by the influence of the militant Industrial Areas Foundation or self-help groups encouraged by the War on Poverty. In some neighborhoods, these organizational forms seem to have persisted despite almost total population change, especially where the Catholic Church has played a hand in their survival (Harris, 1980). Of course, most local neighborhoods do not date back to these early periods of community organizing and a recent report by Bursik and Webb (1982) suggests that the change from white to black did not allow for such a transition, either because of the rapidity of succession or because of the mutual isolation of black and white. Thus, many of the community organizations in black and Hispanic areas have a fairly recent origin, some of them adopting a militant stance associated with the Industrial Areas Foundation, others operating primarily as self-help groups. Generally, groups embracing the ideology of the Industrial Areas Foundation have taken the local school as central to their mission, with local control rather than desegregation being the chief aim. One of the best publicized of these groups is The Woodlawn Organization, and there is clear evidence that it has come to include the local school as part of its own "turf" (Melber, 1974).

Local self-help groups, such as the ones described by Ogbu, seem much more likely to become trapped in the ceremonialism of parent–teacher relations, where the former can do little more than "be cooperative." These groups resemble other community groups formed expressly to mollify conflict during the early stages of school desegregation (Barrows, 1973, Berry, 1979). When they are biracial groups, they do seem able to control emerging conflict, but apparently they are called on only when there is trouble. As Lortie (1975) implied, this is likely always to be the case where school staff can set the agenda. In any event, such groups are usually so preoccupied with their maintenance within a delimited neighborhood that a concern with school desegregation would uproot them by dispersing their activities over a wider area. The few private or alternative schools emerging in minority neighborhoods do not seem to be accompanied by strong relations to local organizations, but the staff and students may be so self-selected that some sort of diffuse bond exists between parents and the school (Wagner, 1977). The dramatic accomplishments and leadership attributed to Marva Collins may rest on this general sense of a shared mission rather than direct parental or community involvement. Both her supporters and critics seem to interact primarily through the mass media.

The best general treatment of classroom behavior is Jackson's (1968) *Life in Classrooms*. In my own observations on classrooms, I have found it difficult to go beyond Jackson without getting out of the classroom. To be sure, there was the visible if unintentional mutual selection between teachers and students to produce "tracks" (often of only one or two students). As well there were the usual association choices within racial and socioeconomic groups. The apprehension and caution that these groups employed in their approach to one another was evident. But in many ways it seems misleading to think of the classroom as having its own sharply defined sociometric structure and pattern of segregation. Often relations seem to be highly fluid and individuated. Of course, individuals have their best friends, and there are cliques and isolates. But generally these relations are a matter of degree and they shade off into a gray area that is not well indicated by sociometric studies. In my own interviews and some others (Cottle, 1976), the classroom itself was not the problematic focus of group relations. Students in the classroom knew each other and had made some accommodation to one another. It was outside the classroom, in the hallways, on the playground, or at the time school let out that students began to refer to one another as representatives of groups and to express genuine fears of conflict.

Schofield (1978) was certainly right in asserting that studies of classroom contacts need more theoretical guidance, but one wonders if either equal-status or contact theory is not too primitive an approach. Student relations seem so heavily determined outside the classroom that a more institutional approach may be helpful, particularly one that takes into account how organizations set up situations that seem almost calculated to juxtapose minority and majority students where they are least matched in their abilities. The school itself seems most likely to make its initial test one of academic abilities where minorities may do poorest, whereas recreation agencies may achieve the opposite with competitive sports (Collins, 1979). There is some evidence that blacks and whites are most evenly matched at communication and dramatic performances (Scherer and Slawsky, 1979; Sullivan, 1979). Normative conditions that facilitate or obstruct contact in these various activities would seem to be the most obvious objects of attention for the ethnographer.

Youth culture, especially that of the ghetto, is widely pointed to as one of the main obstacles to a more serious and instrumental approach to education (Anderson, 1979; Ogbu, 1974). Earlier interpretations emphasizing a culture of poverty, however, have been replaced by one emphasizing a widespread awareness of job ceilings. Undoubtedly, the shared perception of job ceilings is important, but it raises the question of how some groups do and some do not overcome peer pressures and the job ceiling. In my own work in Chicago, I could detect only slight differences between the youth cultures of blacks, Mexican-Americans, Puerto Ricans, and Italians, although the Italians clearly had better job prospects (Suttles, 1968). One clue that may throw some light on this is the reestablishment of dominance by the Italian adult males. The young boys had their gangs, but so did the adults. Peer-group development among the adult males was more than a match for that among the young boys. This was not the case among blacks on Chicago's West Side in the 1960s, but I am told that it is increasingly the case both there and on the South Side, where older youth gangs have reached maturity and by trying to control the "gray market" may be helping to confine the "black market" of youth violence. This, of course, does not mean that adult dominance has any direct pedagogic value, but it may mean that the youth culture is sufficiently contained so that they do not "burn their bridges" to school before they attempt to enter the job market.

Still, one doubts that the general efficacy of adult dominance in doing much beyond keeping youngsters in school a bit longer. One of the things that strikes me about practically all the accounts I have read of contemporary ghetto life is the absence of something like the "college boys" described by Whyte (1943). I found no evidence of a similar group in an Italian community in the 1960s, although some individuals did go to college. Possibly the depression created greater socioeconomic diversity during the time Whyte did his work, but most studies of black areas do show considerable diversity of educational background. With the emergence of accessible community colleges and the increase of blacks enrolling in these institutions, some kind of college-bound youth culture with its own group life may develop in the ghetto. Certainly the emergence of a more differentiated peer culture among blacks would be an important factor in helping to overcome the sort of self-defeat that Anderson (1979) described.

7. FAMILY NETWORKS

Despite extensive quantitative studies of schooling and family background (Coleman et al., 1966; Heyns, 1978), certain aspects of family life among low-income minority groups remain problematic. For a while the "culture of poverty" and matrifocal family drew widespread attention (Lewis, 1966; Miller, 1982). But that seems to have lapsed because of an inability to draw close links across income, minority membership, family type, and occupational or school performance.

Several intriguing studies are now emerging which suggest a rather different approach (Stack, 1974; Hannerz, 1969; Miller, 1982), at least to black family structure. What seems to be revealed in these studies is that separate families are embedded in a network of others that vary considerably in their socioeconomic standing, ranging from totally dependent to self-supporting. The core of this network is a group of women who are able to improve somewhat their standard of living and overcome short-term emergencies by pooling some of their resources. This network is surrounded by dependent children and a number of adult males, both kin and nonkin. Some of these males may have stable employment and persistent relations with others in the network, but as a group they are less able to pool resources than are the women. There is some turnover among the adult males; children develop a primary dependency on one or more of the adult women and, sometimes, on some male kin.

Very frequently, these family networks are linked to yet another network composed largely of unrelated individuals periodically involved in street hustling. Sometimes, these linkages are through one or more of the peripheral males in the first network but occasionally through one of the core female members or one of the older children. The social proximity of street hustling and its members appear to bring about a number of reactions and consequences. First, some of the core female members adopt an almost compulsive effort to protect their children from contact with street life. Children are closely confined to the home, cross-sexual relations are proscribed, and great deference is demanded by adults. All these rules may be articulated in a religious vocabulary that is especially rigid. Given the visible proximity and temptations of street life, it is extremely difficult to enforce these normative restrictions, and they may lead to an early deterioration of the relations between children and some of the adults. This promotes a strong desire for early independence and the establishment of a separate household. The frequent failure to impose this rigid normative order may also help explain a second pattern where an earlier defeat leads adults to abandon further efforts to supervise their young children.

The diverse membership and linkage between these networks would seem to imply that the moral climate of any particular nuclear family is considerably diluted as adult discipline and example take on a variety of normative forms. This *averaging effect* would create a great deal of room for the kind of drift that Matza (1964) describes for delinquent boys. For studies of schooling it would suggest that particular nuclear-family traditions of improving education are especially hard to carry over between generations. In turn, it is probably also difficult for adults to establish a bounded group-life that assigns exceptional importance to academic accomplishment: that could only seem like snobbery. There are some obvious parallels here between the absence of a domestic circle that emphasizes academic achievement and a similar omission among college-bound youth in the ghetto.

Reports of these family networks are almost entirely confined to blacks.[22] Because the decisive condition seems to be the relatively stable income of women

---

[22]See Howell (1973) for evidence that similar but more restricted networks prevail among some Southern whites.

as compared to that of men, this may reflect a true concentration. Opportunities for stable (not high) income have usually been less favorable for black males than for females especially if one includes welfare payments. Still, the extent and concentration of these networks is an open question.

8. THE AGENDA FOR ETHNOGRAPHY

In approaching the ethnography of school desegregation, I have found it necessary to examine a wide range of literature, only a little of it completed by ethnographers. The aim has been to map out a hierarchy of topical areas and variables that would provide a more cumulative and comparative execution of ethnographic studies not only of school desegregation but of the general process of status negotiation among primordial groups. At the top of this hierarchy is the cultural level, including our founding myths of national membership. This level focuses on those selective elements of group history and identity that are incorporated in our folk beliefs about group differences. It extends as well to the ceremonial embodiments of these beliefs (Thanksgiving, Fourth of July, etc.) and popular taxonomies for distinguishing among groups. It recognizes that this cultural level is not static but a social construction, that is in the process of change as new events become eligible for mythic enlargement—not just things that have happened but things that are regarded as expectable and archetypical. These changes imply that one should find variants of this founding myth with the most likely division occurring between "fundamentalists" who adhere to a restrictive interpretation and "revisionists" who adopt a more inclusive interpretation. This debate does not automatically resolve itself in favor of the more inclusive variant, but depends on the conditions indicated in the remainder of this hierarchy (see Appendix).

Probably the most important of these conditions is the relative threat posed by a minority. A small group poses very little threat; a large one poses much more adjustment in terms of perceived loss of jobs, housing, and numerical superiority in a range of institutions including the school.[23] For most Americans the relevant unit is probably their own jurisdictional community within which they share such collective goods as education. Sometimes the threat is more diffuse, as when the possible loss of public sector jobs alarms suburbanites as well as central-city dwellers. Countless studies of invasion and succession document this process and provide at least an initial approach to this problem.

The heightening of group consciousness and efforts at resegregation do not seem to leave the cultural level unchanged. Forcing the debate into the open,

---

[23]These perceptions, of course, may be wrong in at least two ways. They may overestimate the size of the group or the consequence of its presence. It would appear that most Americans think in terms of a "zero sum" encounter between minority groups and their competition for resources. But what unit they use and what markers they employ in estimating group numbers is unclear.

into a more public arena, does seem to give the revisionists some advantage because the expression of brute, simplistic prejudice tends to discredit the fundamentalists. Moreover, the threat posed by a rapidly increasing minority group may make the distinction among previous competitors seem trivial and lead to the acceptance of new myths of incorporation.

However, the extent to which revisionists hold the edge does seem to depend very much on how public the debate is; a quiet process of succession or simply rioting probably leaves things much as they were. Generally, school desegregation has been accompanied by widespread, often national, debate. In large part this is because of the prevalence of court-ordered school desegregation accompanied by irresolute political leadership, the former assuring that it will be seen as coercive, the latter fueling hopes for resistance. For this reason there may have been more change at the cultural level than at some of the subsequent levels. That is, people are willing to entertain new definitions of one another, but the structural conditions (e.g., population balance) for acting on them are not available. Caplow and his associates (1982) comment that amid the pervasive stability revealed in their study of Middletown, the increase of tolerance is the most exceptional. This increase in tolerance does not seem traceable to any local structural condition but to local participation in a national debate.

There are many variations at the level of the wider community, its political leadership, and the school administration. Where local authorities have actually taken the initiative, they seem to have enjoyed a good deal of freedom in how they desegregated their schools. Indeed, some may have practically avoided it altogether, whereas others may have accomplished results well worth publicizing. Court and federally ordered school desegregation seems to result in a more random mixture of students or one that places a particular hardship on specific schools. People may become more sophisticated about how they talk about minority groups—and this should not be discounted—but the coercive character of court-ordered desegregation makes it especially difficult to mobilize public support. Even in the countywide school districts of the South, desegregated schools may have little staying power as private schools and metropolitanization reduce the white student enrollment.

Local political and administrative leadership obviously can be important here, and one might expect there to be a growing number of school administrators who have had enough experience with desegregated schools to have some confidence in their management. Frequently, however, they will find themselves paired with political leaders who are opposed to taking any action. The way in which administrative and political leaders line up is an obvious avenue of investigation.

The wider community also figures into this hierarchy in such obvious ways as its population composition, minority division of labor, the cosmopolitanism of group life, and the presence of visible minority leadership. The larger of our cities continue to be important here if only because they are the most newsworthy. The persistence of in-migration to these cities will surely change the context of school desegregation, possibly making it almost entirely a "black issue" as diverse other minorities seek alternative avenues of acculturation or try to avoid it altogether.

The school itself represents a focus of extensive past research, so much so that the opportunity to examine variations around the typical public school now exists. Alternative schools, schools with special programs, and even private schools can be examined from the perspective of a reasonably well established baseline. The local community and its interface with the school take on additional importance because school desegregation is so often accompanied by a public outcry over the "loss of community"; such an outcry that one wonders if the consequences are not almost the reverse of those claimed. The linkage of local groups to more cosmopolitan centers, the character of youth cultures, and the apprehension of personal abuse would seem to bear on this issue.

Studies of minority family and kinship structure have probably been too narrowly focused on the nuclear family to the neglect of kin and nonkin networks with their competing normative frameworks. Undoubtedly, there are minority populations in which the nuclear family is a relatively self-contained unit that can transmit most if its norms to its children. Indeed, some of these families may be grouped in networks where the accomplishments of children can receive recognition as a continuation of "characteristic achievement." But we must be prepared as well to find very open-ended networks that intersect diverse moral worlds and leave their younger members to drift between alternatives.

This attempt to develop such a broad conceptual framework has two aims for ethnographers. First, it provides a mapping within which the ethnographer can position his study and relate it to the wider literature. Ethnographic studies are especially limited in their range of immediate observation. They can become comparative only by drawing on a wider literature and placing it alongside their own findings in a scheme of plausible theoretical relations. The reader may not want to draw on this particular framework, but he will have to devise something like it if his study is to be more than an isolated case study.

Second, this kind of mapping out of levels and dimensions of variation provides us with a reasoned judgment about where ethnographic effort is most appropriate and strategic. My reading of the literature leads me to the following injunctions. Ethnographic studies are probably best directed to that range of variation that lies to either side of the mainstream of past studies of school desegregation. The exploratory advantages of ethnographic studies are well recognized, but it also appears that a replication of past studies of school desegregation, even if done in far greater depth, is not going to uncover much more. As St. John (1981) pointed out, there is a great deal of continuity in these findings and the general need is to examine a wider range of variations.

Also, the cultural, community, and family levels seem the most opportune for ethnographic exploration. The cultural level is generally something that ethnographers are attuned to and trained to recognize. But more importantly, its expression in ceremonies, in folk taxonomies, in popular culture, in fashions, and in fads is highly situated. Of course, there is a documentary repository for much of this material, but it is at ground level that we can see how culture comes into use—almost always selectively—rather than being simply acted out in stereotypic form. People make use of their culture, they don't just obey it. A knowledge of our founding myths of national memberships may not tell us much about school desegregation in the short run, but it is vital for an understanding of minority relations over the long run. This is not as some would claim, a radical subjectivist review, for like Geertz (1973) and Prager (1982) I take culture to be what is "out there" and available to analysis, rather than something buried in peoples' private thoughts.

The level of threat of racial change, the locus for the initiative of school desegregation, compositional effects, and the stance of political leadership will usually enter ethnographic studies as data rather than as objects of intense investigation. This is usually because the ethnographer cannot spread across enough research sites to find much meaningful variation. Team efforts are possible, but they represent an enormous investment in time and a prodigious effort for more than one investigator to keep abreast of each other's work. But the simplest reason these issues are not of high priority to the ethnographer is that most are susceptible to elaborate quantitative analysis. This would seem to be especially so for assessing compositional effects or the comparative analysis of several cities.

The school and its administration represent a marginal case for the ethnographer. There is always something to be learned from the observation of classrooms, the use of students and staff as informants, and the examination of curricular material. But at some point, decisive examination of most of the issues that emerge at this level requires a fair degree of sampling and quantitative measurement (e.g., measures of achievement, sociability, resource input, teacher skills, etc.). This is already a reasonably well established research tradition among social psychologists, and if ethnographers are to engage in it they must certainly master the canons of research that have developed in that subdiscipline.

In any case, the ethnographer who begins work within the schoolhouse walls is likely soon to be drawn beyond them. The holistic aims of ethnography make the weakness of the school's boundaries something easy to cross, and it will be difficult to avoid the youth culture that exists both inside and outside the school, the actions of community groups, political decisions in the wider community, and a persistent dialogue about problem families and problem groups. It is at this level that ethnographers are in their natural milieu, sorting between what informants say and what can be observed, juxtaposing voiced norms with situated action, tracing out a series of events to see if they are closely linked, comparing images with observations. Such a procedure is clinical in its initial steps, only gradually drawing out the boundaries that circumscribe what is to be investigated. Its direction is informed by opportunism—stumbling on something obviously important—and by an awareness of investigative priorities.

The interface between the school, the local community, and its constituent parts is an appropriate ethnographic site because so much of what is interesting about it is poorly indexed for the purposes of more quantitative research: the importance of a situated action, the presence of an underlife that few know about in its totality, and the emergence of local and particular traditions, images, understandings, and deals. All this can eventually be placed in a comparative framework. Indeed, I have attempted to do so. But first it must be disinterred by the ethnographer.

REFERENCES

Alexander, J. C. Core solidarity, ethnic outgroup, and social differentiation: A multidimensional model of inclusion in modern societies. In Jacques Dofny (Ed.), *National and Ethnic Movements*. London: Sage, 1980.

Anderson, E. Some Observations on Youth Unemployment. In B. Anderson and I. Sawhill (Eds.), *Youth Unemployment and Public Policy*. Englewood Cliffs, NJ: Prentice Hall, 1979.

Baltzell, E. D. *Puritan Boston and Quaker Philadelphia*. New York: Free Press, 1979.

Barrows, F. School busing: Charlotte, N.C. In N. Mills (Ed.), *The Great School Bus Controversy*. New York: Teachers College Press, 1973.

Berry, J. L. *The Open Housing Question: Race and Housing in Chicago 1966–76*. Cambridge, MA: Ballinger, 1979.

Bidwell, C. The School as a Formal Organization. In I. March (Ed.), *Handbook of Organizations*. Chicago: Rand McNally, 1965.

Blauner, R. *Racial Oppression in America*. New York: Harper & Row, 1972.

Bonacich, E. A theory of Middleman minorities. *American Sociological Review*, 1973, *38*, 583–594.

Bossert, S. Education in urban society. In D. Street (Ed.), *Handbook of Contemporary Urban Life*. San Francisco: Jossey-Bass, 1978.

Braddock, J. H., Crain, R. L., and McPartland, J. M., A long-term view of school desegregation. *Phi Delta Kappan*, 1984 (December), 259–264.

Bursik, R., and Webb, J. Community change and patterns of delinquency. *American Journal of Sociology*, 1982, *88*, 24–42.

Caplow, T., Bahr, H. M., Chadwick, B. A., Hill, R., and Williamson, M. H. *Middletown Families*. Minneapolis, MN: University of Minnesota Press, 1982.

Clement, D. C., Eisenhart, M., Harding, J. R. The Veneer of Harmony. In R. Rist. (Ed.), *Desegregated Schools*. New York: Academic Press, 1979.

Cole, S. *The Unionization of Teachers*. New York: Prager, 1969.

Coleman, J. S. The role of incentives in school desegregation. In A. Yarmolinsky, L. Liebman, and C. S. Schelling (Eds.), *Race and Schooling in the City*. Cambridge, MA: Harvard University Press, 1981.

Coleman, J. S., Campbell, E. R., Hobson, C. J., Partland, J. M., Mood, A. M., Weinfeld, E. D., and York, R. L. *Equality of Educational Opportunity*. Washington, DC: U.S. Government Printing Office, 1966.

Collins, T. W. From courtroom to classrooms: Managed school desegregation in a deep south high school. In R. Rist (Ed.), *Desegregated Schools*. New York: Academic Press, 1979.

Cottle, T. *Busing*. Boston: Beacon Press, 1976.

Crain, R. *School Desegregation in the North*. Chicago: National Opinion Research Center, 1966.

Crain, R. *The Politics of Desegregation*. Chicago: Aldine, 1968.

Crain, R., and Mahard, R. The effects of research methodology on desegregation-achievement studies: A meta-analysis. *American Journal of Sociology*, 1983, *88*, 839–854.

Damerell, R. G. *Triumph in a White Suburb*. New York: William Morrow, 1968.

Ellis, C. S. *Community, crabs and capitalism*. Unpublished doctoral dissertation, State University of New York, Stony Brook, 1980.

Gazeway, R. *The Longest Mile*. Baltimore: Penguin, 1974.

Geertz, C. Thick description: Toward an interpretative theory of culture. In C. Geertz (Ed.), *The Interpretation of Cultures*. New York: Basic Books, 1973.

Glazer, N. and Moynihan, D. P. *Beyond the Melting Pot: The Negroes, Puerto Ricans, Jews, Italians and Irish of New York City*. Cambridge, MA: M.I.T. Press, 1963.

Goodwin, C. *The Oak Party Strategy*. Chicago: University of Chicago Press, 1979.

Goody, J. R. *Literacy in Traditional Societies*. Cambridge, England: Cambridge University Press, 1968.

Gordon, E. W. *The Social System of the High School*. Glencoe, IL: Free Press, 1957.

Gronbjerg, K., Street, D., and Suttles, G. *Poverty and Social Change*. Chicago: University of Chicago Press, 1978.

Gurin, P., and Epps, E. *Black Consciousness, Identity and Achievement*. New York: Wiley, 1975.

Hannerz, U. *Soulside: Inquiries into Ghetto Culture and Community*. New York: Columbia University Press, 1969.

Harris, J. D. *Grass roots organizing in Chicago*. Unpublished doctoral dissertation, University of Illinois, 1980.

Hawley, W. D. Developing adaptive schools and the limits of innovation. In S. Nagel (Ed.), *Policy Studies Annual Review, 1977*. Beverly Hills, CA: Sage, 1977.

Heyns, B. *Summer Learning and the Effects of Schooling*. New York: Academic Press, 1978.

Hill, P. T. Comment. In S. Nagel (Ed.), *Policy Studies: Annual Review, 1977*. Beverly Hills, CA: Sage, 1977.

Howell, J. H. *Hard Living on Clay Street*. Garden City, NY: Anchor Books, 1973.

Issacs, H. R. The one and the many. In A. Yarmolinsky, L. Liebman, and C. S. Schelling (Eds.), *Race and Schooling in the City*. Cambridge, MA: Harvard University Press, 1981.

Jackson, K. *Differences in factors that influence black and white achievement in public schools*. Unpublished doctoral dissertation, University of Chicago, 1982.

Jackson, P. *Life in Classrooms*. New York: Holt, Rinehart, & Winston, 1968.

Janowitz, M. Observations on the sociology of citizenship: Obligations and rights. *Social Forces*, 1980, *59*, 1–24.

Kornblum, W. *Blue Collar Community*. Chicago: University of Chicago Press, 1973.

Lewis, H. *Blackways of Kent*. New Haven, CT: College and University Press, 1964.

Lewis, O. The culture of poverty. *Scientific American*, 1966, *215*, 19–25.

Lieberson, S. *A Piece of the Pie: Blacks and White Immigrants Since 1880*. Berkeley, CA: University of California Press, 1980.

Light, I. H. *Ethnic Enterprise in America: Business and Welfare Among Chinese, Japanese and Blacks*. Berkeley, CA: University of California Press, 1972.

Longshore, D., and Prager, J. The impact of school desegregation: A situational analysis. In R. Turner (Ed.), *Annual Review of Sociology 11*. Palo Alto: Annual Reviews, 1985.

Lortie, D. C. *School Teacher*. Chicago: University of Chicago Press, 1975.

McPherson, R. A study of teacher turnover in two elementary schools. Unpublished doctoral dissertation, University of Chicago, 1970.

Matza, D. *Delinquency and Drift*. New York: Wiley, 1964.

Mayer, M. The local board in New York City: A personal document. In D. Street (Ed.), *Innovation in Mass Education*. New York: Wiley, 1969.

McConahay, J. Reducing racial prejudice in desegregated schools. In W. D. Hawley (Ed.), *Effective School Desegregation: Equity, Quality and Feasibility*. Beverly Hills, CA: Sage, 1981.

Melber, B. *Intervention for education: Community participation in the Chicago public schools*. Unpublished doctoral dissertation, University of Chicago, 1974.

Miller, E. *The recruitment of young women to deviant street networks*. Unpublished doctoral dissertation, University of Chicago, 1982.

Molotch, H. *Managed Integration: Dilemmas of Doing Good in the City*. Berkeley, CA: University of California Press, 1972.

Noblit, G. W. Patience and prudence in a southern high school: Managing the political economy of desegregated education. In R. Rist (Ed.), *Desegregated Schools*. New York: Academic Press, 1979.

Ogbu, J. U. *The Next Generation*. New York: Academic Press, 1974.

Ogbu, J. U. *Minority Education and Caste: The American System in Cross-Cultural Perspective*. New York: Academic Press, 1978.

Orfield, G. Why it worked in Dixie: Southern school desegregation and its implications for the north. In A. Yarmolinsky, L. Liebman, and C. S. Schelling (Eds.), *Race and Schooling in the City*. Cambridge, MA: Harvard University Press, 1981.

Patchen, M. *Black-White Contact in Schools*. West Lafayette, IN: Purdue University Press, 1982.

Patchen, M., Davidson, J. D., Hoffman, G., and Brown, W. R Determinants of students' interracial behavior and opinion change. *Sociology of Education*, 1977, *50*, 55–75.

Perry, C. A., and Williams, M. P. *New York School Centers and Their Community Policy*. New York: Russell Sage Foundation, 1931.

Prager, J. American racial ideology as collective representation. *Ethnic and Racial Studies*, 1982, *5*, 99–119.

Queeley, M. Nongrading in an urban slum school. In D. Street (Ed.), *Innovation in Mass Education*, New York: Wiley, 1969.

Rossi, P., and Dentler, R. A. *The Politics of Urban Renewal*. New York: Free Press, 1961.

St. John, N. *School Desegregation: Outcomes for Children*. New York: Wiley, 1975.

St. John, N. The effects of school desegregation on children: A new look at the research evidence. In A. Yarmolinsky, L. Liebman, and C. S. Schelling (Eds.), *Race and Schooling in the City*. Cambridge, MA: Harvard University Press, 1981.

Scherer, J., and Slawski, E. J. Color, class and social control in an urban desegregated school. In R. Rist (Ed.), *Desegregated Schools*. New York: Academic Press, 1979.

Schofield, J. W. School desegregation and intergroup relations. In D. Bar-Tal and L. Saxe (Eds.), *Social Psychology of Education: Theory and Research*. New York: Wiley, 1978.

Schofield, J. W. *Black and White in School*. New York: Praeger, 1982.

Schofield, J. W. and Sagar, H. The Social Context of Learning in an Interracial School. In R. Rist (Ed.), *Desegregated Schools*. New York: Academic Press, 1979.

Sowell, T. *Ethnic Americans: A History*. New York: Basic Books, 1981.

Sowell, T. *The Economics and Politics of Race*. New York: William Morrow, 1983.

Stack, B. *All Our Kin: Strategies for Survival in a Black Community*. New York: Harper & Row, 1974.

Street, D. (Ed.). *Innovation in Mass Education*. New York: Wiley, 1969.

Sullivan, M. L. Contacts among cultures: School desegregation in a polyethnic New York City high school. In R. Rist (Ed.), *Desegregated Schools*. New York: Academic Press, 1979.

Suttles, G. D., *The Social Order of the Slum*. Chicago: University of Chicago Press, 1968.

Suttles, G. D. *The Social Construction of Communities*. Chicago: University of Chicago Press, 1972.

Suttles, G. D. *The social uses of community*. Paper presented at the Annual Meeting of the American Sociological Association, Boston, August 1979.

Wagner, J. *Misfits and Missionaries: A School for Black Dropouts*. Beverly Hills, CA: Sage, 1977.

Waller, W. *The Sociology of Teaching*. New York: Wiley, 1932.

Whyte, W. G. *Street Corner Society: The Social Structure of an Italian Slum*. Chicago: University of Chicago Press, 1943.

Wilson, K. The effects of integration and class on black attainment. *Sociology of Education*, 1979, *52*, 84–89.

Wilson, W. J., Turner, C. B., and Darity, W. A. Racial solidarity and separate education. *School Review*, 1973, *81*, 365–373.

Institutional Levels and Priorities for Ethnographic Research

This appendix makes no effort to be exhaustive but aims to provide a comparative framework within which ethnographic studies can be placed. Each institutional level is indicated along the left-hand margin. The center heading indicates the most general objects of research, followed by a series of more concrete examples. Two dimensions are given for each level to indicate important ranges of variation. The following hypotheses illustrate both the linkage between levels and relationships within each level. Relevant readings are indicated on the right.

INSTITUTIONAL LEVEL	OBJECTS OF RESEARCH	READINGS
Culture	Folk beliefs (e.g., explanations of groups' character)	Alexander (1980)
	Slogans of typification (e.g., the Cuban "economic miracle")	
	Ceremonies (e.g., St. Patrick's Day parade)	
	Taxonomies (e.g., slang terms of ethnic groups) Obgu (1974)	
Fundamentalist-------- adherence to fixed version of group histories	Public opinion---------	Revisionist------- acceptance of new versions of group differences

INSTITUTIONAL LEVEL	OBJECTS OF RESEARCH	READINGS
Essentialist--- explanations of group differences	Public Rheotric---	Voluntaristic vocabulary of motives

Hypothesis 1: Mythic enlargement of the historic accomplishments of one group occurs when (a) they are favorably compared to another negotiating for incorporation, and (b) the accomplishments of that group are used to justify the incorporative claims of another.

Hypothesis 2: Myths of incorporation are constituted by a set of binary distinctions in which the core solidarity is the benchmark against which other groups are compared.

Demographic-Ecological	Population ratios (e.g., percent black)	Lieberson (1980)
	Labor force (e.g., one industry town) Housing (e.g., block-by-block succession)	Ogbu (1974)
Parochial----------	Civic Culture----------	Cosmopolitan
Mutual--------	Level of conflict--------	Accommodation

Hypothesis 1: The more nearly people accept essentialist explanations of group differences, the higher the threat they will assign to an increase in minority population.

Hypothesis 2: The more diversified the economic base of a community, the more likely it is to have a cosmopolitan civic culture.

Political-Administrative	Party Leadership (e.g., desegregation, a partisan issue)	Crain (1968)
	Courts (e.g., level of initiative in desegregation)	
	Administration (e.g., board of education)	
Avoidable-------------	Perception of-------- desegregation	Inevitable
External----------	Origin of------ desegregation plan	Local

Hypothesis 1: The more public the debate over desegregation, the more likely

INSTITUTIONAL LEVEL	OBJECTS OF RESEARCH	READINGS

parties to that debate will adopt a voluntaristic vocabulary of motives to describe group differences.

Hypothesis 2: The more divided and irresolute local political leadership, the more likely the general public will see desegregation as avoidable.

School	Programs to accommodate desegregation (e.g., efforts to broaden intergroup contacts)	Schofield and Sagar (1979)
	School supervision (e.g., extends beyond immediate school grounds)	
	Partnership with community groups (e.g., ceremonial only)	Ogbu (1974) Lortie (1975)
Formal compliance---- -	Response to------- desegregation	Innovative compliance
Ceremonial-- -	Relation to community---- groups	Equalitarian

Hypothesis 1: The more coercive administrators see desegregation, the more likely they are to adopt formal compliance.

Hypothesis 2: The more equalitarian the school administration's relationship with communty groups, the more likely the school administration is to adopt new innovations.

Community	Community Organization (e.g., property owners associations)	
	Adult subcultures (e.g., male tavern groups	
	Youth subcultures	
Parochial--------	Orientation of community---- groups	Cosmopolitan
Street----------	Orientation of youth------ groups	College

Hypothesis 1: The more cosmopolitan local community groups, the more likely they are to support innovative compliance on the part of the local schools.

Hypothesis 2: College-bound youth who have visible groups will be more influential in providing leadership than those who lack corporate group identities.

INSTITUTIONAL LEVEL	OBJECTS OF RESEARCH	READINGS
Family	Bounded nuclear family (e.g., male dominated family)	
	Network of nuclear families (e.g., extended family)	
	Network of kin and nonkin (e.g., child–parent pairs in a larger network)	
Competing---- moral orders	Moral order of--- family or network	Unified moral order
Avoiding--- trouble	Discipline---	Positive injunctions

Hypothesis 1: Street hustling is most able to recruit its members from child–parent pairs in a larger network, including nonkin.

Hypothesis 2: Networks of nuclear families are more able to exercise social control over their children than are isolated families or child–parent pairs in a larger network.

Part **III**

NEW THEORETICAL DIRECTIONS

Chapter 3

The Micro-Structure of School Desegregation

MARK GRANOVETTER

Studies of the effects of desegregation have produced a confusing array of inconsistent results. It is the general theme of this volume that this inconsistency derives from the actual wide variety of disparate situations too sweepingly sub sumed under the vague rubric of desegregation. In retrospect, this should not be surprising. The literature on intergroup relations is replete with studies show-ing that highly specific details of a situation rather than global attitudes toward other groups mainly determine behavior. Easy commingling in the workplace coexists with unyielding residential segregation; written request for reservations from identified ethnic groups or mixed parties are frequently refused by estab-lishments that accept such patrons readily when they appear in person (Pettigrew, 1971).

This chapter explores in detail one of the most crucial situational deter-minants of behavior in desegregated settings: the structure of social relations among participants. Because desegregation is centrally defined around concern with such relations, one might suppose they would always have been a central focus of attention. I would argue that this has not been the case, and that failure to appreciate the complexity of issues related to the social structure of deseg-regation situations is a major cause of confusion.

Much of the chapter analyzes the meaning and determinants of the structure of social relations in desegregated schools. This is justifiable in part because one frequently expressed goal of desegregation is an improvement in intergroup relations. I believe also, however, that even when other outcomes are considered,

MARK GRANOVETTER • Department of Sociology, State University of New York, Stony Brook, NY 11794.

such as academic achievement and later socioeconomic success, school social structure plays an important mediating role. Sections 1 to 3 of the paper thus concentrate on social structure as such, and section 4 considers that structure's role in other outcomes. A final section sketches how this relatively microscopic-level analysis of social structure and its outcomes is affected by the broader societal environment.

1. ANALYZING SOCIAL STRUCTURE: PROBLEMS IN THE LEVEL AND UNIT OF ANALYSIS

It is hardly controversial to say that one ought to study social structure in desegregated schools. But what does this consist of? Have we studied social structure if we have all the students in a classroom name their three best friends, and then use a multivariate analysis to determine the correlates of number of choices received? (See, e.g., Gerard and Miller, 1975, Chap. 10.) *Structural* analysis refers not only to relations among individuals but also, and very crucially, to the structure of those relations. Focus on individual popularity yields an atomized view of social structure. If the classroom is a social system, one cannot see its structure in this way any better than one can imagine the outlines of a cow by looking at a hamburger. At the least one requires some attention to cliques, blocks, and linkages among such units.

If individuals are too low a level of analysis for exclusive focus, much the same can be said for classrooms. With rare exceptions, they are not isolated from one another, and what happens in one class affects what may happen in others. Desegregation studies frequently emphasize how strongly classroom teachers affect outcomes. But teachers interact with other teachers, aides, and school officials. Students' subordinate position in the school pecking-order probably explains why only they, not adults, are given sociometric tests, but it is clear that this practice systematically discards information on one of the most important aspects of school social structure—that of adults. Where such structure involves hierarchy or cliques, much of what occurs in classrooms may be shaped by these, and in turn affect teachers' social relations.

Where a teachers' clique is dominated by a particular teaching philosophy, for example, one might expect classroom practices consistent with this philosophy to receive strong social support. Metz (1978) studied two junior high schools. In one, faculty "culture" was "divided into two bitterly opposed factions," one devoted to traditional classroom practices, the other more "modern." She reported that teachers in this school were much less flexible in their approach than those in the other school she studied, who, though they had similar philosophies, were not members of cliques defined by adherence to a set of ideas. What I suggest here is that teachers in the first school received social support for their practices and felt social pressures to maintain them, whereas neither support nor pressure was felt in the second. The result was a great difference in school climate and classroom practice.

The classroom is not only too low a level of analysis to give a rounded structural picture—it is also a highly artificial unit for the study of children's social relations. Because the classroom physically structures school activity, it is usually the main focus of desegregation analysis. But is it a natural or reasonable sociometric unit? Karweit *et al.* (1979, p. 13) comment that "we have no empirical evidence on whether most student friendships are actually formed and maintained inside or outside of classrooms."

What level of desegregation actually obtains depends on one's definition of what unit of analysis constitutes the desegregation situation. Schools nominally integrated may have classrooms that are *de facto* segregated; this classroom resegregation occurs more "in localities and educational levels where school desegregation has progressed most" (Morgan and McPartland, 1981, p. 13). But even where classrooms are "resegregated," one needs to know also whether out-of-class interactions are comparably divided. Conversely, though classes are integrated, desegregation may be less than meets the eye. Rist (1978) noticed that black students from several first-grade classes congregated on the playground, apparently because there were so few of them within each class. Segregation was thus reconstituted at an extra-classroom level that would escape the purview of classroom sociometrics. Ethnographic observations also make clear that considerable interaction occurs in the interstices of formal school activity—in hallways, bathrooms, stairwells, courtyards, and playgrounds, only the last of these easily observable by teachers or researchers. "You better walk with me. I've been through this before. The hallway's the worst, and whatever you do, don't go to the bathroom." So advised an experienced black student, counseling a friend at her first day in South Boston's newly desegregated high school (Bullard and Stoia, 1980, p. 30; see also Huckaby, 1980). Though it may account for a quantitatively small part of the day, time spent out of classrooms in school is opportunity for spontaneous, unsupervised social interaction among children, and may thus be more important for shaping social relations than what happens in the classroom, particularly when teaching is carried out in traditional lecture style, each student interacting with the teacher, and with one another only at the risk of penalties for deviant behavior.

In junior high and high school settings, extracurricular activities become a particular focus of out-of-class student interaction, and may take on greater significance for many students than the formal educational process. Though it is frequently noted that these activities tend to sort by race and sex—so that segregation is recreated at the small-group level—we have little insight into how this occurs, a question I return to later.

Even the school itself does not fully bound children's social interaction; yet, what happens out of school is persistently neglected. This occurs in part because of the traditional division of labor between sociologists/psychologists of education and other researchers, and in part because classroom sociometry is so enormously more manageable and convenient than pursuing children into their neighborhoods, where there is no natural unit comparable to the classroom, no predictable place of assembly, and little chance of appending the school's authority to one's research. Students consequently vanish from view when they cross the school–neighborhood boundary. Little is known about the social networks of children outside of school settings. (See Foot *et al.*, 1980, for accounts of recent research.)

But this may be important. Though anthropologists are aware of the significance of "multiplex" ties—relations reinforced by appearing in more than one setting or type of interaction—classroom sociometrics abstract away from this. Thus we have no way of knowing to what extent observed relations result from interactions outside of class or of school. Once this issue is taken seriously, a whole new constellation of questions arises, which links the school and its students to broader levels of social structure. We know, for instance, if we have children, that parents inevitably meet the parents of their children's friends. Do children also meet the children of their parents' friends? If this is a significant source of sociality, then whatever forces impact parents' social worlds spill over also into their children's. How school relations link up with those outside is strongly conditioned by where the school fits in a neighborhood ecology. An extreme case is where ethnically defined "turfs" bear heavily on the formation of out-of-school friendships (Suttles, 1968), so that intergroup contacts, even if initiated in school, cannot progress to multiplex contexts. All these factors in turn affect children's summer social structure, of which almost nothing is known. Heyns' (1978) evidence suggests for Atlanta that most organized summer activities are more segregated by both class and race than are the public schools. One might suppose then that informal activities would be all the more so. But how this relates to the overall urban ecology or to school-year friendship ties can only be guessed. Heyns' data are too indirect and too aggregated to shed light on such questions.

Patchen's (1982, pp. 62–66) data on 11 Indianapolis high schools in 1971 show that school-year interaction across races outside of school was "far from unusual. Almost half the students of each race said that they had done things together with other-race schoolmates outside of school at least once or twice that semester." About one out of nine reported that this had occurred ten or more times. About one-third had visited the home of an other-race student or had been so visited—compared to about half for same-race students—a much smaller differential than one might have expected. In answer to a question about the composition of the "informal group of friends . . . with whom you hang around a lot, or with whom you do things pretty often," of those who acknowledged belonging to such a group (about two-thirds of students) more than one in four reported the group to be racially mixed. If these data are in any way typical of other cities, it is hard to escape the conclusion that much of what happens to race relations within the school is intertwined with out-of-school social structure.

There is still another boundary that observers of school social structure do not cross: that between students and teachers. The obvious fact that the two groups are part of the same social system does not intrude on the practice of studying the two groups quite separately. But which students like which teachers and vice versa have crucial effects on what happens in the classroom. When Mr. Brown expects the worst from James because he heard from Mrs. Green, who had him in class last year, that he is a "trouble-maker"—and such conversation is a staple of teachers' lounge gossip—we have hard evidence that the co-presence of teachers and students in the same system of social relations must be taken seriously. The fate of James in Mr. Brown's classroom will depend not only on his IQ or his motivation, but also on which other teachers Mr. Brown talks to when he is puzzled about how to interpret James' behavior, and what relations those teachers have had to him and to James.

It is not only students who have reputations. Student gossip at all levels of education has as a choice topic the relative abilities, habits, and eccentricities of teachers. There are few classes where students begin the year with no preconceptions about the new teacher. "Information" from older siblings and friends sets up initial conditions that may have year-long effects. Teacher training emphasizes the importance of setting the right "tone" in the first few days (the "don't smile until Christmas" strategy), but little research has addressed the question of how students' behavior and preconceptions shape these outcomes.

In everyday school activity, then, students and teachers continually assess and rank-order one another by various criteria, and these rank-orders affect behavior. But researchers only ask children how they rank-order one another. Perhaps it is time to ask children which teachers in the school they like best, and to combine this information with teachers' assessments of children, of one another, and with the traditional children–children information, to get a more rounded picture of what happens in the school.

2. THE PRACTICE OF STRUCTURAL ANALYSIS

The difficulties of choosing appropriate units and levels of analysis are severe, and my comments in the previous section are only a beginning of their solution. Nevertheless, I want now to abstract away from those difficulties, to discuss in more detail the practice of structural analysis in the desegregated school setting.

A preliminary comment is in order on measurement: There has been almost no attempt to measure the actual segregation of school social relations with any procedure comparable across settings. Investigations have instead contented themselves with off-hand statements to the effect that there was very little inter-racial interaction, without reference to any clear baseline expectation. Where measures of segregation have been used, they are of a highly aggregated kind; these indexes of "dissimilarity" or "exposure" do not indicate actual levels of cross-race interaction.

Where sociometric data exist, it would be logical to use them to indicate such levels. Freeman (1978) suggested an index of segregation based on the extent to which actually observed relations between groups exceed what one would expect, given actual absolute numbers of each group, if choices were made without regard to race. (See also Blau 1977, Chaps. 2 and 4, for extensive analysis of the significance of relative numbers for interaction between members of two groups.) If, for example, we had 20 blacks and 80 whites in a group, each of the blacks could interact with any of the whites, and so there are 1600 possible cross-race pairs. In the total group of 100, there are $(100 \times 99)/2$ possible pairs, which is 4950. If relations were random, therefore, we would expect 1600/4950 to be cross-race, that is, 32%. Suppose we observe 120 social relationships in this group. If race were not a factor in choosing, we would expect 32% of these 120 relations to be cross-race, or 38.8. Suppose we observe that only 12 are. Freeman proposes that we take as the extent of segregation the proportional deviation from random expectation, that is, $(38.8\text{-}12)/38.8 = .69$. This measure can be used to compare groups. It reaches 1.0 only when segregation is complete, and is 0.0 when the number of cross-race links is exactly what would be expected by chance. Negative values indicate cross-group choosing in excess of chance: that is, a preference for other-group members rather than one's own. Formally, if N is group total size, B the number of blacks, W the number of whites, C the number of observed cross-race relations, T the observed total number of relations, and S the segregation index, we have

$$S = 1 - \frac{(C)(N)\,(N-1)}{(T)(B)(W)2}$$

Such a measure presupposes the existence of sociometric data, but there are a number of complex methodological and substantive issues concerning the collection of such data that need to be discussed. I now turn to these.

Consider first the use of fixed-choice sociometric procedures, where respondents must name some exact number of others (usually three). Despite ample evidence that such procedures distort the data of actual relations in ways that are difficult to correct (Holland and Leinhardt, 1973), they are commonly used in desegregation research. Distortions are of two kinds: overstatement of the number of relations for isolated individuals, and understatement for those with many friends and acquaintances. In effect, this format homogenizes data that may actually be rather heterogeneous.

It also makes the discovery of weak ties unlikely. This is consistent with the rather narrowly atomized theoretical focus that I criticized in the previous section, because weak ties are of less interest at the dyadic level where they occur than at the level of a larger social system where they have more profound consequences. As I have argued elsewhere (Granovetter, 1973, 1983), weak ties play a crucial role in structural cohesion because our acquaintances are less likely to know one another and more likely to know strangers to us than our close friends. They are thus our bridge to social circles different from our own. From a larger perspective, this implies that insofar as various social circles are connected, it is precisely through weak ties. It may therefore be a tactical error to focus exclusively on strong dyadic interracial ties as the sociometric criterion for successful desegregation (as in, e.g., Clement et al., 1979). Following this line of argument, Karweit et al. (1979) suggested that the key to successful desegregation may, in fact, lie in the stimulation of weak rather than strong interracial ties—promising, if true, because the former are easier to stimulate than the latter (see, e.g., Hansell et al., 1981). Karweit et al. (1979, p. 20) raised the possibility that "racial integration in the classroom can be achieved by arranging classroom structures to produce enough weak contacts to connect black and white cliques, rather than by encouraging strong biracial friendships," and they suspect that the emphasis on strong ties is related to the view that assimilation is the desired end of desegregation. "A more realistic and sensitive result," they suggest,

> given existing cultural diversity, would be to foster diversity without conflict and isolation. Thus an alternative, perhaps more desirable peer structure would be one in which diverse cultures can exchange information and support without necessarily becoming more similar. (Karweit et al., 1979, p. 19)

I would add that a related difficulty with the use of strong cross-race ties as a success criterion is that blacks who become close friends with whites may do so at the expense of their ties to other blacks, becoming integrated into white cliques (see Granovetter, 1973, pp. 1368–1369). St. John (1975, see also Leinhardt, 1972) has observed that the tendency to form cliques among adolescents makes desegregation more difficult than among younger children. Cliques tend to be homogeneous and exclusive in membership, and the addition of a black to a formerly all-white clique on the assimilationist terms I have suggested does not really connect the races. Stable acquaintanceship ties between blacks and whites may be less likely to generate this outcome and thus be more valuable as actual intergroup links.

Adolescent cliques that might bring great pressure against a member with "too many" other-race friends, and that might ultimately break off relations with such a member, should be more tolerant to the extent these relations are seen as acquaintanceships. Even more important, as the number of such weak ties grows, one would expect norms on the permissibility of other-race friends to moderate. Such norms are not etched in stone, but evolve as function of previous behavior and existing social structure. Where no one in a group has other-race friends, the first person to do so stands out rather sharply and is especially vulnerable to peer pressure. As such friendships become more common, the level of deviance involved is arguably less, and the individual can find more social support. Norms on racial contact may be more fragile than they appear, and even the establishment of ties so weak as to be barely perceptible may shake them. In his *Children of Crisis* (1964), Coles describes an Atlanta high school, early in school integration, where only two black girls were enrolled in an otherwise all-white school. The girls were ostracized by the white students until late in the year. Coles' interview of George, a white student, includes the following account:

> One day in April she dropped her lab notebook . . . and before he could think about it he had picked it up. One of his friends ridiculed him and called him a traitor . . . He reminded his friend what it was like for her every day of the year . . . The friend was glad that George had talked to him, because like George he had not been without secret sympathy for Lois. He confessed to George that recently he had let her go before him . . . and then he looked around nervously; if seen he would be known to everyone as a "mixer" . . . Only a month or two earlier pointed rudeness to Lois in just such situations was a virtual necessity. (Coles, 1964, p. 133)

On graduation day, George recalled,

> a couple of girls just felt sorry for her or something. They walked up to her and started talking, and before you knew it they were exchanging autographs . . . Soon a few more came up to her, and then a couple of guys started laughing at them and calling them "nigger lover," but no one moved an inch or stopped talking with Lois, and just about everyone around suddenly joined in and told the guys to shut up and leave. You might have thought Lois was some big star or something.(Coles, 1964, pp. 137–138)

This is not to deny the power of existing peer-group norms concerning racial mixing. Students often assert that they have few other-race friends on account of pressure from their friends against such relationships, and there is no reason to doubt their account. Patchen (1982) reports, for example, that the amount of friendly contact with blacks reported by whites in Indianapolis high schools increases sharply with the proportion of blacks in the classes—except for those whites that report negative racial attitudes among their peers. Similarly, the number of classes in which whites were members of small interracial student groups working together on some project was highly correlated with friendly contact and with friendship between the races, but the effect was strong only when whites' peers had positive racial attitudes, much weaker for intermediate attitudes, and almost negligible for those whose peers were negative. These findings indicate that, other things equal, the proportion of other-race people available to interact with will have strong impact on how many cross-race friendships and acquaintanceships form. This is hardly surprising, because the more members of one's own class or work group are other-race individuals, the more trouble it is to confine own's interaction to those who are not. In the absence of any strong motivation for such confinement, it is easier to become friendly with those just at hand. This is the underlying rationale for random baseline measure of interactional segregation like Freeman's (1978), discussed earlier. Strong peer-group norms against such interactions can impose a sufficient cost to motivate whatever effort is necessary to avoid them.

Patchen's data make clear, however, that not all adolescent groups *have* such norms, and I have already suggested that those which do may not continue to indefinitely. The really interesting theoretical and practical question is what kinds of circumstances, situations, and behaviors lead such group norms to change or to develop in one group and not another. To argue as I have that norms are modified by social contact, as well as affecting such contact, is not new in the study of intergroup relations (see, e.g., Pettigrew, 1971). But the general principle offers little guidance in the crucial task of demonstrating in detail how this occurs. I return later to this theme in my discussion of the dynamics of mixing and sorting.

Thus far I have argued that the use of free-choice sociometric procedures and analysis of weak as well as strong ties will broaden the structural picture beyond that of the individual and pair. Another related route to this result is to consider the impact of indirect ties. Who is known by one's friends significantly conditions relationships and activities. If black students, for example, have white friends who are isolates, the impact is quite different from where the white friends have themselves a rich set of other white contacts. The possible multiplier effects of a friendship are much greater in the latter case.

The existence of such multiplier effects should be taken into account in planning interventions intended to increase cross-race contact. There is, for example, considerable evidence that breaking students up into teams within the classroom, that work together in some way, helps to generate more cross-race friendships. This finding seems more or less independent of whether the teams are structured internally in a cooperative or competitive way (Slavin and Hansell, 1981). Little is known in detail, however, about how this sociometric outcome develops. Slavin and Hansell (1981, p. 28) pointed out that the "impact of cooperative learning almost certainly involves networks of friendship rather than simply dyadic friendships." They report one particular intervention analyzed in unusual detail, indicating that "many of the new cross-racial friendships . . . formed between students who had never been in the same cooperative group" (1981, p. 29). "In theory," they comment, this should not happen; after all, the teams are usually in competition with each other. . . . However, once a cross-racial friendship is formed, the new friend's friends (of his or her race) become likely candidates as friends as well. In other words, if a white boy makes his first black friend, this relationship bridges formerly isolated black and white peer groups, and opens up an entirely new pool of potential black friends, even possibly reaching beyond the confines of a particular classroom. (1981, p. 29)

Because the original research design was not geared to such considerations, the authors could only speculate. It is important to understand indirect effects of these kinds more systematically.

In another interesting speculation on indirect effects, Karweit *et al.* (1979, p. 26) suggested that the "path distance" between a student and school-activity leaders—that is, the smallest number of links needed to connect the two—may have significant impact on the ultimate likelihood of participation. Black students with white friends who are not themselves central in extracurricular activities, but whose friends are, may be less likely to be alienated from such activities than those with no indirect contact at all.

Standard sociometric procedures may also be faulted for reducing the richness of social life to a single relation: friendship. Multiple types of relations characterize real situations and must be considered. Enmity is as important as friendship, in real life, and figures prominently in ethnographic accounts of some desegregated schools. Yet, I know of only one study that studies negative relations systematically. Patchen (1982) found that unfriendly contact between races was common but was uncorrelated with friendly contact. That is, students reporting unfriendliness were just as likely also to report friendly cross-race contact as were those with no unfriendly experiences.

These findings help us see a more complex picture of social relations than our simple stereotypes. It is not that some white and black students have friendly cross-race relations and that others are hostile. In reality, students make much more refined differentiations than "other-race person," as the myriad details of other individuals' personalities overwhelm the initially more salient racial difference. "Time after time," Patchen notes, "a student would describe a warm and friendly relationship with one schoolmate of the other race and then go on to describe a fight or argument with another of that race" (1982, p. 73). Moreover, it may be hasty to interpret hostile cross-race relations as mainly race related. Patchen found that

by far the strongest predictor of unfriendly contact was the student's general aggressiveness. Put another way, those students who fought and argued most with schoolmates of their own race also fought and argued most with students of the other race. (1982, p. 221)

Many other kinds of relations contribute to the rich texture of actual everyday interaction in schools: bullying, dominating, provoking, or "testing" (e.g.,

Hanna, 1982; Schofield and Sagar, 1979), tutoring and mutual helping, tattling (Rist, 1978), and respecting. As compared to "best friend" questions, many of these more specific relationships may be comparatively weak, and one way of capturing the importance of weak ties, in addition to allowing students to name as many friendship choices as they like, is also to be sensitive to the rich array of actual, specialized relationships.

Until recently, data on several types of relationships in one group could only be analyzed one relation at a time. The advent of "block-modeling" techniques makes it possible to treat multiple relations simultaneously rather than separately (Arabie et al., 1978; White et al., 1976). These techniques partition the population into mutually exclusive "blocks" of people. People in each block have similar patterns of relations with other blocks and within their own. People in Block A, for example, might all be similar in that they like people in Block B but not those in C, and are liked by those in C and A, but not B. In other words, similarity in relations given and received is the criterion for being put together into a block.

This is superior to the usual clique-finding in two ways. First, it is more general. Members of a block may have relations to one another and in this respect be indistinguishable from a more conventional clique, but this is only a special case. Block-modeling recognizes that the more general issue is whether individuals are in a structurally similar position. Second, the same partition is used for more than one relation. When passing from positive to negative relations, for example, it is unlikely that the same cliques would persist. But it is common to be able to find a block-model—a partition of the population into blocks—which is valid for both relations. An example from White et al., 1976 (also discussed in Arabie et al., 1978), will illustrate the procedure. The data come from 17 men studied by Newcomb (1961). Block-modeling techniques reduced the 17 into 3 sets, with data on both liking and antagonism. In the matrices below, a 1 in the ij cell indicates that members of block i have the given relation to members of block j; a 0 indicates no such relation between the two.

	LIKING				ANTAGONISM		
	Block				Block		
	1	2	3		1	2	3
1	1	0	0	1	0	0	1
2	0	1	0	2	0	0	1
3	1	0	0	3	0	0	1

Inspection of the block-models makes the underlying sociometric pattern clear. Blocks 1 and 2 report liking only within their own blocks; these are cliques in the traditional sense. Both report disliking only members of Block 3. Members of Block 3 like only members of Block 1, not one another, suggesting that Block 1 has somewhat higher status in the group than 2; Block 3 members share the other two blocks' low opinion of themselves and are thus by all accounts low on the totem pole in this group, the only set of people disliked by anyone. What is interesting about this example is how quickly one can get a picture of this group's social structure by observing the block-model pattern on both kinds of relationship. It is the combination that fleshes out the picture and gives a much more accurate feeling of what is happening than could be gotten from the analysis of one relationship alone. When three, four, or more relationships are used, the picture obtained may be that much richer, albeit more complex and ambiguous. Reading off the block-model information allows the analyst to recover the kind of insight about the group that ordinarily requires intense and prolonged enthnographic observation.

There is no simple prescription for exactly which relationships ought to be put into block-models for a given group. That decision requires the investigator to have enough familiarity with the group to be able to classify all observed interactions into a manageable set of relational types. In one setting, helping, encouraging, and handslapping might all be assimilable to the more general notion of "liking" or "positive affect." In another, the distinctions might be significant. Some relations, like teasing, are ambiguous as to whether they are mainly positive or negative. The observer must make a judgment of what kinds of interaction are most significant in shaping the social structure at hand and which are sufficiently similar to be classified together, before further analysis is possible. It is not profound to say this, but is nevertheless important, because researchers who simply use "best friends" as the sociometric criterion are implicitly making a decision about what relations are important in that group. Such decisions must be made explicitly, and recognized as real decisions.

3. THE HISTORICITY OF SOCIAL STRUCTURE

Thus far I have talked as if it were sufficient to analyze properly the present situation to understand desegregation outcomes. But appearances can be misleading when one does not know from what historical sequence they derive. Social structure does not come out of the air. It is in constant flux and results from previous social structure. Nevertheless, historical and dynamic considerations are typically neglected in favor of snapshots. I will try to demonstrate, in what follows, some of the hazards of this neglect.

Analyses of the desegregation situation often report that within classrooms and in extracurricular activities, students sort themselves into racially separate groups. The detailed dynamics of how this occurs, however, are not reported and probably not observed, though it is often noticed that students who attempt to contravene already-established patterns of sorting, by joining an extracurricular activity dominated by the other race or sitting with members of the other racial group in the classroom or cafeteria, are subjected to strong pressures from their own-race friends. It is easy to conclude from this that the sorting, supported by norms against mixing, also resulted from such norms. But, as I observed above, such norms are easiest to uphold precisely in the extreme segregated situation, and other norms might operate if the sorting had not occurred.

What I want to suggest here is the possible value of extremely detailed observation of the process by which school spaces and activities get sorted—a process akin to that described as "tipping" in studies of neighborhood segregation. Models constructed by Schelling (1971, 1978) and by myself (Granovetter, 1978; see also Granovetter and Soong, 1983) suggest that the interplay between individual motives and preferences, and collective outcomes, can be quite complex, and that it may be extremely misleading to try to infer motives from outcomes, because a given outcome may result from a wide variety of different distributions of motives. Conversely, sets of people with almost identical preferences may generate entirely different outcomes.

In my 1978 article, I give the following example. Imagine that 100 people are milling around in some potential riot situation, and that each person can be characterized by a *threshold*—a number of others one would have to see join a riot before one would also join. Suppose further that these 100 people had thresholds distributed uniformly, as follows: one at Threshold 0 (the "instigator"), one at Threshold 1, one at 2, one at 3, etc., up to one at 99. The final outcome here is that all 100 riot, because the person with Threshold 0 begins, which activates the person with Threshold 1, which activates the person with Threshold 2, etc. Now, change the crowd as follows. Remove the person with Threshold 1 and replace this person by someone with Threshold 2. This new crowd is almost identical, but now, after the instigator riots, there is no crowd member with a threshold as low as 1, so no one further joins. Observers of the two incidents would probably assume that the crowds were completely different: the first made up of "radicals" or "troublemakers" or "riffraff" (depending on the situation and one's prejudices), and the second of solid citizens—with one exception, presumably an outside agitator. But we know, instead, that the crowds were essentially identical, and that it was only a peculiarity in the exact shape of the distribution of thresholds that led to such different outcomes. In my paper, and in Granovetter and Soong (1983), it is shown that this phenomenon is quite general, not confined to the particular numbers chosen here for illustration.

Schelling's (1971, 1978) related analysis of segregation can be adapted to the case of extracurricular activities as follows. Suppose an activity starts out 50% white and 50% black, and that although different students have different levels of tolerance for being in the racial minority, most would be quite happy to take part in an activity that was moderately integrated. Suppose the activity becomes 51% white and 49% black. The problem is that if there are even a handful of black students who have *no* tolerance for minority status in the activity, and who therefore now leave, their leaving reduces the proportion of blacks still further—perhaps to 40%. There may now be blacks who were content at 49% but leave at 40%, further reducing the proportion of blacks. As this occurs, whites who were not willing to join an activity 51% white, but to whom 60% is acceptable may now join, increasing the proportion white. The "domino effect" described here may not end until a very high level of segregation has occurred, even though hardly anyone in the initial group wanted such a level. Again, it is not the attitudes or preferences of participants in this model that generate segregation, but rather the exact distribution of these preferences and how they are implemented over time. Schelling's (1978) analyses of segregation in hypothetical neighborhoods yielded similar results, but with a spatial dimension that may be relevant to classroom seating patterns when students are given freedom to sit where they like.

Not all activities or schools experience racial tipping. Most extracurricular activities in Indianapolis high schools that Patchen (1982) studied were, by teachers' reports, integrated. Only 12% were all white or black, though another 17% were reported to be more than 95% one race. It appears, moreover, that those activities that were integrated made some difference in social relations, because "greater extra-curricular participation is one of the very best predictors of more friendly contact with other-race schoolmates," and is associated with friendship as well (Patchen, 1982, p. 191). For whites, the larger the average proportion black in their activities, the more friendships they report with blacks.

Certain activities recur in ethnographic reports as unusually likely to be integrated. In Memphis, Collins (1979) reported that the band was unique in its easy racial mixing and that friendships even carried over to the lunchroom—the only consistent racial mixing there. In a northern high school, Scherer and Slawski (1979) reported that most activities were segregated, but the band was a marked exception, showing high levels of interracial contact. In a New York City high school, Sullivan (1979) reported ethnic mixing especially in the theater club.

One cannot rule out the possibility that these patterns occur because of self-selection of students with relaxed racial attitudes into "arty" activities. But the discussion of tipping may also be relevant. If students are sensitive to the proportion of their own racial group involved in an activity, then the size of the overall group is significant. Activities with small numbers might tip more easily and, for this reason, be more prone to be tipped as a matter of deliberate political manipulation by an ethnic group that feels that it must "capture" activities to assert status in the school. Band and theater groups, by contrast, may be among the larger activities in a high school.

Furthermore, partly on account of size, partly from the intensity of the activity, band and theater groups are relatively closed and self-sustaining islands of interaction in the school. Once integrated, such groups can therefore sustain norms which permit integration to continue. Scherer and Slawski (1979, p. 146) commented that the "high levels of interracial contact in the band are possible because of the high status that band members have . . . and because the band constitutes a closed society . . . that supports its own norms," in a school where there are generally strong norms against crossing racial lines.

The idea of relatively self-contained "islands" of interaction within the school structure, where genuine integration can flourish, may be quite important. This point can be illustrated by the dynamics of sorting in classroom seating. Schofield and Sagar (1979, p. 187) noticed that there was more interracial interaction among children who "share a table than among the same children when they are assigned to sit next to one another in individual chairs with writing arms." I suggest that this may occur because some such tables become self-defined "neighborhoods," islands of integration.

Consider a classroom with no tables, only individual seats, where children choose their own. Suppose, as Schelling does in his model of neighborhoods, that children are mainly sensitive to the racial proportions in a "neighborhood" that each defines with him- or herself at the center—that is, who sits in front, in back, and to the sides. Even if most children are satisfied with the racial balance in their vicinity, just a few malcontents can have enormous impact. As they leave their previous seats to find an area with more of their own race, they make both their old and new neighborhood more racially homogeneous. Doing so may create a situation where some who were previously content now are in too much of a minority for their taste, and these will now also shift. Each such shift, perhaps one day at a time, not only creates more segregation in seating, but also leads to more such shifts, until segregation may be complete. This may occur even if there was initially only a single area of the classroom where anyone was dissatisfied; the "wave" of tipping originating in this area has rippled through the room.

This is possible because each student's neighborhood overlaps that of each other student, which can happen only where such neighborhoods are self-defined. Where tables define the relevant neighborhood, however, and all students at a table are satisfied with the racial balance, what happens at other tables is irrelevant. As tables become small social systems, they may discourage entry by individuals dissatisfied at other tables, especially to the extent they have an already satisfactory equilibrium and have begun to generate their own norms for interracial behavior, corresponding to their own actual situation. Thus, even if a few tables do undergo racial tipping, the effects will be confined to those, rather than ovewhelming the entire room.

My argument here was suggested in part by Boorman and Levitt's (1980) mathematical treatment of a problem in population biology: How is it possible that there exist species whose members act altruistically toward one another, given that such behavior will decrease one's own survival possibilities except in situations where most other species members also behave the same way? Genes favoring such behavior would be selected against in the early stages of evolution because they would not be dominant in the population. They point out that the usual models are based on a homogeneously mixing population, in which case the initial frequency of such a gene would indeed have to be improbably high before it could spread. They note, however, that real populations do not mix homogeneously, but rather are split up into more or less closed islands of interaction, with some connections among islands. The conditions for the social gene to become dominant in just a few such small islands are less stringent, and so a few may tip in this direction. Then, if the level of contact among islands is just right—neither too small nor too large—the social trait may spread to other islands and eventually become dominant in the overall population. What is crucial is that the decoupling of the population breaks the process down into two steps: the fixation of sociality on islands, and then the cascade of the trait through the *set* of islands. The possibility of such a cascade arises for far smaller concentrations of the relevant genes than would be the case if the population were homogeneous.

The Boorman–Levitt model is not only mathematically complex but depends for its exact results on various assumptions that are specialized to genetics and obviously not appropriate in our context. Nevertheless, the general line of argument has a certain plausibility in a wide variety of situations. They suggest, for example, that one

> area that invites cascade analysis is the historical development of social structures in late feudal Western Europe, where extreme barriers to other than local communication tended to make each town an island weakly connected to other islands by exchange of migrant travelers. For reasons familiar from the present cascade analysis, this pattern may have set boundary conditions making possible social changes that would not have been realized in political or social systems of a more centralized or freely communicating type. (Boorman and Levitt, 1980, p. 363)

In the context of school desegregation, the argument would be similar. It is unlikely, beginning from a situation of social segregation and norms against cross-race friendships, that a school with no clearly defined or bounded activities could generate a substantial level of integration. Any subgroup that veered in that direction would be subject to intense pressure because of its completely open and permeable boundaries. Only relatively well-defined islands of interaction—be they defined by spatial relations in a classroom, by assignment to cooperative work groups, or by the contents of a particular extracurricular activity—would be likely to swim against the stream and develop real social integration. If such groups were truly islands—in the sense that members were quite out of contact with nonmembers—there would be little overall effect on the school at large. But with a moderate level of contact among such islands and the rest of the school population—perhaps divided into other islands with the more typically segregated peer groups—this new situation might spread. The mechanism for spread would be related to my earlier discussion of multiplier effects and to the likely attenuation of strong norms that are placed into intimate contact with other norms wholly inconsistent.

From a policy viewpoint, the implication of this argument would be that creating small integrated structures of interaction might have a ripple effect far greater than that which might be expected only from changes in individual attitudes within those structures. For the analyst trying to understand the process of sorting racially segregated or mixed groups, the lesson is the necessity of observing in some detail the exact historical sequence of social structures within a school, with special sensitivity to the existence of sheltered enclaves that may then spread social change. Snapshots of this process at some end point, or even at successive points in time, are unlikely to yield much insight without some explicit argument about the nature of the dynamic process in operation.

The time element introduced thus far in this section is one of relatively brief duration. Indeed, the fact that tipping phenomena occur so quickly probably accounts for their invisibility in the analysis of school desegregation. But the historicity of social structure extends further into the past as well, in ways that need to be taken account of. Though some studies of desegregation situations have been longitudinal, they have still not taken the historical imbeddedness of social structure seriously enough. The social structure of students and teachers, in a school which begins desegregation, already has a history, one which affects future outcomes.

Collins (1979, p. 102) pointed out, for example, that in the Memphis high school he studied, when the black students arrived there was already in place a "clique of [white] students who had been together from first grade on, and they were well organized. Even the white students who arrived from a different junior high school had difficulty gaining any prominence." Standard sociometric procedures would identify such a clique but miss the historical dimension that gave it its strength and meaning.

How common such long-standing structures of relations are is worth asking, as it may affect desegregation results in important ways. Understanding this issue requires detailed attention to the extent and patterns of children's mobility between schools and school systems over a period of some years before the desegregation situation to be analyzed (see St. John, 1975, p. 5). This is inextricably linked to patterns of residential mobility and to administrative policies concerning which lower schools feed into which higher ones and how school boundaries are drawn. Such factors are obscured by a focus on one point in time or on a period beginning with but not antedating desegregation.

The intent of these comments is not to argue that longstanding social structures in place at the outset of desegregation necessarily impede that process, though that seems to be the case in Collins' account. If that long-standing structure were one already desegregated, the opposite might well be true. Patchen (1982, p. 219) found that

> for students of both races, . . . friendly interracial contact in the neighborhood prior to high school and in grade school contributed to more friendly interracial contact in high school . . . the combined effect of friendly contact in the neighborhood and in grade school was substantial.

Unfortunately, because this study did not ask students about *specific* relationships, we cannot determine to what extent this correlation results from the impact of early integration on attitudes, as against the simple possibility of continuation into high school of the same interracial friendships begun earlier. Now that the importance of this historical dimension has been established, future studies should ask more explicitly whether existing interracial ties are newly created or held over from earlier experience.

Existing structures of relations, then, may have either negative or positive impacts. In either case they closely constrain what outcomes are likely. Students who know each other already will not respond mainly to such abstract matters as racial proportions, as suggested in models of racial tipping, but will instead be more closely attuned to individual identities and previous relationships, in deciding where to sit or what activities to join. Where existing relations are absent, as in a new town, outcomes might be more volatile and unpredictable. Everything must be sorted out from scratch, and the dynamics of mixing and sorting take place in their purest form, with all the complexity I have suggested they can entail.

4. THE IMPACT OF "SUCCESSFUL" DESEGREGATION

Suppose that by "successful" desegregation we mean at least some moderate amount of interracial friendship and reduction of cross-racial intolerance. It hardly needs belaboring that a reduction in ethnic animosity—an increased openness to individuals and cultures of other groups—is intrinsically a benefit worth pursuing. In this section I will focus, rather, on some more concrete possible outcomes.

4.1. Effects on Academic Success

Looking at the short run, there is much interest in whether blacks' achievement levels rise when they enter a school where white levels are higher. Findings on this question are mixed and ambiguous, and theoretical arguments on what one ought to expect are underdeveloped. Miller (1980) notes that expectations of increased minority achievement were originally rooted in what he calls the "lateral transmission of values" hypothesis: that certain values facilitate achievement; that white children are more likely to have them than black; and that desegregation can therefore result in an increase of black achievement by the transmission of these values. His review of the evidence offers little warrant for these assumptions, which he concludes are a drastic oversimplification.

I believe that we need to understand much better the extent to which interaction among students affects learning. Interaction might affect skills by changing behavior even without any change in "values." It is a commonplace in the social psychological literature that individuals who interact frequently become more alike in various relevant ways (Homans, 1950).

Hallinan (1977) pointed out the need to distinguish this from the reverse causal process—selection rather than influence: those who are similar are more likely to become friends to begin with. In a longitudinal study, Epstein (1978, pp. 63, 65) was able to sort out selection from peer influence, and concluded that

> students with initially low and high standardized test scores can be influenced in positive ways by friends with high scores . . . choice of high-achieving friends has positive and continuous influence on student achievement, even when controls are placed on students' own initial scores.

These statistical data do not give us detailed insight into the mechanisms by which these changes occur, but she speculates that for reciprocated friendships, effects result from "directly communicated expectations, and unreciprocated friendship selections influence behavior through modeling or emulation" (1978, p. 68; see also Epstein and Karweit, 1983).

We have little information on whether it is common for blacks with lower scores to be influenced in this positive way by whites with higher ones. Patchen (1982) reported a high frequency of blacks and whites doing school work together. About 1 in 7 reported doing so 10 or more times in the semester, as compared to 1 in 3 who reported this for students of their own race. But because these data do not include the identity of those with whom one worked, there is no way to determine the relative scores of pair members.

It remains to inquire why influence does not operate in the opposite direction, to lower the scores of high achievers. An understanding of this puzzle requires us to consider the complex relations among values, situations, and behavior, and to clarify how the influence noted by Epstein may differ from that pictured in the "transmission of values" argument. An analogy of low achievement to delinquent behavior may be helpful. Sykes and Matza (1957) argued, in their study of delinquent boys, that the boys' values were not significantly different from those of nondelinquents, but the delinquents' peer groups had developed various "techniques of neutralization"—rationales for asserting that the relevant value was not actually applicable to the situation in which the delinquent act occurred. Matza (1964) later elaborated this argument by suggesting that group dynamics were such, among these boys, that for one of them to assert the conventional value (which he held) would be disadvantageous in status competition, because ranking was contingent on more and more daring action. A process of escalation thus occurred in which participants' actions strayed farther and farther from their privately held values. Penalties for stating these values explicitly made it difficult for each boy to be aware of the others' concurrence with his own, resulting in "pluralistic ignorance."

High achievement may be a similar case. It is obviously praised and rewarded by official authorities and at least alleged to be related to higher status later in life. Its connection with official ideology, however, makes it a natural target for adolescent rebellion. There are no doubt adolescents who genuinely despise the notion of high achievement. But there are probably also those who privately aspire to it but cannot express or pursue this within a peer group hostile to it. (Gans, 1963, has made this point dramatically for Italian peer groups in Boston.) For such students the selection of higher-achieving peers may be a groping to escape from this dilemma, by fuzzing over and ultimately restructuring the boundaries of their own peer groups, in ways which will allow them the situational freedom to pursue their preferred goals. An account of this kind suggests how behavior may alter dramatically with no real change in values, only in situational pressures. It has the advantage also of seeing students not merely as passive recipients of influences from elsewhere, but as active shapers of their interpersonal environment. It is probably oversimplified in assuming that any students actually hold only one or another clearcut set of values, when the actual mental constructs affecting behavior are surely more complex and in flux. But it has at least the important quality of freeing the notion of values from its usual status as a tautological renaming of observed behavior.

The structural aspect of this discussion consists of the observation that the extent to which one is influenced by others of higher achievement is not merely the result of dyadic interaction, but is rather imbedded in the social structure of the groups in which the two individuals participate and in the ways these groups generate and change norms for what levels of achievement are permissible. It is surprising, in fact, that the processes outlined here have never been viewed as closely analogous to the often-studied situation in industrial sociology where groups of workers develop definite norms of what constitutes acceptable levels of output (e.g., Homans, 1950). Industrial sociologists have long known that it would be a crude atomization to suppose worker output determined by each worker's "output values."

My discussion thus far concerns the effects of interaction on one's willingness and freedom to pursue academic goals. Some changes in achievement, however, may result more directly from the conveying of specific ideas and techniques among friends. Tutoring relationships as such are rarely reported by classroom observers, perhaps because such an exchange is viewed by students as being so asymmetric. Yet, Blau's (1963) account of an office setting suggests that the tutee may be able to make up his side by engaging in sufficient deference. Tutoring is an activity that may be logistically difficult to manage within school boundaries and schedules and may thus take place mainly in students' neighborhoods and free time, thereby having a genuine but invisible impact on both achievement and status structures.

Mutual helping seems more frequent, requiring either that students be at comparable levels or that there be some skill in which each is better than the other. The latter is made substantially less likely by what Cohen (1980, p. 264) has called "single-ability classrooms," where only one skill, typically reading, is the basis for teachers' and thence students' evaluations of students' competence.

Bossert (1979) studied in detail the effects of classroom organization on social relations. He noticed that in traditional as compared to open classrooms, students were much more likely to choose as friends those similar in academic ability, as demonstrated in competitive recitation, resulting in cliques homogeneous in ability. In open classrooms, where ability was less public and salient, choices seemed much more random in this respect. In the traditional classrooms, furthermore, students seemed much less willing to help one another, presumably because the competitive atmosphere made help to another seem detrimental to one's own position (Bossert, 1979, pp. 82–83). Consistent with this, Hallinan (1980, p. 338) found less cliquing and smaller cliques in open than traditional classrooms, noting also that most "cliques are homogeneous with respect to sex and ethnicity." Neither study explicitly concerned cross-ethnic helping, but Johnson et al. (1981, 1983) summarize a number of other studies that do point to more cross-ethnic helping in cooperative than in competitive or individualistic learning situations.

These ideas may help explain the striking findings of Klein and Eshel (1980) in their study of the integration of Jerusalem elementary schools (between Jews of European and Oriental origins). Integration as such did not improve the achievement of Oriental Jews, but those in integrated classrooms that were open as compared to traditional did considerably better than other Oriental Jews and were closer to European Jews in arithmetic achievement scores. Effects on reading comprehension were smaller, though in the same direction. (It is worth noting that children of European Jewish background also scored higher in integrated, open classrooms than in other settings.)

There is much room here for theoretical speculation and empirical study of what kinds of skills can be expected to change as the result of students' interactions. Klein and Eshel's finding that scores in arithmetic were more responsive than those in reading is consistent with the argument of Mayer *et al.* (1974, p. 42) who suggest that

> social structural change is more likely to work in performance areas that are narrow and depend on recently acquired skills, than in performance areas that depend on more pervasive skills built up over a larger time period.

St. John (1975) refered to this comment to help explain evidence that the proportion of white students in a classroom seems to have a positive impact on the mathematics, but not the other skills, of black students. Intensive observation of interaction may shed light on this question. One supposes, for example, that much of students' mutual help consists of offering answers to problems, without much thought about whether the principle behind the answer has been conveyed. Under what circumstances *do* students attempt to communicate the basic principle? Or are such principles communicated unintentionally, in subtle ways? (See Perret-Clermont, 1982.)

4.2. Effects on Later Socioeconomic Status

In the longer run, Crain and Weisman's (1972) findings, based on a 1966 survey, are tantalizing: Northern blacks who had attended integrated schools were more likely to complete high school and attend college, enter occupations with high status and income, have stable marriages, own homes, live in integrated neighborhoods, have white friends and acquaintances, and say they are happy. McPartland and Braddock (1981, p. 149) reported more recent results based on large longitudinal samples (see also Braddock *et al.*, 1984).

> School desegregation affects the movement of minority students into desegregated settings after high school graduation. . . . Those from earlier segregated school settings are more likely at later stages in their lives to be in segregated colleges and segregated work groups, while those who graduated from desegregated schools are more likely to enter desegregated colleges and work groups.

This is consistent with my (Granovetter, 1974) finding that strong ties are less useful in finding jobs than one might expect, compared to weak ones. School desegregation studies frequently show that cross-racial ties formed are not very strong. But even such weak ties may significantly affect later economic success. Because employers at all levels of work prefer to recruit by word-of-mouth, typically using recommendations of current employees, segregation of friendship and acquaintance means that workplaces that start out all white will remain so.

Becker (1979, pp. 15–16) noted that a 1973 Current Population Survey found that a

> much higher proportion of black youth (16–24) than of whites found certain of the formal intermediaries most useful in their recent job hunt. . . . The other major racial difference . . . is that a much higher proportion of white youth obtain their job by being offered one without taking any actions to find one! This is perhaps the best indication in these data of the superiority of personal networks for young white job-seekers in comparison to young blacks.

He went on to point out, however, that little direct and compelling evidence applies to this data.

> We will not really know how the social network of job-relevant information functions to allocate a disproportionate share of youth employment to whites, or to what extent black youth's lack of employer-respected references makes a difference until more detailed research is done in this area. (Becker, 1979, p. 20)

Research is urgently needed in which the outcome variable is not number of friendship choices received or changes in test scores, grades, or other short-term data, but rather ultimate socioeconomic results. The essence of the *Brown* decision was that segregated education is inherently unequal. Social science research on whether desegregated education is indeed more equal has focused on relatively narrow measures of this equality. It is worth recalling that the philosophical justification for quality of education has been, through much of American history, the notion that it is related to equal life chances. Though there may be overwhelming evidence that schools have not typically equalized life chances (e.g., Persell, 1977), such equalization remains a criterion worth using in asking the value of school desegregation. The research question that arises directly from this criterion is whether the life chances of blacks who attend desegregated schools are significantly improved over those of comparable blacks who do not. Because there is ample evidence that test scores and grades in school do not explain much of the variance in later income or status (Jencks *et al.*, 1979), these latter results must be studied directly.

5. THE MACRO CONTEXT OF MICROSTRUCTURAL ANALYSIS

In the preceding, I have blithely ignored the larger social context, while suggesting how one might better understand and manage the structures of social relationships within desegregated schools. Despite the value of intellectual division of labor, the analyst making arguments about this microstructural level is also obliged to step back and ask whether the macro context in which schools are embedded is such as to nullify or make irrelevant his or her theories and recommendations.

One of the best established findings on desegregation, for example, is that how easily and peacefully it is carried out depends heavily on the stance of local political leaders and elites (Crain, 1968; Rossell and Crain, 1982). Huckaby's (1980; see also Record and Record, 1960) blow-by-blow account of school desegregation in Little Rock in 1957–1958 makes it clear that the vast majority of students would have accepted the situation in a relatively quiet and dignified way. Early in the year, some efforts were made by white students to ease the way for their new black schoolmates, but this majority was ultimately intimidated into inaction by a small number of racist students who would not ordinarily have commanded any influence, had they not been closely linked to vociferous and powerful political forces in the city and state.

Another crucial macro-level factor impinging on desegregation is the relation of neighborhoods to schools. I have talked here as if "desegregated schools" had ample numbers of both black and white students to work with, so that substantial integration would be at least a statistical possibility. In many central cities this is increasingly unrealistic. In the 1976 school year, Detroit had 19% white students; in 1978–1979, Atlanta had 10%; and in 1980–1981, Chicago had 18.6%, and St. Louis 22% (Orfield, 1981). These numbers have been declining consistently. In such cities, even if every school had the average percentage of whites for the city as a whole, this percentage is small enough that within each school resegregation can easily be affected by tracking or other administrative practices, multiplier effects of cross-racial friendship diminish quickly, and tipping effects occur more readily.

One of the first stumbling blocks school desegregation must overcome is, of course, the tendency of students' relationships out of school to be within-race, which may result largely in turn from existing patterns of housing segregation. Cities that have nearly no white students are only an extreme example of this general pattern. Furthermore, it is typical for schools to be more segregated than neighborhoods because changing neighborhoods

> generally have older white families with relatively few children in school, but they attract young successful minority families with school-age children. In any case, minority families normally send a higher proportion of their children to public as opposed to parochial or private schools. This means that a 25% black neighborhood can easily have a 50% black school. (Orfield, 1981, p. 206)

It is a commonplace observation that residential segregation makes school integration difficult. Less often noticed is the role of school segregation or integration in shaping the residential situation. This reverse connection has been noted primarily in connection with claims that "excessive" desegregation would lead to white flight. But more subtle processes are also at work. Epps *et al.* (1980, p. 235) noted that the racial composition of a school and its staff tends to stamp that identity on the surrounding neighborhood. In many urban areas, the attendance zone of a school defines the only effective boundary between "neighborhoods." Homebuyers use school attendance zones as a guide in their selection of a residence. Realtors take particular pains to "sell" the school as they sell the home; the school zone is listed in many newspaper classified advertisements for homes and often serves to identify the racial character of the "neighborhood."

Orfield (1981, p. 205) summarized a number of recent studies showing that

a significant number of whites continue to move into integrated neighborhoods until the transition is well advanced. The basic problem is that minority families move in faster, thus gradually making the community more and more heavily minority until virtually all whites stop considering it as a possible place to live.

This suggests that even relatively small increases in the number of whites entering such neighborhoods might have large impacts in preventing residential tipping (see also Taub et al., 1984). If local schools and their racial composition are a significant factor in moving decisions, it may follow that any policy that insures stably integrated schools may have unexpectedly powerful effects in stabilizing neighborhood integration. This possibility should be entered into the cost/benefit considerations surrounding school integration plans.

Another example of the way broad macro-features of a school system impinge on the behavior of actors in the school desegregation situation is the relation of this situation to the society's labor market and manpower needs. It is clear, for instance, that one of the main mechanisms of resegregation in nominally integrated schools is curriculum tracking. The obvious recommendations are to reduce such tracking, make track assignment more easily changeable, track by subject but not by entire curriculum, etc. These recommendations would be easier to implement if tracking were only what it appears to be: an attempt to deal efficiently with academically heterogeneous populations. But an increasing literature on tracking suggests that there may also be a more subtle and pervasive factor supporting it: the need for the economic system to fill positions at all levels, low as well as high. In her comprehensive review of this literature, Persell (1977, Chap. 6) pointed out that tracking was promoted originally by industrialists early in the 20th century. As businessmen became increasingly influential on boards of education, controlling appointments and helping shape educational practice with ideas and philanthropic contributions, their quite explicit concern that education be geared to meeting the manpower needs of business came to be the dominant conception. Emphasis on testing and sorting was given a scientific cast by the increasing use of psychometrics, with test development heavily supported by major industrial foundations.

The use of tracking increased greatly in the 1920s and 1930s, "when large numbers of foreign immigrants needed to be incorporated into the labor force"; it fell into disuse until the late 1950s when it was revived in conjunction with the outcry raised by Sputnik but also with "increasing migration of rural Southern blacks to Northern cities and an influx of Puerto Rican and Mexican American immigrants" (Persell, 1977, p. 85). In all periods and settings, one result of tracking seems to have been classroom resegregation of ethnic groups in schools nominally integrated. Persell (1977, p. 162) commented that education

> contributes to the reproduction of structures of dominance in two major experiential ways: through the isolating and insulating of experiences; and the correspondence between the experiential nature of education and the requirements of work. Education occurs in relatively segregated and isolated groups, divided along wealth-owning, occupational and racial lines . . . Under such conditions, members of all groups fail to experience each other . . . Once groups with different pasts or different futures are identified and separated, they are exposed to quite different experiences that prepare them most appropriately for their respective futures.

To the extent this is correct, resistance to changes will be far greater than might be expected on educational grounds alone. Note that this analysis does not assert that the educators directly in charge of tracking are themselves mainly concerned with economic outcomes; their beliefs may indeed be based purely on a philosophy of education. It is rather argued that the strong influence of business on what research is funded and on who is appointed to school administrative positions makes more likely the development of this particular philosophy of education and the appointment of those who hold it. Such a process operates over a long period of time and in ways not obviously and explicitly visible. Proponents of changes in our system of tracking and sorting can have more effect if they attend not only to the pure educational issues in isolation but also the broader socioeconomic context in which tracking is set.

It has also been argued that labor market characteristics have quite direct effects on student behavior and performance. It is a commonplace of American ideology that education is the royal road to economic success, and that those who fail in schooling are thereby doomed to economic failure as well. In his study of a small town high school, Stinchcombe (1964, p. 6) turned this argument on its head, asserting that when

> a student realizes that he does not achieve future status increment from improved current performance, current performance loses meaning. The student becomes hedonistic because he does not visualize achievement of long-run goals through current self-restraint. He reacts negatively to a conformity that offers nothing concrete. . . . The future, not the past, explains adolescent rebellion, contrary to the hypothesis that deviant attitudes are the result of distinctively rebel biographies.

In this study, Stinchcombe assumed that low school achievers, who become rebels because they see that the labor market holds little promise for them, are "less intelligent," and that this explains their low achievement. Ogbu (1978 and this volume) takes the argument a step further, asserting that for whole categories of people, particularly the ones he refers to as "caste-like minorities," low school achievement is the direct result of their perception of a "job ceiling" in the labor market that assures that the return on any efforts they put into the educational process will be smaller than if they were members of the dominant group. The opportunity structure forces blacks

> to rely on white patronage to achieve jobs and other necessities of life. And competence in winning their objective through patronage requires the skills of dependence, compliance and manipulation. Thus, the caste system requires blacks to renounce such white motivational skills as autonomy, independence, initiative and competitiveness in order to "make it" in the wider society. (Ogbu, 1978, pp. 211–212; see also Ogbu, this volume)

He argues that black females typically perform better in school than do males because they understand that their opportunities are better. His review of the literature in five other societies confirms that, in all cases, subordinate ethnic groups do worse in school and face labor market discrimination. Ogbu's argument that the perception of a "job ceiling" makes academic striving seem like wasted effort is plausible. But there are very few studies that assess this proposition directly, and formidable methodological problems would be encountered.

To the extent this argument is valid, attempts to equalize achievement between ethnic groups and to reduce stereotypical and status-oriented intergroup behavior will face barriers that cannot be properly understood with reference only to an isolated micro-level situation.

The examples in this section make no pretense of being a complete catalogue of ways in which the small-scale situation is embedded in a larger societal context that has substantial if sometimes subtle and hidden impact on personal interactions and behaviors. The purpose here has only been to sensitize the reader to the importance of taking this context into account in any attempt to understand what is happening and what can and cannot be done by attending only to a micro-level of analysis.

ACKNOWLEDGMENTS

The author is indebted to Jomills Braddock, Robert Crain, Robert Liebman, Jeffrey Prager, and Stanley Katz for their detailed comments and suggestions.

REFERENCES

Arabie, P., Boorman,S., and Levitt, P. Constructing blockmodels: How and why. *Journal of Mathematical Psychology*, 1978, *17*(1), 21–63.

Becker, H. *Personal networks of opportunity in obtaining jobs: Racial differences and effects of segregation* (Report No. 281). Baltimore, MD: Baltimore Center for Social Organization of Schools, Johns Hopkins University, 1979.

Blau, P. *The Dynamics of Bureaucracy*. Chicago, IL: University of Chicago Press, 1963.

Blau, P. *Inequality and Heterogeneity*. New York: Free Press, 1977.

Boorman, S., and Levitt, P. *The Genetics of Altruism*. New York: Academic Press, 1980.

Bossert, S. *Tasks and Social Relationships in Classrooms*. New York: Cambridge University Press, 1979.

Braddock, J. H., Crain, R. L., and McPartland, J. M. A long-term view of school desegregation. *Phi Delta Kappan*, 1984, *66*(4), 259–264.

Bullard, P., and Stoia, J. *The Hardest Lesson: Personal Accounts of a School Desegregation Crisis*. Boston: Little, Brown, 1980.

Clement, D., Eisenhart, M., and Jarding, J. The veneer of harmony: Social-race relations in a southern desegregated school. In R. Rist (Ed.) *Desegregated Schools*. New York: Academic Press, 1979.

Cohen, E. Design and redesign of the desegregated school. In W. Stephan and J. Feagin (Eds.), *School Desegregation: Past, Present, and Future*. New York: Plenum Press, 1980.

Coles, R. *Children of Crisis*. Boston: Little, Brown, 1964.

Collins, T. From courtrooms to classrooms: Managing school desegregation in a deep south high school. In R. Rist (Ed.), *Desegregated Schools*. New York: Academic Press, 1979.

Crain, R. *The Politics of School Desegregation*. Chicago: Aldine, 1968.

Crain, R., and Weisman, C. *Discrimination, Personality and Achievement*. New York: Aldine, 1968.

Epps, E., Taylor, D. G., Farley, R., Pearce, D., Loewen, J., and Orfield, G. School segregation and residential segregation. In W. Stephan and J. Feagin (Eds.), *School Desegregation: Past, Present, and Future*. New York: Plenum Press, 1980.

Epstein, J. *Friends in school: Patterns of selection and influence in secondary schools* (Report No. 266). Baltimore, MD: Center for Social Organization of Schools, Johns Hopkins University, 1978.

Epstein, J., and Karweit, N. *Friends in School*. New York: Academic, 1983.

Foot, H., Chapman, A., and Smith, J. (Eds.). *Friendship and Social Relations in Children*. New York: Wiley, 1980.

Freeman, L. Segregation in social networks. *Sociological Methods and Research*, 1978, *6*(4), 411–429.

Gans, H. *The Urban Villagers*. New York: Free Press, 1963.

Gerard, H., and Miller, N. *School Desegregation*. New York: Plenum Press, 1975.

Granovetter, M. The strength of weak ties. *American Journal of Sociology*, 1973, *78*(6), 1360–1380.

Granovetter, M. *Getting a Job: A Study of Contacts and Careers*. Cambridge, MA: Harvard University Press, 1974.

Granovetter, M. Threshold models of collective behavior. *American Journal of Sociology*, 1978, *83*(6), 1420–1443.

Granovetter, M. The strength of weak ties; A network theory revisited. In R. Collins (Ed.), *Sociological Theory* (Vol. 1), San Francisco: Jossey-Bass, 1983.

Granovetter, M., and Soong, R. Threshold models of diffusion and collective behavior. *Journal of Mathematical Sociology*, 1983, *9*, 165–179.

Hallinan, M. *The peer influence process: A reconceptualization*. Unpublished manuscript, 1977.

Hallinan, M. Patterns of cliquing among youth. In H. Foot, A. Chapman, and J. Smith (Eds.), *Friendships and Social Relations in Children*. New York: Wiley, 1980.

Hanna, W. Public social policy and the children's world: Implications of ethnographic research for desegregated schooling. In G. Spindler (Ed.), *Doing the Ethnography of Schooling*. New York: Holt, Rinehart, & Winston, 1982.

Hansell, S., Tackaberry, S., and Slavin, R. *Cooperation, competition and the structure of student peer groups*. Unpublished manuscript, 1981.

Heyns, B. *Summer Learning and the Effects of Schooling*. New York: Academic Press, 1978.

Holland, P., and Leinhardt, S. The structural implications of measurement error in sociometry. *Journal of Mathematical Sociology*, 1973, *3*, 85–111.

Homans, G. *The Human Group*. New York: Harcourt, 1950.

Huckaby, E. *Crisis at Central High: Little Rock 1957–1958*. Baton Rouge, LA: Louisiana State University Press, 1980.

Jencks, C., Bartlett, S., Corcoran, M., Crouse, J., Eaglesfield, D., Jackson, G., McClelland, K., Mueser, P., Olneck, M., Schwartz, J., Ward, S., and Williams, J. *Who Gets Ahead?* New York: Basic Books, 1979.

Johnson, D., Johnson, R., and Maruyama, G. *Interdependence and cross-ethnic relationships in the desegregated classroom* (Final Report NIE-G-80-0192). Washington, DC: National Institute of Education, 1981.

Johnson, D., Johnson, R., and Maruyama, G. Interdependence and interpersonal attraction among heterogeneous and homogeneous individuals. *Review of Educational Research*, 1983, *53*, 5–54.

Karweit, N., Hansell, S., and Ricks, M. The conditions for peer associations in schools (Report No. 282). Baltimore, MD: Center for Social Organization of Schools, Johns Hopkins University, 1979.

Klein, Z., and Eshel, Y. *Integrating Jersualem Schools*. New York: Academic Press, 1980.

Leinhardt, S. Developmental change in the sentiment structure of children's groups. *American Sociological Review*, 1972, *37*(2), 202–212.

Matza, D. *Delinquency and Drift*. New York: Wiley, 1964.

Mayer, R., King, C. E., Borders-Patterson, A., and McCullough, J.S. *The Impact of School Desegregation in a Southern City*. Lexington, MA: Lexington Books, 1974.

Metz, M. H. *Classrooms and Corridors: The Crisis of Authority in Desegregated Secondary Schools*. Berkeley, CA: University of California Press, 1978.

McPartland, J., and Braddock, J. Going to college and getting a good job: The impact of desegregation. In W. Hawley (Ed.), *Effective School Desegregation*. Beverly Hills, CA: Sage, 1981.

Miller, N. Making school desegregation work. In W. Stephan and J. Feagin (Eds.), *School Desegregation. Past, Present, and Future*. New York: Plenum Press, 1980.

Morgan, P. R., and McPartland, J. *The extent of classroom segregation within desegregated schools* (Report No. 314). Baltimore, MD: Center for Social Organization of Schools, Johns Hopkins University, 1981.

Newcomb, T. *The Acquaintance Process*. New York: Holt, Rinehard and Winston, 1961.

Ogbu, J. *Minority Education and Caste*. New York: Academic Press, 1978.

Orfield, G. Housing patterns and desegregation policy. In W. Hawley (Ed.), *Effective School Desegregation*. Beverly Hills, CA: Sage, 1981.

Patchen, M. *Black-White Contact in Schools*. West Lafayette, IN: Purdue University Press, 1982.

Perret-Clermont, A. N. Approaches in the social psychology of learning and group work. In P. Stringer (Ed.), *Confronting Social Issues: Applications of Social Psychology, Vol. 2*. New York: Academic Press, 1982.

Persell, C. *Education and Inequality*. New York: Free Press, 1977.

Pettigrew, T. *Racially Separate or Together?* New York: McGraw-Hill, 1971.

Record, W., and Record, J. C. *Little Rock, U.S.A.* San Francisco: CA: Chandler, 1960.

Rist, R. *The Invisible Children*. Cambridge, MA: Harvard University Press, 1978.

Rossell, C., and Crain, R. L. The importance of political factors in explaining northern school desegregation. *American Journal of Political Science* 1982, *26*(4), 772–793.

St. John, N. *School Desegregation: Outcomes for Children*. New York: Wiley, 1975.

Schelling, T. Dynamic models of segregation. *Journal of Mathematical Sociology,* 1971, *1*, 143–186.

Schelling, T. *Micromotives and Macrobehavior*. New York: Norton, 1978.

Scherer, J., and Slawski, E. Color, class and social control in an urban desegregated school. In R. Rist (Ed.), *Desegregated Schools*. New York: Academic Press, 1979.

Schofield, J., and Sagar, H. The social context of learning in an interracial school. In R. Rist (Ed.), *Desegregated Schools*. New York: Academic Press, 1979.

Slavin, R., and Hansell, S. *Cooperative learning and intergroup relations: Contact theory in the classroom*. Unpublished manuscript, 1981.

Stinchcombe, A. *Rebellion in a High School*. Chicago, IL: Quadrangle Books, 1964.

Sullivan, M. Contacts among cultures: School desegregation in a polyethnic New York City high school. In R. Rist (Ed.), *Desegregated Schools*. New York: Academic Press, 1979.

Suttles, G. *The Social Order of the Slum*. Chicago, IL: University of Chicago Press, 1968.

Sykes, G., and Matza, D. Techniques of Neutralization. *American Sociological Review*, 1957, *26* 644–670.

Taub, R. P., Taylor, D. G., and Dunham, J. D., *Paths of Neighborhood Change*. Chicago, IL: University of Chicago Press, 1984.

White, H., Boorman, S., and Breiger, R. Social structure from multiple networks. *American Journal of Sociology*, 1979, *81*(4), 730–780.

Chapter 4

A Model for Racial Contact in Schools

H. M. BLALOCK

The primary objective of this chapter, as well as others in the volume, is to examine the literature on school desegregation with a view to providing theoretical insights, guidelines, and frameworks that will improve the quality of research in this area. Presumably, our most important objective is not only to improve research quality, but to make a series of recommendations that will be useful to school administrators and teachers regarding the quality and quantity of interracial and interethnic interaction patterns, as well as ways in which the learning environment for all students may also be improved. Yet, scholars who have examined the literature have concluded, rather pessimistically, that in general research findings are inconclusive and that, where empirical relationships have been found, they are both very weak in magnitude and also difficult to "add up" because of their complexity and seeming inconsistency.[1]

Even with good theories, studies may continue to find weak and inconclusive relationships that make it impossible to provide really useful policy guidelines. One reason is that the dependent variables we are trying to predict may be determined by an extremely large number of variables, only a few of which can be identified, accurately measured, and brought under control. Another is that, within the context of American education, there may not be enough real

---

[1]For literature reviews, see St. John (1975), McConahay (1978), Schofield (1978), Longshore and Prager (1985), and Patchen (1982). Patchen's study represents by far the most detailed and theoretically oriented investigation of interracial contacts that the writer has encountered. For more general discussions of interracial contacts, see Allport (1954), Amir (1969), and Blalock and Wilken (1979).

H. M. BLALOCK • Department of Sociology, University of Washington, Seattle, WA 98195.

variation in important causes to afford any chance of explaining variability in the dependent variables of interest; many factors may be virtually constant across our own educational system or even those that have been tried in other countries. Because one must always take some factors as givens, we will not attempt to account for such constancies, the nature of the American educational system, or how it is linked with other major social institutions.[2]

It goes without saying that there must be multiple theories about school desegregation, according to the nature of the dependent variables one wishes to explain. Some such theories could be stated in strictly macro-level terms. For instance, one might attempt to explain community outcomes such as unemployment levels, racial tensions, or occupational distributions in terms of school desegregation levels or educational policies relating to minorities. The dependent variables that seem to be of greatest practical interest, however, tend to be aggregated individual-level variables: such things as the performances of minority and majority children, their aspiration and achievement levels, their self-esteem, or their friendship choices. Given the diversity of such dependent variables, one could hardly expect a single overarching theory of school desegregation to provide a satisfactory explanation of all such variables. Nor would one expect policy decisions affecting, say, the percentages of each group within a particular school or curriculum to have uniformly favorable consequences in all dimensions and under a variety of circumstances.

The strategy employed in the present chapter is designed to illustrate a mode of attack that, I believe, can be employed in connection with a variety of micro-level dependent variables, although the specific explanatory variables introduced will necessarily vary according to the phenomenon being explained. In brief, the aim is to attempt to locate a reasonably small number of general variables that operate at a very proximate level to the actors concerned, in this case school children or adolescents. If the list of such variables is reasonably complete, we may then make the working assumption that all macro-level variables operate through one or more of these proximate variables to affect the behaviors concerned. Thus macro-level variables are brought into the picture as contextual variables in a micro-level explanatory system, with the objective being to work outward from the individual actor to increasingly remote factors that have indirect effects through the intervening mechanisms specified by the theory.

There will be no attempt, in the present chapter, to summarize the growing body of empirical literature dealing with friendship patterns and sociometric choices in school settings.[3] Although most of these studies have not involved data collected in such a manner to permit formal network analyses, their general

---

[2]For a critique of the American educational system and its linkage to our economic and political institutions, see Ogbu (1978 and this volume).

[3]For such summaries, see Patchen (1982) and Epstein and Karweit (1983).

orientation is highly compatible with that developed in Granovetter's chapter on network analysis. The focus of the present chapter is intended to complement such network orientations and is intended to specify a number of different contact dimensions and link these to characteristics of settings that may influence the nature of cross-racial or cross-ethnic contacts. There will be several points, however, at which it will be relevant to comment briefly on some of the findings of these empirical studies.

Nor will there be any effort in this chapter to theorize about the social processes that may affect other types of outcome variables, such as the status attainments of minority members, the general level of community conflict, personal adjustments to later discrimination, or feedbacks to the school desegregation process at a later point in time. The reason is rather simple. Each of these separate outcome variables requires a distinct explanatory theory at least as complex as the one considered in this chapter and involves a set of intervening mechanisms that refer to the experiences and decisions of a variety of actors, each motivated in different ways. For instance, any reasonably complete theory of occupational attainment would have to contain variables relating to the minority actor, the actor's peers, those responsible for hiring decisions, and the actions of competitors. These rather immediate variables would, in turn, be affected by a set of contextual factors, such as the nature of the local economy, union policies, the mix of population characteristics, governmental regulations enforcing affirmative action, and so forth. Such a theory would take us far beyond the school desegregation issue but—I would argue—could employ basically the same strategy of attack as exemplified in the present chapter.

1. A THEORETICAL MODEL FOR CROSS-GROUP CONTACTS

We have noted that one should not necessarily expect to salvage a host of negative findings or confusing patterns of weak relationships merely by producing a theory in the form of a causal model, because there may be a diversity of reasons for these empirical results. Even so, it does seem important to attempt to formulate a theory of intergroup contacts that is reasonably general in that it is applicable not only to school settings but to numerous other contact situations as well. One may then investigate the degree to which the general explanation accounts for interaction patterns within these school settings and explains the behaviors of that special category of persons we refer to as adolescents. We will assume, then, that interaction processes are sufficiently similar that the general model may serve to guide our thinking about school settings.

The theoretical position that we (Blalock and Wilken, 1979) have taken in a much more general work is that macro-level analyses should be based on micro-level theories that begin with a series of assumptions about individual actors. Our formulation stresses two kinds of subjective variables, namely utilities, or values attached to outcomes or goals, and subjective probabilities that multiply with these utilities to produce expectancies or subjective expected utilities (SEUs). Space considerations to not permit an elaboration of this position, which is discussed in considerable detail in Blalock and Wilken (1979). I will, however, take a general model from that work that is designed to explain the frequency and duration of cross-group interactions. The model is given as Figure 1. Most of the variables in the model will be discussed in the remainder of this section. For the sake of concreteness, I will illustrate its essential features by referring specifically to the interracial or interethnic contacts of children or adolescents in school settings, and I will attempt to link the rather abstract concepts in the theory to these settings and to empirical findings, where relevant.

Although we will proceed by moving from the top of the figure downwards, and from left to right, it is perhaps wise to focus initially on the bottom two rows of the diagram. The dependent variable with which we will be concerned is the frequency and duration of intergroup contacts of various kinds, but the reader will notice two arrows with wiggles leading from this box to segregation at time $t + 1$ and to cultural and status similarity at $t + 1$. The wiggly arrows are intended to represent an aggregating function of some kind, indicating that individual contacts, when aggregated, may feed back to affect later segregation levels and similarities or differences on status and cultural dimensions. Of course, the magnitude of this feedback effect may be very small in some instances, as for example the impact of such school contacts on residential segregation the next year. But, in the longer term, such feedback effects may be considerable. The essential point, in this connection, is that micro-level variables, such as contacts among individual children, may have important consequences at the macro level. For instance, if such contacts involve a high degree of conflict and violence, the policies of school boards, parent associations, and even legislative bodies may be affected. Thus a dependent variable at the micro level may, when aggregated, become independent at the macro level.

1.1. Segregation

In any causal model there will be certain variables that must be taken as predetermined in the sense that, at a given time t, none of the remaining variables in the system can influence these particular variables. This does not mean, however, that prior levels of some of the endogenous or mutually interdependent dependent variables may not have affected some of these predetermined variables, as we have just suggested may be the case when individual behaviors at an earlier point in time have been aggregated. In the model of Figure 1 there are three kinds of such predetermined variables: levels of segregation, cultural or status similarities, and requirements of the external system. In this section,

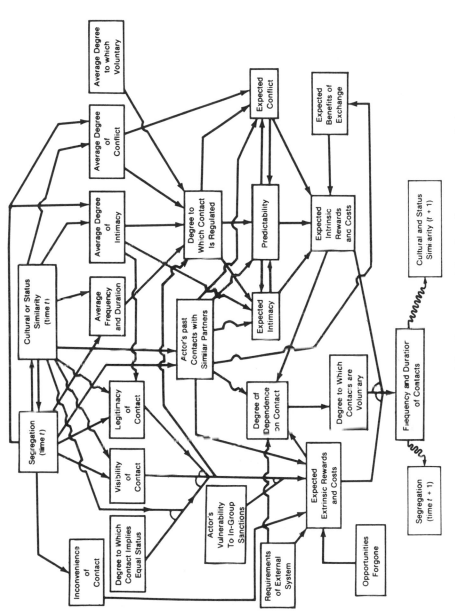

Figure 1. Causal model explaining frequency and duration of cross-group contacts.

we will confine our attention to the first of these variables, though noting that both segregation and similarity affect a number of macro variables that are located on the second line of the figure: the visibility of the contact, its legitimacy, and three average level variables, namely, the average frequency and duration of contacts, the average degree of intimacy, and the average degree of conflict.

By *segregation* we will refer to spatial and/or organizational separation, as is done in the extensive literature on residential segregation (Duncan and Duncan, 1955; Lieberson, 1963; Taeuber and Taeuber, 1965). Residential segregation is defined in terms of departures from a *uniform* distribution, independently of the relative sizes of two (or more) groups. A city or other larger unit is subdivided into subunits, such as census tracts or city blocks, and the percentages of each group are recorded for each subunit. An index of segregation, such as the Gini index or the index of dissimilarity, is then calculated in terms of the distribution of these percentages across the subunits. The index of dissimilarity, for example, provides a measure of the proportion of one group that would need to be redistributed to other subunits in order to produce a uniform distribution having exactly the same percentage of each group in all of these units. Such a measure of segregation can, of course, be applied to other sorts of units and subunits, such as organizations and departments within these organizations or school districts and schools within them. Furthermore, the subunits may be divided internally, so that measures of segregation may be obtained for differing types of units. For instance, a school (having a given minority percentage) may be subdivided into classrooms to assess the degree of internal segregation, but the classrooms themselves may be subdivided, say, into areas of the room, to obtain additional insights into departures from uniformity at varying levels of aggregation.

Several things should be noted about such measures of segregation. First, the results will depend on the sizes of the subunits selected. In the case of residential segregation it has been found that segregation scores using city blocks as subunits tend to be higher than those using census tracts as subunits. Second, none of these measures is designed to tap locational *patterns*, as for example the tendency for blacks to concentrate near the central zones of a city or, perhaps, for white students to be concentrated in specific kinds of classes rather than others. Third, none of the measures gets at interaction patterns directly, though in many instances it is reasonable to assume that interactions will be more common in very small subunits, such as city blocks or classrooms, than in larger ones, such as tracts or entire schools.

Of considerable importance from the standpoint of the school desegregation literature, these measures of uniformity do not take into consideration the possibility of rather extreme racial distributions for the larger units. Thus if a school system contains 90% minority, a score of zero segregation simply means that the 10% nonminority are uniformly distributed across all schools (or within each classroom). Thus, someone who claims that an overwhelmingly black school district is already highly segregated is either using a different criterion for segregation or, more likely, is implicitly using a much larger area unit, such as the entire SMSA, as the criterion. If the suburbs have only 5% minority population, whereas the central city is overwhelmingly minority, either or both of these separate areas may be highly segregated or not, whereas a measure based on the total area (city *and* suburb) might provide a very different result. Similarly, a single school that is 95% black may be internally unsegregated, whereas the school system itself may be highly segregated.

We must also recognize that the *exposure* of one group to the other ordinarily will depend on their relative sizes. Thus, if we hold constant the number of intergroup contacts, it is obvious that members of the numerical minority will, on the average, experience a larger proportion of cross-group contacts than will the typical member of a larger group. It is especially important to keep this fact in mind when we are dealing with instances of extreme racial or ethnic imbalance, whether within schools or individual classrooms. If there are only a very small number of blacks in a much larger class of whites, then virtually all of the black students will be exposed to whites, whereas a substantial proportion of the latter group may have negligible contacts with the much smaller minority. From the standpoint of the individual actor, the exposure rate may be a much more important factor than a measure of contacts that standardizes for the relative sizes of the two groups. Also, of course, whenever the absolute sizes of both groups are large, it becomes possible for almost all actors to confine at least their more important contacts to members of their own group. Thus, both the relative and absolute sizes of each group become potentially important factors influencing the nature of contacts between them.

There appear to be three important kinds of segregation immediately relevant to school contacts. First, residential or neighborhood segregation will obviously affect students' *opportunities* for contact both prior to school entry and also in the case of many activities that occur outside the school setting and during the summer months. Second, segregation of schools within a school district will obviously be dependent on neighborhood segregation, though busing and various incentive systems (e.g., magnet schools) may also affect the degree to which percentages of racial and ethnic groups depart from uniform distributions across schools. Finally, there will be the level of segregation within schools, and in particular the degree to which classrooms and organizations (e.g., school band, athletic teams, or social clubs) have uniform distributions.

Patchen (1982), who asked black and white Indianapolis high school students whether or not they intentionally avoided members of the other race, found that the three factors most closely associated with such avoidance were (a) negative parental attitudes toward the other race, (b) the nature of neighborhood contacts, and (c) the nature and quality of interracial contacts at schools previously attended.

Clearly, the absence of residential segregation is a necessary condition for neighborhood contacts and also is linked to primary school desegregation and thus indirectly contributes to avoidance through several mechanisms. Patchen also found that the extent of friendly contact across races was most clearly related to the exposure that students had, through classroom contacts and extracurricular activities, to members of the other race. These findings are not at all surprising, of course. They are perhaps a statement of the obvious fact that when contacts are inconvenient they are less likely to occur, but they also suggest that not all types of prior or outside contacts will affect those that occur within a specific school setting.

Segregation also affects contacts through other mechanisms that will be discussed in the remainder of the chapter. There is obviously a reciprocal causal linkage between spatial separation and various types of cultural or status similarity variables. Two groups that have very different cultural characteristics or income levels are likely to self-select themselves into different sections of a community or school campus. But once they have done so, the spatial separation further inhibits contact and therefore the very communication that might, over time, reduce these same cultural or status differences. Therefore, we have drawn in a double arrow between these two types of macro-level variables.

Two additional mechanisms will be discussed in appropriate places in what follows. First, segregation will affect the degree to which intergroup contacts are defined to be legitimate and the extent to which they will be visible or readily noticed, and perhaps sanctioned. Secondly, and perhaps most important, segregation is often an effective tension- or conflict-reducing mechanism, so much so that whenever there are strong pressures to keep violence and tension to a minimum, the most practical expedient may be to encourage a high degree of spatial separation. Once such separation becomes accepted, and once each group has staked out its own territory—say in a cafeteria or playground—the path of least resistance may be to look the other way and to rationalize a high degree of segregation as being necessary for maintaining order.

1.2. Cultural or Status Similarity

Whenever contacts are primarily voluntary and there are a sufficiently large number of potential contact partners that each person has a wide range of choice, we may expect "sifting" to occur. By this we mean that there is likely to be a gradual process through which individuals select their friends and acquaintances according to criteria of similarity, selecting as closest friends those who are most compatible in a number of respects: convenience, similar interests and habits, acceptability to one's other friends and parents, and—as the child matures—approximately equal status with oneself. Such a sifting will of course never be complete, but it will be facilitated whenever a sharp line has been drawn between two categories, as for example, blacks and whites, boys and girls, or persons with distinctly different linguistic backgrounds.

Thus, we may expect cultural and status similarity to play an important role in both the spatial segregation and interaction processes, even though the processes involved may be gradual and undramatic. Children, like their parents, find it easy to amplify or exaggerate rather small differences, such as those involving dress or unusual mannerisms. Norms develop to the effect that one should keep a certain distance from those who are stigmatized because of these characteristics. The latter persons then must select partners among their own group, or perhaps among outcasts from the majority or dominant group. This process, being gradual or natural, may go unnoticed by persons in authority, or it may be very difficult to counter where it has been called to their attention.

In the case of minorities, there are a number of such differentiating factors: racial features, differences in physical aggressiveness, language or dialect, learning skills and self-confidence, or competitiveness. Children who play rough are not likely to be attractive to those who fear aggressiveness, a factor that may partly account for the segregation of the sexes in elementary school. Those who do well in their school work, and whose behaviors are most acceptable to their teachers, will tend to avoid and be avoided by those who are obvious problem students. Those minority students who have been socialized to avoid competitive situations can also expect to be avoided by mainstream white students who have been taught at an early age to compete, compete, compete. And those who have had their competitiveness channeled into athletics, and who have developed athletic skills at an early age, can also be expected to shun those who have other interests. The familiar pattern of black domination of certain sports undoubtedly begins at a very early age and then becomes reinforced in the school setting.

Metz (1978) made the important point that heterogeneity, *per se*, may lead to difficulties in the control process that spill over into other aspects of school life. She notes two major types of control exercised by school authorities. The simplest involves rigid discipline and strict authority, which also are somewhat characteristic of lower-class families and that, at least until recently, used to be common in all-black segregated schools. The second form of control is much more subtle and relies on what she terms the "institutionalization of ignorance." If properly socialized, young students will simply not realize that rules may be broken or that adults may be disobeyed. They take their teachers' word for it that learning is in their best interest and that certain things must or must not be done.

If students come to school with drastically different backgrounds, however, neither type of control mechanism may work. Students socialized to respond positively to a flexible atmosphere may rebel against strict authoritarian measures, particularly if they see others similarly tempted to rebel. Those who are primarily used to authoritarian methods may take advantage of the flexibility that often goes along with the "institutionalization of ignorance" approach. Once a significant number of students challenge either type of control system, its weaknesses will become apparent. Deviations from authoritarian controls will lead to the realization that only a few students can be controlled at any one time, not only because of the students' superiority of numbers, but also because of the very real limitations placed on school authorities in terms of punishments that can be meted out. And it will be impossible to maintain students' ignorance or acceptance, once a significant number of others have challenged their elders. A compromise resolution, we may infer from Metz's argument, may be very difficult to achieve.

Of course it may only be a few specific kinds of socialization factors that are related to the above differences in reactions to these two kinds of control practices, and it appears as though social class differences may be at least as important as racial or cultural ones. Certainly, however, there will be important differences in family socialization with respect to the degree to which preschool children are taught to obey authorities without question, and with the expectation that deviance will be met by almost certain punishment. Such socialization differences will carry over to the school setting, where students may experience either what they perceive to be a license to misbehave with impunity or a more authoritarian atmosphere than that to which they are accustomed. Although these differences may not become translated into spatial segregation and avoidance, we expect that the gradual sifting process will result in a self-selection of friends and acquaintances along the lines of how students react to the control structure of the school system. Those who actively rebel, or who are defined as troublemakers and poor students, are likely to be differentiated from those who conform or who may be defined as "goodies" or "suckers" by those who perceive this system as being counter to their immediate interests.

In general, people will tend to avoid situations in which they expect failure and, conversely, will self-select themselves into settings in which their competitive skills give them an advantage. Where racial or ethnic groups differ with respect to socialization patterns that emphasize the development of very different skills, we would therefore expect that as students enter school they will begin to sort themselves out by setting and type of activity. But they may also attempt to place roadblocks in front of others, so that the latter's skills may not be used as effectively.[4] Thus students who lack, for any reason, the intellectual tools to compete successfully in a classroom setting may engage in diversionary tactics that disrupt this learning environment. They may also attempt to create peer pressures designed to inhibit the competitive display of intellectual skills. The serious student, in such a setting, may be encouraged to keep quiet, to appear

---

[4]A similar process, of course, occurs in the case of occupational discrimination. We would anticipate that propositions appropriate to occupational competition could, with suitable modification, suggest conditions applicable to school situations. See Blalock (1967).

inattentive and disinterested, and even possibly to make a sufficient number of mistakes so that this student's superiority is hidden from view. A member of a minority group characterized by relatively low achievement levels may be especially vulnerable to such peer pressures lest one be labeled as too "white" or middle-class in orientation.

As students age and gain increasing flexibility with respect to opportunities to choose among alternative behaviors, we may therefore expect these choices to result in a sifting process through which members of different groups sort themselves by engaging primarily in those activities in which they have, in the past, been successful. The drift of black students to athletics and away from college preparatory programs is a case in point, as is the avoidance of mathematics and science by girls and most racial minorities, except Japanese- and Chinese-Americans. This selectivity among programs and activities will then obviously tend to reduce the frequency and duration of intergroup contacts, not necessarily because of prejudice and discrimination, but simply as a result of differential skills brought into the school setting and then reinforced by subsequent performance levels and sanction patterns. Unless such patterns of differential skills and sorting can be countered during the very early grades, when adult authorities have greater control over students' behaviors and choices, it may be virtually impossible to block their occurrence later on.

Thus, although the maximization of unrestricted choices may be desirable from the standpoint of the maturation process, it may also have important side effects that warrant systematic study. In particular, more research is needed on how choice patterns vary by age and sex, and how these are affected by both the absolute and relative sizes of racial and ethnic groups. For example, it has been suggested by Miller (1983) that girls' play groups tend to be smaller than those of boys, largely because boys are more likely to engage in competitive sports in which relatively large numbers of participants are needed. In a group of boys choosing up sides for a softball game, for instance, black or other minority boys will be needed to make a complete team. Given individual differences in abilities, this will ordinarily result in teams that are approximately similar in racial composition. Although the choices may be free ones, the very nature of the activity tends to restrict the options to a much higher degree than those that are available for two or three person games. Teacher interventions, perhaps in the form of encouraging larger team activities on the part of girls, may indirectly affect these otherwise free-choice patterns, as noted by Miller.

1.3. Equal-Status, Visibility, and Legitimacy of Contacts

As we move down the left-hand side of Figure 1, we note that most of the arrows feed into a box titled "expected extrinsic rewards and costs." By extrinsic rewards and costs we refer to actions that may be taken by *others* (not immediately involved in the contact) either to reward or to punish the actors involved. We exclude, however, actions taken by the interacting partners themselves, considering these to be intrinsic to the interactions. Toward the top of the left-hand side there are three important variables: the degree to which the contact implies equal status, the visibility of the contact (to various other parties), and its legitimacy. The arrows directed from these three variables to expected extrinsic rewards and costs intersect before reaching that box, representing the assumption that they may interact nonadditively in their joint effects on rewards and costs. Small arcs drawn between such intersecting arrows indicate that such joint effects are assumed to be *multiplicative*, implying that the two factors must both be present for an effect to occur. In particular, unless a contact is visible to others it cannot be sanctioned either negatively or positively. Thus, if a contact is defined as illegitimate, it must also be witnessed by the relevant sanctioning party, or at least be reported to that party.

In considering visibility and legitimacy, we must specify a list of types of actors who will be relevant as third parties to the contact. First, there will be the students' parents, many of whom may disapprove of interracial or interethnic contacts of specified kinds. We assume, however, that in most instances parents will be unaware of the myriad of contacts that take place in these school settings, so that the visibility factor will be near zero in these instances. Two important kinds of contacts will be visible to parents, however. Close friendships, especially those involving opposite sexes, are much more likely to be monitored by parents, especially in instances where friends are brought home after school or during weekends.

The second type of contact likely to come to the attention of parents involves overt friction and conflict, especially of an organized variety. We assume that many school administrators place a very high priority on preventing such conflictful contacts from coming to the attention of the wider community, and on playing down their significance as "nonracial" whenever the public has become aroused.

Many contacts (or lack of contacts) will be visible to teachers and administrators, but they may either take them for granted or consider them relatively unimportant as long as they appear to have no bearing on the main objectives related to learning. Thus it may be noted that whites and blacks sit in separate sections of the cafeteria or congregate outside of school in different areas. Or they may even enter different doors and use different corridors or bathrooms. If such patterns are defined as neutral, being neither legitimate nor illegitimate, then regardless of whether or not they are observed, we expect sanctions from these sources to be negligible. Indeed, it may be difficult in most such instances to reward those students who do make an effort to increase intergroup contacts because, as long as behaviors are within certain bounds, they are defined as irrelevant to the major objectives of teachers and administrators.

Students' peers are another matter, however, and as children age and become increasingly sophisticated about norms relating to legitimacy, we may expect them to become more and more concerned about possible peer sanctions resulting from deviations from these norms. I am unaware of any definitive studies that deal specifically with student norms regulating different kinds of interracial contacts or how these norms change as students age, but if such norms approximate adult norms as students progress through the grade levels, we may expect something of the following to emerge. Rather casual friendly contacts across races will be encouraged, particularly as a hedge against conflict and aggressive behaviors. But certain lines will be drawn, rather subtlely, such that students learn not to become too friendly with others of a different race, or at least not to display overt signs of such friendships, thereby making them highly visible to peers of their own group.

Such norms defining which behaviors are and are not legitimate will probably be more sharp when they relate to cross-sex interactions and when they refer to contact situations that imply near status-equality among the partners. Thus certain "social" events, such as out-of-school parties or school dances are likely to be more segregated than are events, such as band concerts or football games, where contacts are more casual and where the status equality of partners is not implied. The argument is that, if a contact implies that partners are nearly equal in status, the person of higher status will have more to lose than that person would in situations where status is irrelevant. This assumes, of course, that the contact is visible to relevant others. And it also assumes that such contacts are, at least to a degree, defined as illegitimate or "off limits."

An additional variable that we assume interacts with all three of these contact variables is the degree to which the partners concerned are *vulnerable* to peer-group sanctions. Ever since Hollingshead's (1949) classic study of "Elmtown" and Coleman's (1961) analysis of adolescent society, sociologists have been sensitized to the extreme importance of peer-group pressures, particularly among high school students. But students vary in their degree of dependence on other students. Especially in larger schools they are often able to locate large groups of persons with similar orientations, so that for all intents and purposes, they are relatively immune to at least certain kinds of peer pressures. We may distinguish two nearly opposite kinds of relatively invulnerable persons: those who, for whatever reason, have become isolates or who are defined as deviant from peer norms, and those who are sufficiently popular that they may in some instances rise above these pressures without fear of major sanctions.

In the first instance, certain of these isolates or deviants may be perceived as "solid citizens" according to adult norms. They may be rejected by their peers because they refuse to drink at parties, openly disapprove of drug use, or are defined as too intellectual. Or they may be defined as queer or too "arty" or unusual in some other way. Such isolates may then deliberately seek out others like themselves, including members of other racial or ethnic groups. For instance, a "hard rock" group may consist of blacks and whites, as did many jazz musician groups long before integration became fashionable among intellectuals. Such deviant or isolated students, however, are seldom in a position to affect student norms, though they may gain a certain amount of notoriety or popularity if their skills are sufficient to compensate for their deviant behavior.

In the second instance, perhaps exemplified by the star white athlete whose closest friend is a black teammate, school authorities are provided with a potential mechanism for modifying student norms, provided that the cooperation of such popular individuals can be obtained. If it is "OK" for the superstar athlete to associate with members of another race, then this obviously sets an example that may be exploited by those who wish to increase interracial contacts. But if there is a perception that such students are being used, or that their own interracial friendships are not genuine, such an approach to modifying student norms could very well backfire.

1.4. Extrinsic Rewards and Costs and Demands of the External System

Homans (1950) stressed that most groups engage in activities and inter-actions over and above those demanded by their environments, but he also noted that as these demands from the external system decrease one may also expect many of these additional activities and interactions to decrease. Furthermore, certain kinds of external demands will be more effective than others in increasing the extent of interaction relative to the total amount of activity. We would generally expect that the nature of the tasks one is assigned may affect the amount of cooperation and division of labor required to complete them, as well as the mutual dependence of each actor on the others. For instance, teachers may assign tasks in such a fashion that some but not all students are highly dependent on certain types of contacts, thereby also affecting the degree to which these contacts are voluntary or involuntary and thus their frequency and duration (see lower left-center portion of Figure 1). It has also been shown that situations requiring task interdependence are more likely than those that do not to encourage members to distribute rewards on an egalitarian basis, rather than strictly in terms of input or the importance of their individual contributions (Yamagishi, 1981).

It is in this area of reward and task manipulation that school authorities and teachers may have their greatest opportunity directly to affect the nature of intergroup interactions. Presumably, there is little that they can do, in the short run, about residential segregation, parental attitudes and behaviors, or status and cultural differences among groups. But the learning situation may be structured in a number of different ways, and rewards and punishments may also be manip-ulated so as to encourage or discourage intergroup interactions. This is especially the case in classroom settings and, perhaps, certain of the more structured extra-curricular activities (such as sports, cheerleading, and band) that are likely to be attractive to members of all racial and ethnic groups.

Bossert (1979) noted the effects of the standard type of lecture-recitation classroom environment, in which students learn to compete with one another for the teacher's favor (and attention) and in which they become exceedingly well aware of just where each student stands in the competitive game. He contrasts this traditional type of learning situation with one in which students proceed relatively independently and at different paces, but without this being explicitly called to their attention via the mechanism of the teacher's calling for a public performance of one's abilities or lack of them. A series of interesting experiments by Slavin (1979, 1980) and his associates suggests, as did the research of Bossert, that interracial contacts of a more than casual nature are more likely whenever there are cooperative learning environments that reward all members of a team, perhaps in terms of their average score or even one that gives the greatest weight to the performance levels of the slowest members.[5] The idea here is certainly not new and, in fact, was an essential part of Allport's (1954) thesis to the effect that cooperative, equal-status contacts of an enduring nature are needed to bring about extensive interracial contacts in other types of situations. The indication is that cooperative classroom activities of this nature do have a positive impact on intergroup contacts in the classroom and that these also spill over into school cafeterias, informal interactions, and out-of-school activities.

In addition to urging the study of potential side effects of such cooperative learning, we can introduce several notes of caution. First, one wonders whether American parents and most teachers and school principals can be expected to encourage a really concerted program to replace the traditional competitive learning atmosphere within the classroom. In spite of lip service to the contrary, the overwhelming stress in our society on individually achieved success may be far too strong. Those parents who are most active in school affairs may be the very same parents who want their children to enter an Ivy League college and to achieve high honors. Once they've become aware of a reward system that gives equal rewards to slow learners and faster ones, would they tolerate such a system, even if it could also be shown that it led to improved race relations?

Second, as Cohen (1972, 1975, 1982; Cohen and Rober, 1985) and her associates have emphasized, it may be difficult to achieve situations in which near status equality between racial and ethnic groups can be expected to hold. In most situations, she argues, members of the white dominant groups will "take over" the learning situation, with blacks and other minorities becoming relatively passive. Although her research produced situations in which blacks were able to give help to whites, these were artificially constructed by giving the black students prior practice, so that in effect they began with a head start. For most

---

[5]See especially, Slavin (1979, 1980), Slavin and Madden (1979), Hansell and Slavin (1979), Slavin and Hansell (1983), and Hansell et al. (1981).

classroom learning experiences, however, the shoe will be on the other foot, and we may expect that in interracial teams there will be a preponderance of whites helping blacks, rather than vice versa. For very young children, who are not racially conscious, the nature of this pattern may not be obvious. But as the children age, and as they add up a number of observations, one wonders just how equal these interaction situations can be.

Finally, in all cooperative situations in which members are rewarded by a common good that cannot be withheld from any members, there will be the problem of dealing with the "freeloader" who recognizes that the rational course of action may be to minimize one's costs by reducing effort to near zero, while letting the other members do all the work. If such freeloading were randomly distributed across all ethnic groups, it might have few negative consequences for intergroup contacts. But if it became patterned, the results could be exactly the opposite from those intended. The direction of the pattern could favor either group. Minority members might readily slip into a dependent, lazy role, reaping the rewards of the much greater efforts of their white partners. Or a dominant group could exploit the minority by making it do all the work, perhaps through the application of threats of various kinds, including their ability to capitalize on their more favored position with the teacher. As Olson (1965) argued, such freeloading may be countered by providing all actors with "selective incentives" or differential rewards based on their own unique contributions. This, of course, requires careful monitoring of the interaction process, but may not turn out to be a major source of difficulty, especially in the case of cooperative projects of rather short duration.

There are obviously other ways of encouraging intergroup contacts, and doubtlessly such contacts are reinforced or discouraged in numerous subtle ways. Especially in the elementary grades, one can imagine a systematic effort to apply operant conditioning principles by rewarding each instance of friendly intergroup contact, while either ignoring or negatively sanctioning actions that involve hostile contacts. But unless there were an explicit policy along these lines, and unless teachers were specifically trained to use these techniques, the most common situation is likely to be a mixed one in which some teachers reward such contacts, others are totally indifferent to them, and perhaps still others may actively discourage them.

Most teachers are primarily oriented to imparting knowledge and getting lessons completed. What students do during recess and lunch periods or in the hallways is likely to go unnoticed unless the behaviors create disturbances or are otherwise embarrassing. And, of course, many student behaviors are simply not witnessed by any adults. Informal norms also exist to the effect that many kinds of student behaviors are simply not the business of teachers or school authorities. It is therefore difficult to imagine implementation of major school policies that would dramatically impact most of these informal types of contact situations. Task-related activities would seem to hold much greater promise as mechanisms for deliberately encouraging intergroup contacts.

1.5. Intrinsic Rewards and Costs and the Regulation of Contact

By *intrinsic rewards* and *costs*—the set of variables that appears toward the bottom right of Figure 1—we mean those rewards and costs resulting strictly from the interaction process itself, including the behaviors of one's interaction partners, quite apart from any rewards or costs that may result from products of this interaction. Because one's partner plays a crucial role in connection with these intrinsic rewards and costs, a number of variables that we have already discussed also come into play. In particular, any status or cultural differences that would make the contacts ambiguous, uncomfortable, embarrassing, demeaning, or otherwise unpleasant will tend to increase the costs of such contacts. There are all sorts of informal techniques that can be applied to either party to make contacts costly or unrewarding: the use of subtle insults, snobbery, aloofness, being highly inconsistent and unpredictable, or merely removing oneself so as to make contact inconvenient.

Minorities and other subordinate groups (as well as majorities) thus have a variety of relatively cost-free devices to reduce contact if they so desire, and therefore we may expect them to get back at the dominant group in such a fashion. Indeed, in the case of many interracial contacts, it appears as though really special efforts would need to be made by both parties to compensate for a host of inconveniences and potentially uncomfortable kinds of interactions. We therefore presume that, initially at least, a number of extrinsic rewards would be needed to reinforce those intergroup contacts that do occur and to compensate for negative sanctions that are likely to be applied by dissimilar partners.

It is generally recognized that in many instances spatial segregation is a conflict-reducing mechanism, as is avoidance. Especially when community tensions are high, or when a school previously occupied by one group is being "invaded" by another, we may therefore expect that segregated patterns will not only emerge but will be encouraged as a safety valve by school authorities. Once such patterns have been set, it may then require special incentives to break them down, given the expected costs to any persons who initiate such contacts. Unless two individuals knew each other before entering school, or have had extensive contact in connection with some task-related activity, there is little likelihood that either will take the considerable risk of rebuff or embarrassment.

Furthermore, if there has been overt physical violence or intimidation, any given actor would be taking a decided risk unless the partner and partner's friends were a known quantity, and in a segregated situation this is indeed unlikely.

Even when tension and conflict have subsided, and when desegregation and integration become more feasible, it may be exceedingly difficult to obtain the necessary critical mass of students willing to take the gamble.[6] Therefore, the average level of intergroup conflict, as well as the average amount of previous contact, will impact on any given actor's *expected* intrinsic rewards and costs, quite apart from the ones that might have been realized had the interaction taken place (Blalock and Wilken, 1979). In this sense, segregation and a low level of cross-group interactions become self-maintaining patterns unless outside catalysts can be brought into the equation and unless potentially conflictful contacts can be regulated.

Metz (1978) made the important point that mechanisms used by school authorities to control student behaviors may be counterproductive to the objective of maximizing the learning process. She noted that, in many instances, insecure officials may find it necessary to institute rigid rules designed to prevent dramatic, though rare, outbursts of violence that would produce unfavorable public reaction, and perhaps their dismissal from office. The knifing of a student, a racial brawl, or an incident involving extortion may gain considerably more attention in the mass media than a much larger number of uneventful, peaceful acts of racial cooperation. To the extent that spatial segregation and a very low level of intergroup interaction inhibit both types of contacts, it may be the former rather than the latter that dominates the thinking of school authorities. If so, the rational administrator may have little incentive to attempt to break down patterns of segregation or to encourage a larger number of intergroup interactions, both positive and negative.

A number of macro-level or structural variables may affect the role of school administrators and their accountability to their superiors, an elected school board, or parent groups. In the American educational system, school superintendents are in an extremely vulnerable position, with the result that turnover at this level is extremely rapid. Local school boards often consist of middle-class oriented persons, including a high proportion of those representing the business and banking communities. Not only are such board members socialized to abhor violence and controversy, but they also tend to be motivated to protect their middle-class children from both the threat of violence and also any radical ideas regarding social equality or controversial teaching techniques. Furthermore, most such board members are subject to recall petitions or have relatively short terms of office. To the extent that they have run for office in order to seek status as civic-minded citizens, or to launch a political career, we may expect them to try to avoid controversy and to insist that their administrators act so as to minimize the risk of bad publicity. School boards composed of members less vulnerable

---

[6]See Granovetter (this volume) for a discussion of tipping effects and the distribution of threshold effects, both of which seem relevant to this matter of the size of such a critical mass.

to citizen pressures and school authorities with long-term contracts might be expected to take greater risks.[7]

Students, of course, regulate their own behavior. In situations that ordinarily imply approximately equal status, but where in fact status or power inequalities actually exist, a dominant group will often develop a set of regulations that symbolize this inequality so that it is ever-present in the minds of all actors. For instance, in the South, various deference patterns or a racial etiquette was enforced, so that the inferior position of blacks was continually emphasized. In school settings, however, a role reversal may occur, especially in instances where blacks or other minorities constitute a substantial proportion of the student body. Because it is virtually impossible for school authorities to control minor incidents and relatively subtle forms of student coercion, one group may gain the upper hand in terms of control over the most desirable spatial locations and the ability to extract deference. In particular, in instances where there are substantial class or race differences in the use of physical violence, and therefore also the threat of physical sanctions, there may come to be an understanding among students that, say, white middle-class students are not to use certain facilities, or that they are to give way when approached by those who are in a position to apply such physical sanctions. In another setting in which they are a small numerical minority, black students may fear negative sanctions for similar behaviors.

In situations where control mechanisms differ by racial or ethnic group, we may also anticipate that these devices will encounter differing responses on the part of school administrators and teachers. If, for example, middle-class students rely primarily on subtle devices, such as snobbery and ridicule, they are much more likely to avoid disciplinary measures than are those who employ physical means. In a sense, lower-status students have fewer options and therefore tend to use the kinds of control devices most likely to alienate teachers and administrators. In effect, they get caught and their behaviors are defined as much more serious than are those involving symbolic types of messages. It may actually be the case that black and other minority students do break school rules more often than whites, and this may not be totally due to differences in socialization. They may simply be employing the control mechanisms that are most effective, given their backgrounds. Thus, in school settings where disturbances involving overt physical acts are relatively common, and where there are also important class and racial cleavages, administrators would be well advised to examine the

---

[7]See Crain (1968) for an interesting discussion of the processes by which school board members are selected and influenced. Stanley Lieberson (personal communication, 1982) has pointed out that it may be naive to assume that superintendents with long-term tenure would be any more willing to take risks because they may be subject to other kinds of negative sanctions and also, perhaps, deliberately selected so as to assure their cooperation.

relatively more subtle forms of social control being exercised by middle-class and/or white students to see whether these, too, can be modified. Otherwise, any third-party intervention on the part of adults will be defined as unfair.

Patchen (1982), studying interaction patterns in Indianapolis high schools, found that avoidance was most common among those who perceived a power imbalance, in either direction, between blacks and whites. He also found that avoidance and unfriendly contacts were more common among boys than among girls, and that those who were most likely to indicate that their contacts with members of the other race were unfriendly were also those who tended to have more unfriendly contacts with their own race. Presumably, such persons will play more or less important roles in determining student control mechanisms according to the nature of the school climate, the degree to which physical controls are tolerated, and the ability of other students to sanction them by other means.

The Patchen group also found that changes in a school's racial composition may be more important in affecting the level of tension than the actual racial or ethnic percentages (Davidson et al., 1978). Undoubtedly, such changes present a power threat to whichever group is losing ground, and at the same time provide an opportunity to those in the other group who are most inclined to rely on physical control mechanisms. Metz (1978) also noted some very striking differences between the disciplinary atmospheres in the two schools she studied, one being a school that had experienced a gradual change in racial composition, the other having very recently received a substantial influx of blacks. Although administrative responses also differed between the two schools, making it difficult to unconfound the two types of variables, Metz noted that "discipline" and "behavior problems" were much more prominent in the second of these schools, and teachers were also more polarized.

We assume that virtually all contact behaviors are motivated by short-term considerations of individual expected rewards and costs, regardless of possible long-term consequences for the group as a whole. Racial and ethnic minority students who suddenly find themselves in a situation in which they may become the dominant group may therefore be expected to exercise this dominance, even though it may have negative consequences later on when they may encounter whites (or Anglos) in the outside world, where latent hostilities may be turned against them. At least temporarily, they will have shown members of the hated dominant group what it is like to be in a subordinate position. Even where outright domination cannot be achieved, members of such minorities may at least block voluntary contacts by making it clear that whites are resented. As noted, they may do so through a number of techniques, including rudeness, uncouth behaviors, and overt avoidance.

Toward the bottom of the right-hand side of Figure 1, there is a box referring to the predictability of one's partner's behaviors. Even where contacts are primarily positive or neutral, a moderate percentage of unfriendly behaviors, occurring at unpredictable intervals, may be sufficient to inhibit members of the other group from initiating contacts, especially when these persons have plenty of alternative partners available from their own groups. Or if members of either group tend to be friendly only when their contacts are not visible to others in their group, and become either indifferent or hostile in situations that are more public, this too will introduce a greater element of uncertainty into the picture. It will also call into question the individual's sincerity unless the control mechanisms operating are very obvious, and unless the interracial partners have reached some form of understanding concerning their friendship. As a general rule, the greater the ambiguity and uncertainty involved in a potential contact situation, the less the expected net benefit (Langley, 1977). Figure 1 also implies that previous contacts with similar partners will affect an actor's expected (intrinsic) benefits from any exchange relationships that may occur, with such benefits affecting the total expected intrinsic rewards and costs.

Finally, Figure 1 shows both expected extrinsic rewards and costs and the expected intrinsic ones feeding into the box referring to the frequency and duration of intergroup contacts of various kinds. We do not expect students to make a rational calculation of costs and benefits, especially when possible contacts are relatively instantaneous, numerous, and individually inconsequential. Nevertheless it is important to stress the *expectancy* component in that all actors must make decisions under varying degrees of uncertainty. They will of course base these expectations on their own past experiences, not only with members of the other groups but also in connection with the sanctions expected from members of their own group. These many individual short-run decisions are then aggregated (not necessarily in a simple fashion) to produce a general climate of interaction patterns that then affects later individual behaviors.

2. MACRO-LEVEL SETTING VARIABLES

It has been our thesis that to explain a micro-level process, such as informal interaction patterns among students, it is first necessary to formulate a micro-level theory, even where one is primarily interested in the impact of macro-level variables in a social setting. One may then take each of the causally prior variables within that micro theory and ask about the setting or macro variables that may affect them. In our case, we have focused on the individual student as actor. For a more inclusive formulation we would next need to list the other types of relevant actors: teachers, administrators, parents and siblings, school boards, political figures, judges or others in a position to make rulings on busing, and so forth. Keeping in mind the narrowed focus on children's interactions, we could then ask how the behaviors of each of these other actors impact on variables such as those suggested in Figure 1.[8]

There is also a general context within which these other actors' behaviors are embedded, and in this final section we shall examine a few of the variables that would seem to be important as additional contextual variables. From the standpoint of theory development, unfortunately, many possible variables take on virtually constant values within the American educational system. Thus, in the American setting, such factors should probably be taken as givens, with the realization that the levels of these givens may have a major impact on the levels of desegregation and intergroup contacts, even though variation in these two dependent variables may be only weakly associated with these virtually constant explanatory variables.

Clearly, if residential segregation were negligible, and if preschool children's contacts with members of other races or ethnic groups were both frequent and friendly, one would expect negligible segregation and maximal intergroup contact within school settings. Likewise, if nearly all children were socialized similarly, and if they developed approximately the same levels of skills prior to school entry, we would expect that interaction patterns across groups would approximate a chance distribution. But in virtually all large American cities— and minorities are heavily concentrated in such cities—blacks and whites are highly segregated from one another, with Hispanics and other whites also being spatially separated. American communities contain differing percentages of several minorities, but unfortunately we know too little about how the presence of multiple groups affects the interaction patterns between any two of them.

There are also a number of constraints imposed by the nature of American public education that result in considerable uniformity from community to community, district to district, and even school to school. Although there are a few experimental schools, magnet schools, or schools located within peculiar neighborhoods (e.g., those close to a college campus), the vast majority of American public schools are very uniform with respect to such things as pupil–teacher ratios, modal classroom arrangements, teacher training, autonomy provided to teachers, disciplinary procedures, classroom hours, curricular and governance procedures. Although authors such as Anderson (1982), Davidson *et al.* (1978), McDill and Rigsby (1973), and Metz (1978) have suggested that there may be important differences in school climates, it is often necessary to select highly atypical schools (which differ simultaneously in several ways from the others) in order to locate any school differences at all.

---

[8]For *some* of these actors, it may be fruitful to think in terms of *nested* contexts, such as classrooms within schools, schools within districts, and districts within states. One may then analyze data in terms of several different levels of aggregation, with the context at one level becoming the unit of analysis at the next higher level. See Eulau (1969), Blau (1980), Boyd and Iversen (1979), Blalock and Wilken (1979, Chap. 7), and McDill and Rigsby (1973). Space considerations do not permit us to explore this possibility in the present chapter, however.

This absence of variation does not imply that, if changes were made in any of these variables, substantial changes in children's interaction patterns might not also occur. If, for example, teacher–pupil ratios were improved by a factor of five, so that closely supervised individual instruction were possible, drastic changes might take place. But it is difficult to imagine that the American public would pay for such an expensive system. Nor can we expect parents to be willing to give greater security to school administrators who attempt to make basic reforms of a controversial nature.

With these preliminary remarks in mind, we may list and briefly discuss several kinds of setting variables suggested by the previous analysis, beginning with those that are most closely linked to the students themselves, and therefore being more likely to have immediate impacts on their interaction patterns.

2.1. Classroom Learning Activities

Research findings (see page 125, footnote) are sufficiently encouraging to suggest that if teachers were to modify their classroom techniques, this could have immediate impacts not only on students' interaction patterns but also on the extent to which they perceive group differences in performance levels. To the degree that a student's performance is not made public via recitations, the posting of grades, spelling bees, and so forth, there is at least some evidence (Bossert, 1979) to suggest that friendship patterns are also less likely to be correlated with such performance levels. In instances where minority children enter school with fewer competitive skills, or with weaker motivations to compete in the learning process, openly displaying students' skills or lack of skills for all to see tends to place these students at an initial disadvantage which, over time, will not only cumulate, but will also provide tangible criteria, readily available to students, through which racial and ethnic sorting may take place.

In contrast, evidence suggests that team learning projects, through which students are encouraged to cooperate to achieve a common good, will encourage additional intergroup contacts beyond these immediate ones.[9]

2.2. Competition for Space

Spatial layouts may be important when they are not uniform in quality, convenience, or other factors that affect relative desirability. For instance, if there are two very unequal baseball diamonds or playgrounds, one may find that a dominant group—whether defined in terms of age, sex, or race-ethnicity—takes over the most choice locations, with the result that some form of segregation occurs. In such instances, an age-graded hierarchy of dominance will ordinarily

---

[9]It may also be true that *competitive* team learning projects also increase such contacts, though in slightly different ways. See Hansell *et al.* (1981) and Slavin (1980).

be uncorrelated with one based on race and therefore may work in favor of increased contacts among persons of the same age (or grade) but differing race, and a similar pattern will hold if there is considerable segregation by sex. For instance, in an elementary school fifth and sixth graders may take over the most desirable sports facilities, relegating the others to younger students of all races.

Thus, it is not at all clear just what the implications will be whenever there are crosscutting lines of cleavage, apart from the high likelihood that spatial locations will be nonrandom. School authorities, by a judicious scheduling of recess or lunch periods or by a reallocation of facilities for specific uses, will be in a position to take advantage of whatever patterns of facility use seem most compatible with those intergroup contacts they wish to encourage. It does not follow, however, that the highest priority will be given to maximizing interracial contacts at the expense, say, of discouraging the domination of younger students by older ones or girls by boys. Further research on this important problem is needed so as to provide more useful specific guidelines as to the conditions under which the competition for space will be defined along racial or ethnic lines, rather than in other terms.

2.3. Other Organized Activities and Informal Contacts

Evidence suggests that, as children age, there is a strong tendency toward spatial segregation and a very low level of racial contact in connection with strictly voluntary, unstructured activities (Gerard et al., 1975). It therefore seems much easier to encourage intergroup contacts via those structured activities that are likely to be attractive to a diversity of individuals. Musical groups and athletic teams, for example, seem to provide such opportunities for some students, but there is no reason to restrict efforts to these two kinds of activities. A really conscious and explicit policy of seeking out members of underrepresented groups, persuading students from overrepresented groups to welcome them and allow them to play important roles, and encouraging social events for participants might very well have an important impact, especially where prestige leaders are members of the same groups. What we are concerned with, here, is the creation of a favorable school atmosphere for intergroup contacts. This nebulous concept is more likely to develop a concrete meaning in the context of reasonably structured activities under the supervision of adults sensitized to the objective of improving the quality and quantity of intergroup contacts.

2.4. Reduction of Cultural Differences Relevant to Performance

The other contexts of most immediate importance to students are the family and neighborhood. Here, of course, school officials and other policymakers can have virtually no direct impact, except insofar as practices followed within the school either reinforce, or are incompatible with, experiences in these other, more inclusive settings. We confront a major dilemma for those who believe strongly in the "cultural pluralism" thesis. If children become increasingly aware of minor differences as they age, and if sorting processes involve self-selection on the basis of such differences, then it becomes difficult to increase substantially the amount of intergroup interaction without, simultaneously, reducing these differences.

Ideally, children might be taught to appreciate differences while ignoring them in their day-to-day behaviors. But whenever these differences are relevant to their interactions, they will rarely be ignored. Those students who cannot speak "good" English, who play too roughly, or who adhere to very different values relating to personal property, competitiveness, personal cleanliness, and so forth, can be expected to be shunned by typical middle-class white students. And, as compensations, we may then expect these shunned students to retaliate by engaging in behaviors that further offend middle-class white norms.

Presumably, there are many kinds of cultural differences that are of only minor relevance within the school setting and that can be exploited, positively, to encourage a greater appreciation of cultural diversity. Such things as native costumes, religious beliefs, music, and dietary customs can sometimes be emphasized without affecting contact patterns. But where children have been accustomed to very different familial norms and ways of communicating that are highly relevant to their classroom behaviors and ways of interacting with peers, we may expect these differences to become important criteria as children select their contact partners. Those who idealize the notion of cultural pluralism need to be aware of its negative consequences. It may prove to be exceedingly difficult to have it both ways!

2.5. Neighborhood Contacts

Although what happens outside of school in neighborhood settings and during summer months and other vacation periods almost constitutes a residual category of factors that may influence within-school interaction patterns, it seems important to note the possibility of one factor that warrants further study. Activity groups may be highly homogeneous with respect to age, with little or no contact between children who are a year or more different in age, or there may be hierarchical arrangements in which older children tend to dominate the activities of younger ones, as in the case of gangs of boys that socialize younger members into the activities of the older ones. Age-homogeneous groupings may tend to be more heterogeneous with respect to race in those instances in which there are too few persons (of the same sex) of a given age to "permit" racial sorting as well. But this may be a function of the spatial density of the neighborhood and the relative and absolute numbers of same-sex, same-age children of each racial or ethnic group. Clearly, considerably more research is needed to disentangle the interrelationships among these variables and to study how peer-group norms emerge and are transmitted from one age-group to another.

2.6. Racial and Ethnic Group Numbers

The empirical evidence regarding the relationship between minority percentage and school contacts is ambiguous.[10] Clearly, whenever one or the other group constitutes the overwhelming majority, there will be an obvious imbalance of power among students and also the opportunity for many members of the larger group to avoid interaction with the numerical minority. Especially crucial is the racial or ethnic distribution in classrooms, where friendly contacts and cooperative projects are most frequent. If the current opposition to mandatory busing continues unabated and is combined with movements to suburbs and to private schools, we may soon return to virtually segregated school *systems* in which racial and ethnic percentages within schools become increasingly extreme in one direction or the other. If so, the vast majority of American school children will be able to complete their educations with minimal exposure to other groups.

Whenever there are multiple racial and ethnic groups within the same school, several patterns may emerge. In some instances, a middle-class racial minority, such as Japanese-Americans, may play an intermediary role and lessen the resistance of white parents to the desegregation process. Although this type of situation has apparently not been well studied, it is my impression that a prior period of contact between white and Asian-American students in Seattle schools may have weakened resistance to the various desegregation plans that have been implemented in that city. Multiple ethnic groups may also create tensions within a school system, however, if one ethnic group believes that others are getting more favorable treatment or if student members of the several groups become rivals oriented to increasing the conflict level within a given school. Furthermore, the interests of different minorities may be divergent. Garcia (1981), for example, notes that bilingual education among some Hispanics and Asian immigrants may require a degree of segregation sufficient to provide a critical mass of students to justify such programs in relatively small schools. This, in turn, may place Hispanic and black parents and community leaders on opposite sides of a school busing controversy.

---

[10]See Patchen (1982) for one set of rather complex findings regarding minority percentages. Certain findings by St. John and Lewis (1975) suggest that minority percentages may have different impacts for boys and girls in elementary schools. The picture also seems confusing in connection with the effects of absolute and relative numbers. Karweit (1976) found that increasing the size of a school tends to reduce students' participation rates, their sense of participation, group cohesiveness, and the degree of consensus on esteem networks. However, it is not clear that these possible effects of size have any bearing on the distribution of interactions across racial or ethnic lines.

2.7. Tension Levels in Community Settings

Many factors including increased unemployment, the rise of demagogic political candidates (including persons running for school board positions), housing shortages, or rapid changes in racial compositions of neighborhoods may increase the level of racial or ethnic tension in the community. As we have implied, the impact of such tension on student behavior can be expected to be indirect and therefore not necessarily very pronounced. It may, however, affect students' attitudes through those of their parents. Secondly, a high level of community tension will affect school board and administrative personnel, making them extremely vulnerable to criticism and hypersensitive to the need to prevent embarrassing incidents in their schools. As we have suggested, this may result in a lack of incentive to encourage any form of contact between groups.

2.8. Insecurity of School Officials

We have suggested that the American educational system is generally characterized by short-term office-holding among both school boards and top administrative officials. This, of course, makes these actors especially sensitive to public pressures and unwilling to take risks with programs that may become defined as "controversial" if attention is called to their existence.[11] Normally, in school settings many kinds of activities occur that are virtually invisible to parents and other outsiders, and everyday contacts among students are likely to be among these relatively noncontroversial activities. Thus, administrators generally have considerable flexibility in directing these activities as long as no dramatic and unpopular events are believed to result from them. But the existence of a high level of community tension over racial issues, when combined with a high degree of vulnerability on the part of school officials, can be expected to lead to cautious practices with regard to encouraging cross-group contacts among students. At the same time, this combination of tension and vulnerability may also play into the hands of those few student extremists who wish to stir up trouble between student groups.

2.9. Decisiveness of Action

It has often been pointed out in the race relations literature that unless actions of policymakers are decisive and consistent, there will be an open invitation to pressures from all sides, with a resultant increase in tension levels.

[11]Crain (1968) discussed a number of factors that may possibly account for differences among school boards in their cohesiveness in implementing desegregation plans, noting that boards composed primarily of political appointees or persons aspiring to political office tend to be more sensitive to outside pressures than are those composed mainly of civic and business leaders.

Where a school board indicates, for example, that it is enforcing school desegregation only because of court action and that it favors court challenges or organized resistance, we can naturally expect increased tension and polarization among citizen groups.[12] Decisiveness also seems crucial within schools in situations where potential student conflicts are likely, as for example when a community is already polarized.

Yet, it is obvious that indecisiveness is not just a function of personality characteristics. If a school board is almost evenly divided on an issue, its decisions may shift according to a single vote. In many instances, indecisiveness results from a genuine lack of knowledge and inability to predict the consequences of a given decision. Presumably, officials who are in insecure positions will be less decisive than those whose positions are relatively safe. Thus, the degree of decisiveness may often be an indicator of other factors at work within the larger community setting.

Although not quite the same thing as indecisiveness, it is also clear that vacillating or confused policies may result simply because improved intergroup contacts are low priority goals. If the Seattle schools are at all typical of others across the country, considerably more attention may be given to school desegregation or the transfer of bodies from one school to another than to the nature and quality of interaction patterns that occur, once students of different races and ethnic groups have been placed in the same settings. If so, what may appear to be indecisiveness may instead simply be a combination of confusion based on ignorance of the most effective alternatives and on the low priority given to intergroup contacts. Insofar as school administrators are primarily motivated by the goals of avoiding outside pressures and providing reasonable learning environments, we would expect this kind of inattentiveness to interaction processes of a rather mundane nature.

3. CONCLUSION

In concluding, it is perhaps well to emphasize a point made in the opening paragraphs. It may turn out to be exceedingly difficult to modify the individual behaviors of large numbers of children without making a concerted effort to do so. Yet, it seems very unlikely that the American public will place a sufficiently high priority on increasing pressure on school administrators and teachers to make the needed effort. School personnel often stress that their primary objective is to pass along information to the young and to prepare them for a competitive

---

[12]Lieberson (personal communication, 1982) has suggested that the existence of such a court order may enable a board to deflect hostility away from itself and thus, perhaps, enable it to present a more united front.

adult life. Although lip service may be given to such things as learning to cooperate with others, appreciating cultural differences, and understanding the problems faced by others who may be less fortunate than themselves, it may be too much to expect that an educational system embedded in a society that merely gives lip service to such goals will, itself, be able to induce students to behave very differently from their elders. If so, rapid change with respect to both desegregation and improved intergroup contacts cannot be expected to occur, nor can we realistically hope to locate a few variables or policy changes that will have dramatic effects.

ACKNOWLEDGMENTS

The author is grateful to Nancy S. Landale for her extensive literature review and to Jomills H. Braddock, Stanley Lieberson, and Martin Patchen for their helpful comments on a previous draft of this chapter. Project participants also made numerous useful suggestions.

REFERENCES

Allport, G. W. *The Nature of Prejudice.* Cambridge, MA: Addison-Wesley, 1954.

Amir, Y. Contact hypothesis in ethnic relations. *Psychological Bulletin,* 1969, *71,* 319–342.

Anderson, C. S. The search for school climate: A review of the research. *Review of Educational Research,* 1982, *52*(3), 368–420.

Blalock, H. M. *Toward a Theory of Minority-Group Relations.* New York: Wiley, 1967.

Blalock, H. M., and Wilken, P. H. *Intergroup Processes: A Micro-Macro Approach.* New York: Free Press, 1979.

Blau, P. M. Contexts, units, and properties in sociological analysis. In H. M. Blalock (Ed.), *Sociological Theory and Research.* New York: Free Press, 1980.

Bossert, S. T. *Tasks and Social Relationships in Classrooms.* Cambridge: Cambridge University Press, 1979.

Boyd, L. H., and Iversen, G. R. *Contextual Analysis: Concepts and Statistical Techniques.* Belmont, CA: Wadsworth, 1979.

Cohen, E. G. Interracial interaction disability. *Human Relations,* 1972, *25,* 9–24.

Cohen, E. G. The effects of desegregation on race relations. *Law and Contemporary Problems,* 1975, *39,* 271–299.

Cohen, E. G. Expectation states and inter-racial interaction in school settings. *Annual Review of Sociology,* 1982, *8,* 209–235.

Cohen, E. G. and Rober, S. Modification of interracial interaction disability. In J. Berger and M. Zelditch (Eds.), *Status, Rewards, and Influence.* San Francisco: Jossey-Bass, 1985.

Coleman, J. S. *The Adolescent Society.* New York: Free Press, 1961.

Crain, R. L. *The Politics of School Desegregation.* Chicago: Aldine, 1968.

Davidson, J. D., Hofmann, G., and Brown, W. R. Measuring and explaining high school interracial climates. *Social Problems,* 1978, *26,* 50–70.

Duncan, O. D., and Duncan, B. A methodological analysis of segregation indexes. *American Sociological Review*, 1955, *20*, 210–217.

Epstein, J. L., and Karweit, N. L. (Eds.), *Friends in School*. New York: Academic Press, 1983.

Eulau, H. *Micro-Macro Political Analysis: Accents of Inquiry*. Chicago: Aldine, 1969.

Garcia, H. D. C. *Problems and remedies in Chicano school desegregation and bilingual education* (Report #316). Baltimore, MD: Center for Social Organization of Schools, The Johns Hopkins University, 1981.

Gerard, H. B., Jackson, T. D., and Conolley, E. S. Social contact in the desegregated classroom. In H. B. Gerard and N. Miller (Eds.), *School Desegregation*. New York: Plenum Press, 1975.

Hansell, S., and Slavin, R. E. *Cooperative learning and interracial friendships* (Report #285). Baltimore, MD: Center for Social Organization of Schools, The Johns Hopkins University, 1979.

Hansell, S., Tackaberry, S. N., and Slavin, R. E. *Cooperation, competition, and the structure of student cliques* (Report #309). Baltimore, MD: Center for Social Organization of Schools, The Johns Hopkins University, 1981.

Hollingshead, A. B. *Elmtown's Youth*. New York: Wiley, 1949.

Homans, G. C. *The Human Group*. New York: Harcourt, Brace, 1950.

Karweit, N. L. *School influences on student interaction patterns* (Report #220). Baltimore, MD: Center for Social Organization of Schools, The Johns Hopkins University, 1976.

Langley, C. T. *Structural ambiguity*. Unpublished doctoral dissertation, University of Washington, 1977.

Lieberson, S. *Ethnic Patterns in American Cities*. New York: Free Press, 1963.

Longshore, D., and Prager, J. The impact of school desegregation: A situational analysis. In R. Turner (Ed.), *Annual Review of Sociology 11*. Palo Alto, CA: Annual Reviews, 1985.

McConahay, J. B. The effects of school desegregation upon students' racial attitudes and behavior: A critical review of the literature and a prolegomenon to future research. *Law and Contemporary Problems*, 1978, *42*, 77–107.

McDill, E. L., and Rigsby, L. C. *Structure and Process in Secondary Schools,* Baltimore, MD: Johns Hopkins Press, 1973.

Metz, M. *Classrooms and Corridors: The Crisis of Authority in Desegregated Secondary Schools*. Berkeley, CA: University of California Press, 1978.

Miller, N. Peer relations as the mediator of beneficial desegregation effects. In J. L. Epstein and N. L. Karweit (Eds.), *Friends in Schools*. New York: Academic Press, 1983.

Ogbu, J. U. *Minority Education and Caste: The American System in Cross-Cultural Perspective*. New York: Academic Press, 1978.

Olson, M. *The Logic of Collective Action*. Cambridge, MA: Harvard University Press, 1965.

Patchen, M. *Black-White Contact in Schools*. West Lafayette, IN: Purdue University Press, 1982.

St. John, N. *School Desegregation: Outcomes for Children*. New York: Wiley Interscience, 1975.

St. John, N., and Lewis, R. G. Race and the social structure of the elementary classroom. *Sociology of Education, 1975, 48,* 346–368.

Schofield, J. W. School desegregation and intergroup relations. In D. Bar-Tal and L. Saxe (Eds.), *Social Psychology of Education*. Washington: Hemisphere, 1978.

Slavin, R. E. Effects of biracial learning teams on cross-racial friendships. *Journal of Educational Psychology*, 1979, *71*, 381–387.

Slavin, R. E. Cooperative learning in teams: State of the art. *Educational Psychology, 1980, 15,* 93–111.

Slavin, R. E., and Hansell, S. Cooperative learning and intergroup relations. In J. Epstein and N. Karweit (Eds.), *Friends in School*. New York: Academic Press, 1983.

Slavin, R. E., and Madden, N. A. School practices that improve race relations. *American Educational Research Journal,* 1979, *16,* 169–180.

Taeuber, K. E., and Taeuber, A. F. *Negroes in Cities.* Chicago: Aldine, 1965.

Yamagishi, T. *Development of distribution rules in groups: An experimental study.* Unpublished doctoral dissertation, University of Washington, 1981.

Chapter 5

Trait Theory Revisited

A Cognitive Social Learning View of School Desegregation

WALTER MISCHEL

The theoretical background for studying school desegregation has been a curious mix. On the one hand, sociologists and social psychologists traditionally have been committed to clarifying the role of sociocultural context and "situation" in the analysis and explanation of human behavior. Indeed, recognition of the importance of the situation is a hallmark of both sociology and social psychology. On the other hand, a good deal of desegregation research by psychologists has been implicitly or explicitly modeled on the assumptions of traditional personality psychology. (See Mischel, 1968, for a review.) In that approach, one begins (and ends) not with an analysis of the particular situation but with a focus on the required personal characteristics of the participants in that situation. An illustrative large-scale example is Gerard and Miller's (1975) effort to narrow the achievement gap between Anglo and minority children by exposing them to a desegregation situation. Guided by the traditional personality theory perspective and strategy, Gerard and Miller assumed that ethnic differences in personality and in broad dispositions—such as achievement orientation—underlie differences in the actual academic achievements of the children. Perhaps most fundamental, Gerard and Miller assumed further that certain personality traits (e.g., high self-esteem, tolerance for delayed gratification) are centrally related to academic achievement: change the personality traits (e.g., through the desegregation experience) and achievement changes will naturally follow. For example, a core

WALTER MISCHEL • Department of Psychology, Columbia University, New York, NY 10027.

assumption of their study was that "increased self-esteem will lead to increased achievement" (Gerard and Miller, 1975, p. 285).

The massive and elegant data provided by their study surprised the psychologists who conducted it and profoundly challenged the traditional personality perspective that guided them. For example, the correlations between personality traits and achievement in their data were found to "account for a relatively miniscule amount of the variance in scholastic achievement" (Gerard and Miller, 1975, p. 285). Further, and perhaps as a function of contemporary changes in social structure, it may be that

> individual differences in stable, enduring personality systems of internality, tolerance for delay, and achievement motivation, occupy an increasingly weaker position in their ability to explain what people actually do—their educational achievement and attainment. (Gerard and Miller, 1975, p. 291)

After reviewing the voluminous, enormously costly data collected by them, the authors concluded:

> In sum, our data show that desegregation is no simple panacea for counter-acting the increasing achievement gap between white and minority students as they progress through school. Our findings suggest that major personality changes are not prerequisites for narrowing the gap and point instead toward the potential of situational factors in the educational setting that can be directly altered—teacher behavior and peer acceptance. In this sense they are encouraging; beneficial effects need not await basic changes in personality structures. They further show that simply implementing a bussing or desegregation program will not by itself achieve "integration" in the full sense of the word. Beyond desegregation, additional procedures must be developed to foster integration of the minority child into the classroom social structure and academic program. (Gerard and Miller, 1975, pp. 302–303)

Such a sweeping rejection of the relevance of the traditional personality trait approach to desegregation would be easy to minimize (e.g., as reflecting only methodological weaknesses, deficits, or peculiarities in the studies done so far) if it stood alone. But it does not. It must be seen in the context of the larger challenge to the usefulness of this type of personality approach, a challenge that has been formulated beginning in the 1960s (e.g., Bandura, 1969; Mischel, 1968; Peterson, 1968; Vernon, 1965). To understand that challenge and its possible implications for the desegregation problem, a first step is to review the assumptions and states of the traditional approach more closely.

1. TRADITIONAL PERSONALITY TRAIT APPROACHES

1.1. Assumptions

It has generally been assumed that the basic units of personality study are personality dispositions or traits. They are assumed to be relatively stable, highly consistent attributes that exert widely generalized *causal* effects on behavior.

Thus, personality consists of broad underlying dispositions that pervasively influence the person's behavior across many situations and lead to consistency in his behavior (e.g., Allport, 1937). These dispositions are not directly observed but are inferred from behavioral signs (trait indicators), either directly or indirectly (Mischel, 1968). Guided by this assumption, personality research has been a search for such underlying broad dimensions, in many forms (e.g., basic factors, motives, characteristic coping styles). These trait assumptions are seen in the existence of hundreds of personality tests designed to try to infer dispositions, whereas there are almost no tests to measure situations. The same belief in global traits that manifest themselves pervasively is perhaps best seen in the projective test assumption that responses to vague or minimal stimuli will reveal individual differences in fundamental generalized dispositions (MacFarlane and Tuddenham, 1951). In the context of desegregation, these assumptions are embodied in both the conception and design of the Gerard and Miller study. Namely, ethnic differences in achievement reflect differences in personality dispositions (e.g., the ability to delay gratification, to plan and work for long-term goals) that supposedly underlie successful achievement: The desegregation experience should allow these dispositions to become more equally shared by different ethnic groups, resulting in more equitable achievement.

A main goal of traditional trait psychology has been to discover the individual's position on one or more personality dimensions by comparing a person with other persons tested under similar conditions. It was assumed that an individual's position on these dimensions would be relatively stable across testing situations and over lengthy time-periods, if the test was sufficiently reliable. Therefore, the main focus in trait psychology was on the development of reliable instruments administered under standard conditions. Such instruments were thought to tap accurately the person's presumably stable, highly generalized traits across a relatively large number of situations or settings.

The early psychometricians tended to follow the example of simple physical measurement, hoping that the measurement of traits would be basically similar to such measurements as table length with rulers or temperature with thermometers. They unquestioningly assumed that broad trait structures exist and lead people to behave consistently. Consequently, they did not pay much attention to the role of environmental variables as determinants of behavior. Instead, they concentrated on standardization of measurement conditions in the hope that broad traits would emerge.

1.2. Evidence: How Broad or Specific Are Traits?

Will a person who is "conscientious" about homework also be conscientious about keeping social appointments and honoring obligations to other people? Will an individual who is anxious about school also be anxious about meeting strangers or taking on a new job? How broad (general) or specific (narrow) are traits like conscientiousness and anxiety? Do people have dispositions that reveal themselves consistently in a wide range of behaviors and over many situations? These questions have been asked for years, and the answers remain the subject of intense debate. Perhaps no topic in personality psychology is more controversial—and more important—than the question of the relative specificity versus generality of traits.

Trait theorists have been surprised by a great deal of research indicating that performances on trait measures are affected by a variety of situations or conditions, and can be modified by numerous environmental changes (Masling, 1960; Mischel, 1974; Peterson, 1968; Vernon, 1964). Most important, it has been found that normal people tend to show considerable variability in their behavior even across seemingly similar contexts. A person may delay, for example, all sorts of immediate gratification and work hard and well to prepare for next year's carnival, but be unwilling to wait even one day for a better notebook (Mischel, 1966, 1974). Such behaviors as delay of gratification, or other forms of self-control and planfulness, may be highly specific, varying as a result of slight situational alterations, such as subtle changes in the particular delayed rewards or in the conditions necessary for their attainment. Thus, behavior had be much more situation-specific and discriminative than early trait theorists and thought. Such patterns as "achievement orientation" may hinge on many considerations and depend on many factors (Mischel, 1981a).

Studies of individual differences on common trait dimensions have produced many extensive networks of correlations. These associations tend to be large and enduring when people rate themselves or others with broad trait terms (e.g., Block, 1971). For example, on questionnaires people may describe their traits consistently (e.g., E. L. Kelly, 1955). When ongoing behavior in specific situations is sampled objectively by different, independent measures, however, the association generally tends to be quite modest. Thus, although people often show consistency on questionnaires and ratings, these data tend to have limited value for predicting their actual behavior in specific situations (Mischel, 1973, 1981a).

The correlational research on "delay of gratification," for example, is fairly representative of correlational research on other personality dimensions. Some supporting validity data tend to be easily obtained. The networks of relationships from such research extend far and wide and provide ample evidence that people's tendency to defer immediate satisfactions for the sake of larger, more valued but delayed goals, has some consistency, that it is not totally situation specific, that there are clear threads of coherence and continuity (e.g., Block and Block, 1980; Mischel, 1966). What a person does in one setting is not independent of what he does in other settings, and it is, of course, related to what he did before and to what he will probably do again. In general, however, correlational work on voluntary delay of reward and on other personality dispositions suggests that the strength of the associations tends to be too low for confident predictions about behavior in the individual case. They also may be too low to be the main or exclusive basis for social policy and for major social programs.

We therefore have to be most cautious about generalizing from an individual's test behavior to that individual's personality and behavior outside the test. For example, we cannot safely conclude that a child's unwillingness to work for better grades in arithmetic class precludes his behaving in highly delay-oriented ways under certain life conditions in which, for example, his self-confidence or trust is greater. In the present view, such qualities as self-control are not situation-free attributes. They depend on many modifying conditions and hence are relatively specific across contexts.

Behavioral specificity, or the dependence of behavior on specific situational conditions, has been discovered regularly on character traits like self-control, rigidity, or social conformity, or honesty, or aggression, or on most other personality dimensions (Mischel, 1968, 1981a; Peake, 1982; Peterson, 1968; Vernon, 1964). Specificity tends to be high, for example, among the components of traits like conscientiousness, or attitudes toward authority—although trait theorists originally believed these to be highly generalized dispositions. Results of this kind present a basic problem for approaches to personality that assume the existence of relatively situation-free, broad dispositions. They also present a serious challenge to desegregation approaches that rely on a "large lumps" conception of personality and of social behavior.

The phrase *personality coefficient* has been coined to describe the modest correlation (usually between .20 and .30) typically found in personality research linking responses on questionnaires to other behavior (Mischel, 1968). Such correlations are too small to have value for most individual assessment purposes other than gross screening decisions. The evaluation of all data on trait consistency depends of course on the standards selected to evaluate them. A modest consistency coefficient (of about .30, for example) can be taken as evidence of either the relative specificity of the particular behaviors or the presence of some cross-situational generality (Burton, 1963). Furthermore, one has to infer dispositions from imperfect behavior measurements that involve errors. Nevertheless, it is increasingly being recognized that behavioral fluctuations reflect more than imperfections in measuring instruments (Mischel and Peake, 1982). On most traits most people show only limited consistency across most situations. The utility of describing everyone in broad trait terms (e.g., "impulsive," "achievement oriented") therefore has to be questioned deeply.

1.3. Behavior Stability over Time

The specificity of behavior across situations should not be confused with its stability over time in similar situations. In fact, there is continuity over long periods of time, especially when people rate themselves or when observers rate them (Block and Block, 1980; Epstein, 1979; Mischel, 1968, 1979). And these two types of ratings often are significantly related to each other and to relevant behavior. Consistency over time and agreement among judges in personality ratings are not disputed (Mischel and Peake, 1982). Indeed, there is increasing evidence showing impressive coherence in behavior patterns even when measured over many years (Block and Block, 1980). Lives do have coherence, and we tend to view ourselves and others as relatively stable people, without questioning our basic identity and continuity over time.

What *is* in dispute is the consistency of behavior not over time or in similar situations but across increasingly dissimilar situations; that is disputed especially when one infers personality dimensions from ongoing behavior sampled by methods that go beyond trait ratings, such as direct observations. Studies with objective measures of behavior as it occurs naturally have indicated that a given individual's actions are often rather specific to the particular situation and tend to be patterned uniquely (e.g., Mischel, 1968; Mischel and Peake, 1982; Peterson, 1968; Shweder, 1975; Shweder and D'Andrade, 1979). Objective, specific measures of ongoing behavior tend to yield erratic evidence of consistency across situations. Although the patterns are often coherent and meaningful (i.e., non-random), they also tend to be complex and unevenly related to personality ratings (Block, 1977).

1.4. Defense of Traits

Though many psychologists acknowledge that the specific situation is important, they remain convinced that past research has underestimated the personal constancies in behavior. They note that if we want to test how well a disposition (trait) can be used to predict behavior, we have to sample adequately not only the disposition but also the behavior that we want to predict (Ajzen and Fishbein, 1977; Block, 1977; Epstein, 1979; Jaccard, 1974; Weigel and Newman, 1976). In the past, researchers often attempted to predict single acts (for example, physical aggression when insulted) from a dispositional measure (e.g., self-rated aggression). Generally such attempts did not succeed. But although measures of traits may not be able to predict such single acts, they may do much better if one uses a "multiple-act criterion," that is, a pooled combination of many behaviors that are relevant to the trait.

In this vein, there have been a number of demonstrations that reliability will increase when the number of items in a test sample are increased and combined. It is important to remember that

> there is nothing magical about a correlation coefficient, and its interpretation depends on many considerations. The accuracy of reliability of measurement increased with the length of the test. Since no single item is a perfect measure, adding items increases

the chance that the test will elicit a more accurate sample and yield a better estimate
of the person's behavior. (Mischel, 1968, p. 37)

Making this point empirically, Epstein (1979) demonstrated that temporal stability (of, for example, self-reported emotions and experiences recorded daily,
and observer judgments) becomes much larger when it is based on averages over
many days than when it is based on only single items on single days. Such
demonstrations help by reminding psychologists again that reliability is essential
before one can hope to have validity. However, most of the evidence so far
again is relevant to the temporal stability of traits. It does not suggest broad
cross-situational consistency of behavior in personal domains (Mischel and Peake,
1982).

1.5. Interaction of Dispositions and Conditions

Some investigators have tried to analyze the role of situations and conditions as well as the role of dispositions. In the last decade, sophisticated trait
research has begun to take situations and "stimulus conditions" into account
seriously (e.g., Argyle and Little, 1972; Endler, 1973, 1982; Moos, 1974).
Knowledge of individual differences alone often tells us little unless it is com
bined with information about the conditions and situational variables that influence the behavior of interest. Conversely, the effects of conditions depend on
the individuals in them. Research results consistently suggest that the interaction
of individual differences and particular conditions tends to be most important.

Moos's (1968) studies of self-reported reactions by staff and psychiatric
patients to various settings in the hospital provide a typical example. The findings
were based on ratings in nine settings with regard to a dimension of "sociable,
friendly, peaceful" versus "unsociable, hostile, angry" behavior. These results
revealed, first, that different individuals reacted differently to the settings. Second, a given person might be high on the dimension in the morning but not at
lunch, high with another patient but not with a nurse, low in small group therapy,
moderate in industrial therapy, but high in individual therapy, etc. An entirely
different pattern might characterize the next person. It seems reasonable to believe
that parallel results would be found in an analysis of children's reactions to
school settings and to different components of the desegregation situation.

We might be able to predict many of the things a child will do simply by
knowing something about the particular context of the school desegregation
situation in which the child will be. For example, we might be able to predict
a good deal from information about the proportions of children from the various
ethnic groups present in the situation, their attitudes towards each other in that
context, the specific task structure of the activity (e.g., requiring intergroup
cooperation versus implying competition), and/or the type of task (e.g., highly
valued by one group but not by the other). Indeed predictions based on such

fine-grained specific information about the particular "psychological situation" might be more efficacious than those based on inferences about the children's global dispositions.

The limited utility of inferring hypothesized global trait dispositions from behavioral signs does not mean that situations are more important than persons (Bowers, 1973). Is information about the individual more important than information about the situation? I have persistently refused to pose this question because, phrased that way, it is unanswerable and can serve only to stimulate futile debates. In these debates "situations" are often incorrectly invoked as entities that supposedly exert either major or only minor control over behavior, without specifying what, psychologically, they are or how they function (Alker, 1972; Bowers, 1973; Wallach and Leggett, 1972). But whereas some situations may be powerful determinants of behavior, others are likely to be exceedingly trivial (Mischel, 1977). The relative importance of individual differences will depend on the situation selected, the type of behavior assessed, the particular individual differences sampled and the purpose of the assessment or research.

1.6. Moderator Variables

Many "moderator variables" may influence the correlations found in trait research (e.g., Bem and Allen, 1974; Kogan and Wallach, 1964; Wallach, 1962). That is, the relations between any two variables often depend on several other variables. For instance, correlations between measures of risk taking and impulsivity may be found for males but not for females; they may even be negative for one sex but positive for the other. Similarly, relations between two measures might be positive for children with low IQ but negative for highly intelligent children, or they might occur under relaxed testing conditions but not under anxious conditions. The concept of moderator variables was introduced to trait theory to refer to the fact that the effects of any particular disposition generally are moderated by or dependent on many other conditions and variables. Such variables as the person's age, sex, IQ, the experimenter's sex, and the characteristics of the situation all are common moderators.

Research on dispositions has begun to recognize more fully the extraordinary complexity of the interactions found between person variables and conditions (Mischel, 1981b). When one examines closely the interactions obtained in research on the effects of dispositions and conditions, the number of moderator variables required to predict behavior, and the complexity of their interrelationships (e.g., McGuire, 1960), tend to become most formidable (Cronbach, 1975). For example, to predict a child's voluntary delay of gratification, one may have to know how old he is, his sex, the experimenter's sex, the particular objects for which he is waiting, the consequences of not waiting, the models to whom he was just exposed, his immediately prior experiences—the list gets almost endless (Mischel, 1973). This seems to be another way of saying that what a person does tends to be relatively specific to a host of variables, and that behavior is multiply determined by all of them rather than being the product of widely generalized dispositions. Let me emphasize again that this does not imply that predictions cannot be made from person variables to relevant behaviors, but it does suggest severe limits on the range and level of relationships that can be expected. As a representative example, consider one effort to relate individual differences in young children's expectancies about locus of control to their behavior in theoretically relevant situations (Mischel et al., 1974). To explore these interactions, the Stanford Preschool Internal-External Scale was developed as a measure of expectancies about whether events occur as a consequence of the child's own action ("internal control") or as a consequence of external forces ("external control"). Expectancies about locus of control were measured separately for positive and negative events so that scores reflect expectancies for degree of internal control of positive events $(I+)$, or negative events $(I-)$, and a sum of these two (total I). Individual differences in $I+$, $I-$, and total I then were correlated with the children's ability to delay gratification under diverse working and waiting conditions. The results provided highly specific but theoretically meaningful patterns of relationships. To illustrate, relationships between total I and overall delay behavior were negligible, and $I+$ was unrelated to $I-$. As expected, $I+$ (but not $I-$) was found to be related to persistence in three separate situations where instrumental activity would result in a positive outcome; $I-$ (but not $I+$) was related to persistence when instrumental activity could prevent the occurrence of a negative outcome.

The total results indicated that individual differences in children's beliefs about their ability to control outcomes are partial determinants of their goal-directed behavior, but the relationships hinge on extremely specific moderating conditions, both with regard to the type of behavior and the type of belief. If such moderating conditions had not been considered and all indexes of delay behavior had been combined regardless of their positive or negative valence, the actual role of the relevant individual differences would have been totally obscured. Whereas the results were of considerable theoretical interest, the number and mean level of the achieved correlations were not appreciably higher than those typically found in correlational personality research. Moreover, the ability of these correlations to survive cross-validation remains to be demonstrated empirically.

The more moderators we need to qualify a trait, the more the trait becomes a relatively specific description of a behavior–situation unit. That is, the more highly circumscribed, moderated, and situation-specific the trait, the more it becomes indistinguishable from a specific behavior–situation description. When a great many strings of hyphenated moderator variables are needed, the behavioral signs from which the disposition is inferred may become equivalent to the inferred disposition and make the inference gratuitous. As we increasingly qualify the description of a person to specify the exact response modes and conditions in which a particular behavior will occur, we move from broad characterizations with generalized traits to describing specific behavior in particular forms and under particular conditions.

2. THE COGNITIVE SOCIAL LEARNING VIEW

2.1. Multiple Determinants: "Contextualism"

What, then, are the implications of results like these for how one approaches the study of desegregation and, more generally, the problem of measuring human qualities? In my view, one of the major lessons from the history of personality measurement is the recognition that complex human behavior tends to be influenced by many determinants and reflects the almost inseparable and continuous interaction of a large number of variables both in the person and in the situation. And if human behavior is determined by many interacting variables—both in the person and in the environment—then a focus on any one of them is likely to lead to limited predictions and generalizations. In the context of desegregation, this means that it may be naive to expect any one set of changes (e.g., racially mixed classrooms) automatically to have a broad impact (e.g., on school achievement, intergroup relations, self-concepts). The impact is likely to depend on many other variables, including the details of the specific situation.

This recognition of multiple determinism and specificity has profound implications, and it may be increasingly shared not only across many areas of psychology but even more generally in the social sciences. The same basic conclusion has been reached in analyses of topics as diverse as the impact of teaching practices and classroom arrangements in education, the effects of interview styles in psychotherapy, and the role of instructions to aid recall in memory experiments (Mischel, 1977a). For example, after a survey of research on memory, Jenkins (1974, p. 793) cautioned,

> What is remembered in a given situation depends on the physical and psychological context in which the event was experienced, the knowledge and skills that the subject brings to the context, the situation in which we ask for evidence for remembering, and the relation of what the subject remembers to what the experimenter demands.

The sentence would hold just as well if we substituted action for memory. Thus, what is done (or thought, or felt) in a given situation depends on the physical and psychological context in which the event was experienced, the knowledge and skills that the subject brings to the context, the situation in which we ask for evidence, etc. Identical conclusions probably would be reached for the subject matter of any other area of psychology and perhaps throughout the social sciences. Hence, it becomes difficult to achieve broad, sweeping generalizations about human behavior; many qualifiers (moderators) must be appended to our "laws" about cause-and-effect relations—almost without exception and perhaps with no exceptions at all (Cronbach, 1975).

Specificity (or "contextualism," as Jenkins put it) may occur because there are so many different ways in which different people may react to the "same" treatments and reinterpret them (e.g., Cronbach, 1975; Neisser, 1974) and because the impact of most situations can usually be changed easily by coexisting conditions (Mischel, 1974). Thus, even a relatively simple situation may produce a variety of often unpredictable specific (and weak) effects, depending on a large number of moderating variables and the many different ways in which the particular "subjects" may view them and transform them.

Contextualism suggests the need to specify carefully circumscribed goals. In my view, more modest, specific, highly qualified goals may be refreshing for a field in which false hopes have often produced depression (e.g., Cronbach, 1975; Fiske, 1974; Gerard and Miller, 1975). The need to qualify generalizations about human behavior complicates life for the social scientist and for the social planner alike. But it does not prevent one from studying human affairs scientifically or from generating sensible social policy and plans. It does, however, demand a respect for the complexity of the enterprise and alerts one to the dangers of oversimplifying the nature and causes of human behavior or the "cures" for human problems. It should be clear that this danger is equally great whether one is searching for generalized (global) person-free situational effects or for generalized (global) situation-free personality variables. In the context of personality measurement generally, and the study of desegregation in particular, serious recognition of multiple determinism and interactions has many specific implications. It calls for a careful specification of goals with more modest, clearly circumscribed expectations. For example, although desegregation may be a socially, culturally, and morally desirable objective in its own right, it should not be endowed with global curative powers for enhancing the performance of underachievers. Whether or not children achieve more or less hinges on the learning conditions and support for achievement in the classroom and home, to which desegregation may only be marginally related. So, one might study what enhances better achievement, better interactions, and better group cooperation, in terms of specific conditions within the school culture and its psychological milieu, rather than as the global fallout of a desegregation effort. Many methods for studying such more specific interactions exist and can be applied readily to the investigation of desegregation (e.g., Patterson, 1974; Raush, 1974).

2.2. Studying Persons in the Cognitive Social Learning Approach

A cognitive social learning approach contends that the discriminativeness of behavior and the complexity of the interactions between the person and the situation imply that we must focus more specifically on what the person *constructs* (does, thinks, and feels) in particular situations, instead of attempting to infer the global traits a person generally *has*. A cognitive social learning approach to assessment and research focuses on the individual's cognitive activities and behavior patterns, studied in relation to the specific conditions that evoke, maintain, and modify such activities and patterns and which they, in turn, change (Mischel, 1968, 1973, 1979). Instead of trying to compare and generalize about what different individuals "are like," this approach assesses what the individuals *do*—behaviorally and cognitively—in relationship to the psychological conditions in which they do it and on which the particular investigation focuses. Attention shifts in this approach from describing situation-free people with broad trait adjectives to analyzing the specific interactions between conditions and the cognitions and behaviors of interest. In the context of desegregation this viewpoint implies that the researcher must begin by clearly specifying the particular outcomes that are desired in fine-grain detail. These outcomes need to be specified as concretely as possible (i.e., not in global terms) and anchored to particular contexts. For example, one might want, as a goal, to increase classroom cooperation between minority and Anglo children. If so, clear referents that define such cooperation, its nature and settings, need to be spelled out in terms of the desired actions and attitudes. The conditions in the situation that would increase those outcomes then need to be clarified by a functional analysis in which relations between the hypothesized variables and the desired outcomes are systematically explored. (For example, see Mischel, 1968, 1981b; Patterson, 1974; Webb, 1982.)

Cognitive social learning person variables include the individual's *competencies* to construct (generate) diverse behaviors under appropriate conditions. In addition, we have to consider the person's *encoding* and *categorization* of events and people, including the self. To understand what a person will peform in particular situations we also have to attend to that person's *expectancies*, the subjective values of any expected outcomes, and the individual's *self-regulatory systems and plans*. Although the variables overlap and interact, each may offer some distinctive information about the person and each may alert us to somewhat different aspects of individuality. And each person variable may be seen both as a product of the individual's total history and as a mediator of the impact of any future experiences. The person variables on which a particular investigation focuses should be dictated by the investigator's goals. Thus in the study of desegregation, for example, one would attend particularly to those competencies required for the particular desegregation goals, for example, improved academic achievement. Likewise, one might attend to the ways in which the children from different ethnic groups encode or construe themselves, and each other, within the context of particular desegregation situations. Let us consider each person variable briefly.

2.2.1. Cognitive and Behavioral Construction Competencies

Throughout the course of life, people learn about the world and their relationship to it, thus acquiring an enormous potential to generate a vast array of knowledge and organized behavior. Although the accumulation of this potential seems an obvious product of cognitive development, just what gets learned is not so obvious. The products of such socialization and cognitive growth encompass the social knowledge and rules that guide conduct, the personal constructs one generates about the self and others, and a vast array of social and cognitive skills and competencies. The concept of cognitive and behavioral construction competencies refers to these diverse products and is intended to be broad enough to include the wide range of psychological acquisitions that must be encompassed.

To assess competencies we must create conditions and incentives to encourage optimal performance. The necessary assessment conditions for this purpose are the same as those employed in ability and achievement testing (Wallace, 1966). We can use the same strategy to assess what people know (their available information, comprehension, and construction skills) and what social behaviors they are capable of executing. For example, to assess what children had acquired from observing a model, attractive rewards were offered to them after the observation period. Getting the rewards was contingent on their reproducing the model's behaviors (e.g., Bandura, 1965; Grusec and Mischel, 1966). The findings demonstrated that the children had acquired a great deal of information from observation of the model and could reconstruct the modeled behavior in detail, but did so only when offered appropriate incentives. It seems most likely that children in desegregated situations know many behaviors that would enhance intergroup cooperation for mutual benefit, but fail to do so due to inadequate incentives and opposing pressures (e.g., from peers).

Assessing a person's potential cognitive constructions and behavioral enactments, measuring social, interpersonal, and cognitive skills, requires that we test what the individual *can* do (under the appropriate conditions of interest) rather than what he usually does. One of the most persistent and promising individual-differences dimensions seems to involve such cognitive and behavioral (social) competencies (e.g., White, 1959; Ziegler and Phillips, 1961, 1962). Such competencies may have much better temporal and cross-situational stability, and more pervasive consequences for coping and adaptation, than many of the social and motivational dispositions favored in traditional personality research that ignored cognitive characteristics (Mischel, 1968).

Construction capacities tend to be relatively stable over time, as reflected in the relatively high stability found in performances closely related to cognitive and intellectual variables (Mischel, 1968, 1969). They also may contribute significantly to the impression of consistency in personality. A person who knows how to solve certain problems that require particular self-monitoring and assertiveness skills remains capable of performing skillfully in relevant situations over long periods of time.

Cognitive competencies (as measured by "mental age" and IQ tests) seem to be among the best predictors of later social and interpersonal adjustment (e.g., Anderson, 1960). Moreover, more competent, brighter people experience more interpersonal success and better work achievements and therefore become more benignly assessed by themselves and by others on the ubiquitous evaluative "good-bad" dimension in trait ratings (e.g., Vernon, 1964). In other words, they may tend to have somewhat higher self-esteem and to be esteemed more by others. Likewise, cognitive competencies presumably are a key component of such enduring concepts as "ego strength" and "ego development." Interestingly, the large "first factor" found regularly on tests like the MMPI (Block, 1965), usually given labels connoting "adjustment" at the positive end and maladaptive character structure at the negative end, may reflect the person's level of cognitive-social competence and achievement to a considerable extent. The assessment of competence in response to specific problematic situations in the direct manner developed by Goldfried and D'Zurilla (1969) is one good example. The assessment of social competence is also seen nicely in the social problem-solving approach with young children (e.g., Krasnor and Rubin, 1981; Shure and Spivack, 1978).

2.2.2. Encoding Strategies and Constructs

The recognition that human behavior depends on the "situation as coded" requires that we assess how individuals perceive, think, interpret, and experience the world. By definition, a cognitive orientation to the assessment of persons includes a focus not on the objective situation in itself but on the psychological situation as it is represented cognitively and seen by the perceiver. This focus on the person's perception of the world dictates attention to the individual's own personal constructs or ways of encoding experience. In this vein, George Kelly's (1955) pioneering search for assessments that illuminate the client's personal constructs rather than the clinician's preferred hypotheses provide a most impressive conceptual and empirical milestone. The current impact of Kelly's perspective is still dramatic. (See, for example, Neimeyer and Neimeyer, 1981.)

As Kelly emphasized, the subject (like the psychologist) also groups events into categories and organizes them into meaningful units. People do not describe their experiences with operational definitions. They categorize events in terms of personal constructs that may or may not overlap with those of the assessor. The tendency to categorize things and people into categories, so that nonidentical events can be treated as if they were equivalent (Rosch *et al.*, 1976), is a basic feature of cognition. We continuously sample the flood of information impinging from the world, grouping objects and other people according to their similarities into natural categories of kinds or types (of chairs, of children, of teachers, of blacks and whites, of psychologists). These categorization schemes permit us to structure our general knowledge about events, people, and the social world, yielding coherent expectations about characteristic patterns of behavior. Although research on social cognition has discovered much about the consequence of categorization (as in "stereotyping"), so far much less is known about the structure and growth of people's natural categories about the social world. A comprehensive approach requires that we also consider a variety of questions. What are the basic natural units for the categorization of people and psychological situations? What are the gains and losses of categorizations at different levels of abstraction? What are the rules used to judge that someone does or does not fit a particular "person type" or that "John is (or is not) a typical extravert?" Questions of this kind have guided our recent explorations of natural categories in social cognition (e.g., Cantor and Mischel, 1979; Cantor *et al.*, 1982; Hamilton, 1982), in efforts to assess how individuals categorize types of people (extraverts, social climbers) and types of psychological situations (dates, business meetings, classrooms).

Whereas much of this research is only of theoretical interest to the student of desegregation, there also are some possible practical implications. For example, many methods have been developed to study the "natural categorization" of people into such categories as "good student," "disruptive child," or "angry and withdrawn misfit." (See Cantor and Mischel, 1979; Cantor *et al.*, 1982; Horowitz *et al.*, 1981, for examples.) Such methods may be readily adaptable to study how teachers, children, and other people categorize and stereotype each other—often in disadvantageous ways—in the desegregation situation. Certainly it seems worth studying the perceptions of participants in the desegregation situation as those perceptions bear on the goals of the effort and on the desegregation process itself.

2.2.3. Expectancies

When one turns from what people *can* do and how they categorize the world to what they actually do, one goes from construction capacity and constructs to the selection and execution of performance in specific situations. To analyze or predict behavior in a given situation requires attention to the person's expectancies about alternative behavioral possibilities in that situation. The person's expectancies (hypotheses) guide the selection (choice) of behaviors from among the many that could be constructed in a given context. For example, a child's willingness to cross the physical or psychological barriers between ethnic groups in a particular context (e.g., the gym, the playground) depends on the child's expectations about the probable consequences.

Behavior-outcome expectancies are hypotheses or contingency rules that represent the if/then relations between behavioral alternatives and probable outcomes anticipated for particular situations. Expectancy-value theories predict that people will generate the response patterns that they expect are most likely to lead to the most subjectively valuable outcomes (consequences) in any given situation (e.g., Mischel, 1973; Rotter, 1954). When there is no new information about the behavior-outcome expectancies in any situation, performance depends on previous behavior-outcome expectancies in similar situations. But new information about behavior-outcome relations in the particular situation may overcome the effect of presituational expectancies, so that specific situational expectancies soon become major determinants of performance (Mischel and Staub, 1965). When the consequences expected for performance change, so does behavior, although strongly established behavior-outcome expectancies may constrain an individual's ability to adapt to changes in contingencies. The behavior-outcome expectancy construct has been central in social learning personality theories for several decades, and diverse methods are available for its assessment (Rotter, 1954; Rotter et al., 1972).

A special aspect of expectancy, *self-efficacy*—defined as the person's conviction that one can execute the behavior required by a particular situation—has come into focus more recently (Bandura, 1978). Self-efficacy is assessed by asking the person to indicate the degree of confidence that one can do a particular task that is described in detail. The perceptions of one's own efficacy may importantly guide and direct one's behavior. The close connection between high self-efficacy expectations and effective performance is illustrated in studies of people who received various treatments to help reduce their fear of snakes. A consistently high association was found between the degree to which persons improved from treatment (becoming able to handle snakes fearlessly) and their perceived self-efficacy, assessed by asking people specifically to predict their ability to do each given act successfully (Bandura and Adams, 1977). Results of this kind suggest strong and clear links between self-perceptions of one's competence and the ability to behave competently, and demonstrate again that when the right questions are asked people can be excellent predictors of their own behaviors. These results also indicate that the best way to increase children's specific achievements is by providing concrete, guided opportunities and experiences that enhance the children's self-efficacy expectations for those achievement tasks. Such self-efficacy enhancement is likely to work best one step at a time in a carefully guided sequence until increasing levels of mastery are virtually guaranteed (Bandura, 1982). Such specific mastery training is a most promising way to enhance the achievement potential of disadvantaged children. Such programs to enhance academic self-efficacy and achievement can be adapted readily to also encourage intergroup cooperation by leading the participants to believe they can do so successfully.

Although expectancies seem clearly central person variables, it would be a mistake to transform them into generalized trait-like dispositions by endowing them with broad cross-situational consistency or by forgetting that they depend on specific stimulus conditions, on particular contexts. Empirically, "generalized expectancies" tend to be generalized only within relatively narrow, restricted limits (e.g., Mischel and Staub, 1965; Mischel et al., 1974). We already noted that, for example, "locus of control" may have limited generality, with distinct, unrelated expectancies found for positive and negative outcomes and with highly specific behavioral correlates for each (Mischel et al., 1974). If we convert expectancies into global trait-like dispositions and remove them from their close interaction with situational conditions, they may well prove to be no more useful than their many theoretical predecessors. But construed as relatively specific (and modifiable) subjective hypotheses about behavior-outcome contingencies and personal competencies, expectancies may be readily assessed and serve as useful predictors of both academic and social behavior.

2.2.4. Subjective Values and Preferences

The behaviors people choose to perform also depend on the subjective values of the outcomes that they expect. Different individuals value different outcomes and also share particular values in different degrees. Unless children from different ethnic groups value such goals as desegregated classroom contacts, there is no reason why they should seek them. Therefore it is necessary to assess still another person variable: the subjective (perceived) value for the individual of particular classes of events, that is, an individual's stimulus preferences and aversions, as they bear on the desegregation situation. This requires assessing the major stimuli that have acquired the power to induce positive or negative emotional states in the person and to function as incentives or reinforcers for behavior. Subjective values can be assessed by measuring the individual's actual choices in life-like situations, as well as verbal preferences or ratings for different choices and activities (Bullock and Merrill, 1980). Verbal reports (e.g., on questionnaires) about values and interests also may supply valuable information about the individual's preferences and aversions, and appear to provide some of the more temporally stable data in the domain of personality (E. L. Kelly, 1955; Strong, 1955).

Alternatively, people may be asked to rank actual rewards (Rotter, 1954), or the reinforcement value of particular stimuli may be assessed directly by observing their effects on the individual's performance (e.g., Gewirtz and Baer, 1958). Reinforcement (incentive) preferences may also be assessed by providing individuals opportunities to select the outcomes they want from a large array of alternatives, as when patients earn tokens that they may exchange for objects or activities. The price they are willing to pay for particular outcomes provides an index of subjective value (e.g., Ayllon and Azrin, 1965).

2.2.5. Self-Regulatory Systems and Plans

Still another person variable—one that may be especially relevant to the desegregation researcher—consists of the individual's self-regulatory systems and plans. This person variable may be related closely to successful achievement. It includes a number of components, all relevant to how complex, relatively long-term patterns of goal-directed behavior are generated and maintained even when the environment offers weak supports, barriers, and conflicts. To a considerable degree individuals regulate their own behavior and affect the quality of their performance by self-imposed goals and standards, by self-produced consequences, and by plans and self-statements. Even in the absence of external constraints, people set performance goals for themselves, criticize or praise their own behavior (depending on how well it matches their expectations and standards), and encourage or demoralize their own efforts through their own ideation. Let us consider some of the main components in this process that may be assessed independently even if they are parts of an integral self-regulatory system.

2.2.5a. Self-Imposed Goals and Standards. Studies of goal setting and self-reinforcement (e.g., Bandura and Whalen, 1966; Mischel and Liebert, 1966) have made it plain for many years that even young children will not indulge themselves with freely available immediate gratifications but, instead, set goals and follow rules to delay gratification. Far from being simply hedonistic, they impose standards and contingencies on their own behavior. A key feature of self-regulatory systems is the person's adoption of *goals and contingency rules* that guide behavior. Such rules specify the kinds of behavior appropriate (expected) under particular conditions, the performance levels (standards, goals) that the behavior must achieve, and the consequences (positive and negative) of attaining or failing to reach those standards. Like expectancies and subjective values, self-imposed goals have had a significant place in personality theorizing and research for many years (e.g., Bandura and Walters, 1963; Kanfer, 1971; Mischel, 1966; Rotter, 1954; Rotter *et al.*, 1972). The implications for applied assessment, however, have not been fully realized, and the measures that have been developed in research contexts serve more as readily available prototypes for the future than as well-established, formal instruments in their own right.

2.2.5b. Self-Statements. After the person has selected standards (terminal goals) for conduct in a particular situation, the often long and difficult route to self-reinforcement and external reinforcement with material rewards is probably mediated extensively by covert symbolic activities, such as praise and self-instructions, as the individual reaches subgoals. When reinforcers and noxious stimuli are imagined, they appear to influence behavior in the same way as when such stimuli are externally presented (e.g., Cautela, 1971). Imagined events, self-statements, and other covert activities serve to maintain goal-directed work until the performance matches or exceeds the person's terminal standards (e.g., Bandura, 1977). Progress along the route to a goal is also mediated by self-generated distractions and cognitive operations through which the person can transform the aversive "self-control" situation into one that can be mastered effectively (e.g., Mischel, 1974; Mischel and Moore, 1980; Mischel et al., 1972). Achievement of important goals generally leads to positive self-appraisal and self-reinforcement; failure to reach significant self-imposed standards tends to lead the person to indulge in psychological self-lacerations (e.g., self-condemnation).

Whereas the anticipation of success may help to sustain performance, the anticipation of failure may lead to extensive anxiety. Anxiety interferes most with effective performance when it arouses anxious, self-preoccupying thoughts (e.g., "I'm no good at this, I'll never be able to do it") in the stressed person. These thoughts compete and interfere with task-relevant thoughts (e.g., "Now I have to recheck my answers"). The result is that performance (as well as the person) suffers (Sarason, 1979). The interference from self-preoccupying thoughts tends to be greatest when the task is complex and requires many competing responses. One cannot be full of negative thoughts about oneself and simultaneously concentrate effectively on difficult work. Likewise, as the motivation to do well increases (as when success on the task is especially important), the highly anxious person may become particularly handicapped. That happens because under such highly motivating conditions test-anxious people tend to catastrophize and become even more negatively self-preoccupied, dwelling on how poorly they are doing. In contrast, the less anxious pay attention to the task and concentrate on how to master it effectively. Obviously, high self-efficacy expectations are the foundations for successful performance, whereas intrusive self-doubts can guarantee failure.

When people believe that there is nothing they can do to control negative or painful outcomes, they may come to believe that they are helpless (Seligman, 1975). That is, they may learn to expect that aversive outcomes are uncontrollable, that there is nothing they can do. In that state, they also may become apathetic, despondent, and slow to learn that they actually can control the outcomes. Such states of helplessness may generalize, persist, and involve feelings of depression or sadness. The state of helplessness may have especially negative and persistent effects when one believes that it reflects one's own enduring, widespread internal qualities (e.g., "I'm incompetent") rather than that it is due to more momentary, external, or situational considerations (Abramson et al., 1978). Thus people's attributions have an important part in determining how a state of helplessness affects them, and the measurement of such attributions is an important ingredient of cognitive assessment (see Shaw and Dobson, 1981).

Following frustration in the form of failure on a task, some individuals fall apart and their performance deteriorates. But other people actually improve. What causes these two different types of responses to the frustration of failure? One important cause may be how the person interprets the reasons for the experience. Children who believed their failure was due to lack of ability (called "helpless children") were found to perform more poorly after they experienced failure than did those who saw their failure as due to lack of effort (called "mastery-oriented" children). Indeed, the mastery-oriented children often actually performed better after failure. A most encouraging finding is that training the helpless children (those who attribute their failure to lack of ability) to view outcomes as the result of their own effort results in their improved performance after a failure experience (Dweck, 1975).

When faced with failure, helpless children seem to have self-defeating thoughts that virtually guarantee further failure. This became clear when groups of helpless and mastery-oriented fifth-graders were instructed "to think out loud" while solving problems. When children in the two groups began to experience failure, they soon said very different things to themselves. The helpless children made statements reflecting their lack of ability, such as "I'm getting confused" or "I never did have a good memory" or "This isn't fun anymore" (Diener and Dweck, 1978, p. 458). In contrast, the mastery-oriented children never talked about their lack of ability. Instead, they seemed to search for a remedy for their failure and gave themselves instructions to try to encourage themselves and improve their performance, such as "I should slow down and try to figure this out" or "The harder it gets the harder I need to try" or "I've almost got it now" or "I love a challenge."

In sum, people continuously judge and evaluate their own behavior, congratulating and condemning themselves for their own attributes and achievements. We assess our own characteristics and actions, we praise or abuse our own achievements, and we self-administer social and material rewards and punishments from the enormous array freely available to us. These self-regulatory processes are not limited to the individual's self-administration of such outcomes as the tokens, "prizes," or verbal approval and disapproval that has been favored in most early studies of self-reinforcement (e.g., Bandura, 1969; Kanfer and Marston, 1963; Kanfer and Phillips, 1970; Mahoney, 1974; Masters and Mokros, 1974; Mischel et al., 1968). An especially pervasive but until recently neglected feature of self-regulation is people's selective exposure to different types of positive and negative information (Mischel, 1976), subsequent evaluative self-encoding (Mischel, 1973, 1979), and the information and ideation to which people expose themselves mentally.

Almost limitless "good" and "bad" information about the self is potentially available (for example, in the form of memories), depending on where one looks and how one searches. Individuals usually can find or construct information and thoughts to support their positive or negative attributes, their successes or failures, almost boundlessly. They can focus cognitively, for example, on their past, present, and expected assets or liabilities, and attend either to strengths or to weaknesses by ideating about selective aspects of their perceived personalities and behaviors. Affective self-reactions, as in the enhancement of one's own self-esteem and, in common sense terms, individuals' personal positive and negative feelings, presumably hinge on selective attentional processes through which individuals expose themselves only to particular types of information from the enormous array potentially available. By means of such selective attention, individuals presumably can make themselves feel either good or bad, can privately congratulate or condemn themselves, and in the extreme, can generate emotions from euphoria to depression (e.g., Mischel *et al.*, 1973, 1976; Wright and Mischel, 1982). Other studies have extended this paradigm to demonstrate that success-failure and/or positive-negative affect influence a wide variety of responses (including generosity to self and others, and self-reactions) and also delay behavior in consistent, predictable ways (e.g., Isen *et al.*, 1978; Rosenhan *et al.*, 1974; Schwarz and Pollack, 1977; Seeman and Schwarz, 1974; Underwood *et al.*, 1977). Taken collectively, the data strongly support the conclusion that success and positive affect lead to more benign reactions to the self and to others. The manifestations of this positive "glow" are diverse indeed and they even seem to influence memory for information about the self in the same manner (Mischel *et al.*, 1976; Wright and Mischel, 1982).

Given the central role of selective attention, of mastery versus helplessness ideation, and of other self-statements in determining the nature and quality of performance, it becomes most important in the study of achievement to assess systematically the relevant cognitions, attributional styles, and information preference patterns. Recent contributions to such assessment include think-aloud methods (Genest and Turk, 1981), thought listing (Cacioppo and Petty, 1981), imagery measurement (Anderson, 1981), the assessment of social-evaluative anxiety (Glass and Merluzzi, 1981), and the assessment of depressive schemas (Shaw and Dobson, 1981).

2.2.5c. Plans and the Activation of Metacognitions. Although there has been increasing work on the role of self-instructions in self-control apart from specific reinforcement considerations (e.g., Bem, 1967; Luria, 1961; Meichenbaum, 1977; O'Leary, 1968), less attention has been given to the planning and organization of complex behavioral sequences essential for sustained self-regulation in the achievement context. In recent years, exciting developments have been occurring in the study of heuristics for such cognitive activities as reading and story comprehension (e.g., Brown, 1978). At the same time, more is becoming known about the role of plans in self-control (Meichenbaum, 1977), for example, in resistance to temptation (Mischel and Patterson, 1978) and in delay of gratification (Mischel, 1979, 1981c). We have been finding that even young children develop a remarkable degree of knowledge and understanding about a wide range of psychological principles, including those basic for effective self-control. For example, children's spontaneous delay of gratification strategies show a clear developmental progression in knowledge of effective delay rules (Mischel and Mischel, 1983; Yates and Mischel, 1979). Even the young child has considerable knowledge about the conditions that allow effective self-control. Helping the child to access that knowledge and to put it to good use in the service of the child's own potential achievements is a major challenge for research and for effective educational planning. Such knowledge may also be fruitfully harnessed by the desegregation researcher.

In the present view, our "subjects" are much smarter than many of us thought they were, even when they are children. Hence, if we do not stop them by asking the wrong questions, and if we provide appropriate structure, they often can tell us much about themselves and, indeed, about psychology itself. In some recent pilot work, for example, Harriet Nerlove Mischel and I have started to ask young children what they know about psychological principles—about how plans can be made and followed most effectively, how long-term problems can be organized, how delay of gratification can be mastered. We also asked them to tell us about what helps them to learn and (stimulated by Flavell and his colleagues; e.g., Kreutzer *et al.*, 1975) to remember. We are most impressed by how much even an eight-year-old knows about mental functioning. Indeed, one wonders how well such young children might perform on a final exam in introductory psychology if the jargon and big words were stripped away. (I do not want to imply, incidentally, that psychology knows little. Rather, I believe, people are good psychologists and know a lot. We professionals might be wise to enlist that knowledge in our enterprise.)

The moral, for me, is that it would be wise to allow our "subjects" to slip out of their roles as passive "assessees" or "testees" and to enroll them, at least sometimes, as active colleagues who are the best experts on themselves and are eminently qualified to participate in the development of descriptions and predictions—not to mention decisions—about themselves. Of course if we want individuals to tell us about themselves directly, we have to ask questions that they can answer. If we ask people to predict how they will react to a desegregated situation but do not inform them of the specific situation and the specific criterion measure that will constitute the assessment, we cannot expect them to be accurate. Similarly, it might be possible to use self-reports and self-predictions more extensively in decision making—for example, to help the person to "self-select" from a number of behavioral alternatives (e.g., different types of classroom structure, different assignments). Such applications would require conditions in which accurate self-reports and honest choices could not be used against the people who offer them. We might, for example, expect job candidates to predict correctly which job they will perform best, but only when all the alternatives available to them in their choice are structured as equally desirable. We cannot expect people to deny themselves options without appropriate alternatives. We cannot expect them to get in trouble by going against the implicit demands of the situation.

3. THE ANALYSIS OF ENVIRONMENTS

For many purposes it is useful to focus on the social and psychological environments in which people live and function. The student of desegregation needs to pay as much attention to the specific psychological situations in which desegregation is expected as to the psychological qualities of the participants. Until recently this focus was neglected. The dramatic rise of interest in the environment as it relates to the person is documented easily. From 1968 to 1972 more books appeared on the topic of person–environment relations from an ecological perspective than had been published in the prior three decades (Jordan, 1972). As is true in most new fields, a first concern in the study of environments is to try to classify them into a taxonomy. Environments, like all other events, of course, can be classified in many ways, depending mainly on the purposes and imagination of the classifiers. One typical effort to describe some of the almost infinite dimensions of environments, proposed by Moos (1968, 1974), calls attention to the complex nature of environments and to the many variables that can characterize them. Those variables include the weather, the buildings and settings, the perceived social climates, and the reinforcements obtained for behaviors in that situation—to list just few.

The classification alerts us to a fact that has been slighted by traditional trait-oriented approaches to personality: Much human behavior depends delicately on environmental considerations, such as the setting (e.g., Barker, 1968), and even on such specific physical and psychosocial variables as how hot and crowded the setting is, or how the room and furniture are arranged, or how the people in the setting are organized (e.g., Krasner and Ullmann, 1973; Moos and Insel, 1974). Many links between characteristics of the environment and behavior have been demonstrated. For example, measures of population density (such as the number of people in each room) may be related to certain forms of aggression, even when social class and ethnicity are controlled (Galle et al., 1972). Likewise, interpersonal attraction and mood are negatively affected by extremely hot, crowded conditions (Griffitt and Veitch, 1971).

Depending on one's purpose, many different classifications are possible and useful (e.g., Magnusson and Ekehammar, 1973; Moos, 1973, 1974). To seek any single basic taxonomy of situations may be as futile as searching for a final or ultimate taxonomy of traits. We can label situations in at least as many different ways as we can label people. It will be important to avoid emerging simply with a trait psychology of situations, in which events and settings, rather than people, are merely given different labels. The task of naming situations cannot substitute for the job of analyzing how conditions and environments interact with the people in them.

Although person–condition interactions are never static, sometimes environmental variables can be identified that allow useful predictions. In the present chapter we examined ways to study persons that are compatible with the simultaneous analysis of environments in exactly the same terms. For example, to predict intellectual achievement, it also helps to take account of the degree to which the child's environment supports (models and reinforces) intellectual development (Wolf, 1966). And when powerful treatments are developed—such as modeling and desensitization therapies for phobias—predictions about outcomes are best when based on knowledge of the treatment to which the individual is assigned (e.g., Bandura et al., 1969).

In the present view, the attributes of environments are as important to understand as the attributes of the people in them.[1] A comprehensive psychological approach requires that we move from physical descriptions of the environment—of the climate, buildings, social settings, etc., in which people live—to the psychological processes through which environmental conditions and people influence each other reciprocally. For this purpose, it is necessary to study in depth how the environment influences behavior and how behavior and the people who generate it in turn shape the environment in an endless interaction. To assess properly the interaction of person and environment we must consider both person variables and environmental variables. This goal may be pursued more effectively if we can use the same concepts and language to assess both persons and environments. It seems plausible to try to analyze settings in terms of the competencies, encodings, expectancies, values, and plans they require for effective coping. If so, it may allow us to map the psychological demands of the environment on to the qualities of the person with the same concepts and in the common language of the same underlying psychological processes (e.g., Mischel, 1984).

[1]The perspective presented here of course recognizes the subtle differences that exist among individuals and groups in their response to any situation, but it tries to go beyond that obvious recognition and beyond lip service to the complexity of the interactions between people and their environments. It emphasizes instead the magnitude of the variability that typically exists on virtually any social dimension, within individuals and within any given social group, and attempts to explore the implications. It recognizes within-person and within-group variability as genuine phenomena, rather than as measurement errors to be averaged out in pursuit of the "central tendency" (see Mischel and Peake, 1982). Such within-person and within-group variability, in turn, needs to be taken into account seriously in the assessment of individuals and groups and in the design of programs intended to influence them.

REFERENCES

Abramson, L. Y., Seligman, M. E. P., and Teasdale, J. D. Learned helplessness in humans: Critique and reformulation. *Journal of Abnormal Psychology*, 1978, *87*, 69–74.

Alker, H. A. Is personality situationally specific or intrapsychically consistent? *Journal of Personality*, 1972, *40*, 1–16.

Allport, G. W. *Personality: A Psychological Interpretation*. New York: Holt, Rinehart, and Winston, 1937.

Ajzen, I., and Fishbein, M. Attitude-behavior relations: A theoretical analysis and review of empirical research. *Psychological Bulletin*, 1977, *84*, 888–918.

Anderson, J. The prediction of adjustment over time. In I. Iscoe and H. Stevenson (Eds.), *Personality Development in Children*. Austin, TX: University of Texas Press, 1960.

Anderson, M. P. Assessment of imaginal processes: Approaches and issues. In T. V. Merluzzi, C. R. Glass, and M. Genest (Eds.), *Cognitive Assessment*. New York: The Guilford Press, 1981.

Argyle, M., and Little, B. R. Do personality traits apply to social behavior? *Journal of Theory of Social Behavior*, 1972, *2*, 1–35.

Ayllon, T., and Azrin, N. H. The measurement and reinforcement of behavior of psychotics. *Journal of the Experimental Analysis of Behavior*, 1965, *8*, 357–383.

Bandura, A. Vicarious processes: A case of no-trial learning. In L. Berkowitz (Ed.), *Advances in Experimental Social Psychology, Volume 2*. New York: Academic Press, 1965.

Bandura, A. *Principles of Behavior Modification*. New York: Holt, Rinehart, and Winston, 1969.

Bandura, A. *Social Learning Theory*. Englewood Cliffs, NJ: Prentice-Hall, 1977.

Bandura, A. Reflections on self-efficacy. In S. Rachman (Ed.), *Advances in Behavior Research and Therapy, Volume 1*. Oxford: Pergamon Press, 1978.

Bandura, A. Self efficacy mechanism in human agency. *American Psychologist*, 1982, *37*, 122–147.

Bandura, A., and Adams, N. E. Analysis of self-efficacy theory of behavioral change. *Cognitive Therapy and Research*, 1977, *1*, 287–310.

Bandura, A., and Walters, R. *Social Learning and Personality Development*. New York: Holt, Rinehart, and Winston, 1963.

Bandura, A., and Whalen, C. K. The influence of antecedent reinforcement and divergent modeling cues on patterns of self-reward. *Journal of Personality and Social Psychology*, 1966, *3*, 373–382.

Bandura, A. Blanchard, E. B., and Ritter, B. Relative efficacy of desensitization and modeling approaches for inducing behavioral, affective, and attitudinal changes. *Journal of Personality and Social Psychology*, 1969, *13*, 173–199.

Barker, R. G. *Ecological Psychology*. Stanford, CA: Stanford University Press, 1968.

Bem, D. J. Self perception: An alternative interpretation of cognitive dissonance phenomena. *Psychological Review*, 1967, *74*, 183–200.

Bem, D. J., and Allen, A. On predicting some of the people some of the time: The search for cross-situational consistencies in behavior. *Psychological Review*, 1977, *81*, 506–520.

Block, J. *The Challenge of Response Sets*. New York: Appleton, 1965.

Block, J. *Lives Through Time*. Berkeley, CA: Bancroft, 1971.

Block, J. Advancing the psychology of personality: Paradigmatic shift or improving the quality of research. In D. Magnusson and N. S. Endler (Eds.), *Personality at the Crossroads: Current Issues in Interactional Psychology*. Hillsdale, NJ: Erlbaum, 1977.

Block, J., and Block, J. The role of ego-control and ego resiliency in the organization of behavior. In W. Collins (Ed.), *The Minnesota Symposium on Child Psychology, Volume 13*. Hillsdale, NJ: Erlbaum, 1980.

Bowers, K. Situationism in psychology: An analysis and a critique. *Psychological Review*, 1973, *80*, 307–336.

Brown, A. Development, schooling and the acquisition of knowledge about knowledge. In R. Anderson, R. Spiro, and W. Montague (Eds.), *Schooling and the Acquisition of Knowledge*. Hillsdale, NJ: Erlbaum, 1978.

Bullock, D., and Merrill, L. The impact of personal preference on consistency through time: The case of childhood aggression. *Child Development*, 1980, *51*, 808–814.

Burton, R. V. Generality of honesty reconsidered. *Psychological Review*, 1963, *70*, 481–499.

Cacioppo, J. T., and Petty, R. E. Social psychological procedures for cognitive response assessment: The thought-listing technique. In T. V. Merluzzi, C. R. Glass, and M. Genest (Eds.), *Cognitive Assessment*. New York: The Guilford Press, 1981.

Cantor, N., and Mischel, W. Prototypes in person perception. In L. Berkowitz (Ed.), *Advances in Experimental Social Psychology, Volume 12*. New York: Academic Press, 1979.

Cantor, N., Mischel, W., and Schwartz, J. A prototype analysis of psychological situations. *Cognitive Psychology*, 1982, *14*, 45–77.

Cautela, J. R. Covert conditioning. In A. Jacoby and L. B. Sachs (Eds.), *The Psychology of Private Events*. New York: Academic Press, 1971.

Cronbach, L. J. Beyond the two disciplines of scientific psychology. *American Psychologist*, 1975, *30*, 116–127.

Diener, C. I., and Dweck, C. S. An analysis of learned helplessness: Continuous changes in performance, strategy, and achievement cognitions following failure. *Journal of Personality and Social Psychology*, 1978, *36*, 451–462.

Dweck, C. S. The role of expectations and attributions in the alleviation of learned helplessness. *Journal of Personality and Social Psychology*, 1975, *31*, 674–685.

Endler, N. S. The person versus the situation—a pseudo issue. *Journal of Personality*, 1973, *41*, 287–303.

Endler, N. S. Interactionism comes of age. In M. P. Zanna, E. T. Higgins, & C. P. Herman (Eds.), *Consistency in social behavior: The Ontario Symposium* (Vol. 2). Hillsdale, NJ: Lawrence Erlbaum Associates, 1982.

Epstein, S. The stability of behavior: On predicting most of the people much of the time. *Journal of Personality and Social Psychology*, 1979, *37*, 1097–1126.

Fiske, D. W. The limits of the conventional science of personality. *Journal of Personality*, 1974, *42*, 1–11.

Galle, O. R., Gove, W. R., and McPherson, J. M. Population density and pathology: What are the relations for man? *Science*, 1972, *176*, 23–30.

Genest, M., and Turk, D. C. Think-aloud approaches to cognitive assessment. In T. V. Merluzzi, C. R. Glass, and M. Genest (Eds.), *Cognitive Assessment*. New York: The Guilford Press, 1981.

Gerard, H. B., and Miller, N. *School Desegregation: A Long-Term Study*. New York: Plenum Press, 1975.

Gewirtz, J. L., and Baer, D. M. The effect of brief social deprivation on behaviors for a social reinforcer. *Journal of Abnormal Social Psychology*, 1958, *56*, 49–56.

Glass, C. R., and Merluzzi, T. V. Cognitive assessment of social-evaluative anxiety. In T. V. Merluzzi, C. R. Glass, and M. Genest (Eds.), *Cognitive Assessment*. New York: The Guilford Press, 1981.

Goldried, M. R., and D'Zurilla, T. J. A behavioral-analytic model for assessing competence. In C. D. Spielberger (Ed.), *Current Topics in Clinical and Community Psychology, Volume I*. New York: Academic Press, 1969.

Griffitt, W., and Veitch, R. Hot and crowded: Influences of population density and temperature on interpersonal affective behavior. *Journal of Personality and Social Psychology*, 1971, *17*, 92–98.

Grusec, J., and Mischel, W. Model's characteristics as determinants of social learning. *Journal of Personality and Social Psychology*, 1966, *4*, 211–215.

Hamilton, D. (Ed.). *Cognitive Processes in Stereotyping and Intergroup Behavior*. Hillsdale, NJ: Erlbaum, 1982.

Horowitz, L. M., Wright, J. C., Lowenstein, E., and Parad, H.W. The prototype as a construct in abnormal psychology: A method for deriving prototypes. *Journal of Abnormal Psychology*, 1981, *90*, 568–574.

Isen, A. M., Shalker, T. E., Clark, M., and Karp, L. Affect, accessibility of material in memory, and behavior: A cognitive loop? *Journal of Personality and Social Psychology*, 1978, *36*, 1–12.

Jaccard, J. J. Predicting social behavior from personality traits. *Journal of Research in Personality*, 1974, *7*, 358–367.

Jenkins, J. J. Remember that old theory of memory? Well, forget it! *American Psychologist*, 1974, *29*, 785–795.

Jordan, P. A real predicament. *Science*, 1972, *175*, 944–978.

Kanfer, F. H. The maintenance of behavior by self-generated stimuli and reinforcement. In A. Jacobs and L. B. Sachs (Eds.), *Psychology of Private Events*. New York: Academic Press, 1971.

Kanfer, F. H., and Marston, A. R. Determinants of self-reinforcement in human learning. *Journal of Experimental Psychology*, 1963, *66*, 245–254.

Kanfer, F. H., and Phillips, J. S. *Learning Foundations of Behavior Therapy*. New York: Wiley, 1970.

Kelly, E. L. Consistency of the adult personality. *American Psychologist*, 1955, *10*, 659–681.

Kelly, G. A. *The Psychology of Personal Constructs, Volumes 1 and 2*. New York: Norton, 1955.

Kogan, N., and Wallach, M. A. *Risk Taking: A Study in Cognition and Personality*. New York: Holt, Rinehart, and Winston, 1964.

Krasner, L., and Ullman, L. P. *Behavior Influence and Personality: The Social Matrix of Human Action*. New York: Holt, Rinehart, and Winston, 1973.

Krasnor, L. R., and Rubin, K. H. The Assessment of Social Problem-solving Skills in Young Children. In T. V. Merluzzi, C. R. Glass, and M. Genest (Eds.), *Cognitive Assessment*. New York: The Guilford Press, 1981.

Kreutzer, M. A., Leonard, C., and Flavell, J. H. An interview study of children's knowledge about memory. *Monographs of the Society for Research in Child Development* (Serial No. 159), *40*, 1975.

Luria, A. R. *The Role of Speech in the Regulation of Normal and Abnormal Behavior*. New York: Pergamon Press, 1961.

MacFarlane, J. W., and Tuddenham, R. D. Problems in the validation of projective techniques. In H. H. Anderson and L. Anderson (Eds.), *Projective Techniques*. Englewood Cliffs, NJ: Prentice-Hall, 1951.

Magnusson, D., and Ekehammar, B. An analysis of situational dimensions: A replication. *Multivariate Behavioral Research*, 1973, *8*, 331–339.

Mahoney, M. J. *Cognition and Behavior Modification*. Cambridge, MA: Ballinger, 1974.

Masling, J. M. The influence of situational and interpersonal variables in projective testing. *Psychological Bulletin*, 1960, *57*, 65–86.

Masters, J. C., and Mokros, J. R. Self-reinforcement processes in children. In H. Resse (Ed.), *Advances in Child Development and Behavior, Volume 9*. New York: Academic Press, 1974.

McGuire, W. J. Cognitive consistency and attitude change. *Journal of Abnormal and Social Psychology*, 1960, *60*, 345–353.

Meichenbaum, D. *Cognitive-Behavior Modification*. New York: Plenum Press, 1977.

Mischel, H. N., and Mischel, W. The development of children's knowledge of self-control strategies. *Child Development*, 1983, *54*, 603–619.

Mischel, W. Theory and research on the antecedents of self-imposed delay of reward. In B. A. Maher (Ed.), *Progress in Experimental Personality Research, Volume 3*. New York: Academic Press, 1966.

Mischel, W. *Personality and Assessment*. New York: Wiley, 1968.

Mischel, W. Continuity and change in personality. *American Psychologist*, 1969, *24*, 1012–1018.

Mischel, W. Toward a cognitive social learning reconceptualization of personality. *Psychological Review*, 1973, *80*, 252–283.

Mischel, W. Processes in delay of gratification. In L. Berkowitz (Ed.), *Advances in Experimental Social Psychology, Volume 7*. New York: Academic Press, 1974.

Mischel, W. The interaction of person and situation. In D. Magnusson and N. S. Endler (Eds.), *Personality at the Crossroads: Current Issues in Interactional Psychology*. Hillsdale, NJ: Erlbaum, 1977.

Mischel, W. On the interface of cognition and personality. *American Psychologist*, 1977, *34*, 740–754.

Mischel, W. On the interface of cognition and personality: Beyond the person–situation debate. *American Psychologist*, 1979, *34*, 740–754.

Mischel, W. *Introduction to Personality* (3rd ed.). New York: Holt, Rinehart and Winston, 1981a.

Mischel, W. A cognitive-social learning approach to assessment. In T. V. Merluzzi, C. R. Glass, and M. Genest (Eds.), *Cognitive Assessment*. New York: The Guilford Press, 1981b.

Mischel, W. Metacognition and the rules of delay. In J. H. Flavell and L. Ross (Eds.), *Social Cognitive Development: Frontiers and Possible Futures*. New York: Cambridge University Press, 1981c.

Mischel, W. Convergences and challenges in the search for consistency. *American Psychologist*, 1984, *39*, 351–364.

Mischel, W., and Liebert, R. M. Effects of discrepancies between observed and imposed reward criteria on their acquisition and transmission. *Journal of Personality and Social Psychology*, 1966, *3*, 45–53.

Mischel, W., and Moore, B. The role of ideation in voluntary delay for symbolically presented rewards. *Cognitive Therapy and Research*, 1980, *4*, 211–221.

Mischel, H. N., and Mischel, W. The development of children's knowledge of self-control strategies. *Child Development*, 1983, *54*, 603–619.

Mischel, W., and Patterson, C. J. Effective plans for self-control in children. In W. A. Collins (Ed.), *Minnesota Symposium on Child Psychology, Volume 11*. Hillsdale, NJ: Erlbaum, 1978.

Mischel, W., and Peake, P. K. Beyond déjà vu in the search for cross-situational consistency. *Psychological Review*, 1982, *89*, 730–755.

Mischel, W., and Staub, E. Effects of expectancy on working and waiting for larger rewards. *Journal of Personality and Social Psychology*, 1965, *2*, 625–633.

Mischel, W., Coates, B. and Raskoff, A. Effects of success and failure on self-gratification. *Journal of Personality and Social Psychology*, 1968, *10*, 381–390.

Mischel, W., Ebbesen, E. B., and Zeiss, A. R. Cognitive and attentional mechanisms in delay of gratification. *Journal of Personality and Social Psychology*, 1972, *21*, 204–218.

Mischel, W., Ebbesen, E. B., and Zeiss, A. R. Selective attention to the self: Situational and dispositional determinants. *Journal of Personality and Social Psychology*, 1973, *27*, 129–142.

Mischel, W., Zeiss, R., and Zeiss, A. R. Internal-external control and persistence: Validation and implications of the stanford preschool internal-external scale. *Journal of Personality and Social Psychology*, 1974, *29*, 265–287.

Mischel, W., Ebbesen, E. B., and Zeiss, A. R. Determinants of selective memory about the self. *Journal of Counseling and Clinical Psychology*, 1976, *44*, 92–103.

Moos, R. H. Situational Analysis of a Therapeutic Community Milieu. *Journal of Abnormal Psychology*, 1968, *73*, 49–61.

Moos, R. H. Conceptualizations of Human Environments. *American Psychologist*, 1968, *28*, 652–665.

Moos, R. H. Systems for the assessment and classification of human environments. In R. H. Moos and R. M. Insel (Eds.), *Issues in Social Ecology*. Palo Alto, CA: National Press Books, 1974.

Moos, R. H., and Insel, P. M. (Eds.), *Issues in Social Ecology*. Palo Alto, CA: National Press Books, 1974.

Neimeyer, G. J., and Neimeyer, R. A. Personal construct perspectives on cognitive assessment. In T. V. Merluzzi, C. R. Glass, and M. Genest (Eds.), *Cognitive Assessment*. New York: The Guilford Press, 1981.

Neisser, U. Review of "Visual Information Processing." *Science*, 1974, *183*, 402–403.

O'Leary, K. D. The effects of self-instruction on immoral behavior. *Journal of Experimental Child Psychology*, 1968, *6*, 297–301.

Patterson, G. R. Interventions for boys with conduct problems: Multiple settings, treatments, and criteria. *Journal of Consulting and Clinical Psychology*, 1974, *42*, 471–481.

Peake, P. K. Searching for consistency: The Carleton student behavior study. Unpublished doctoral dissertation, Stanford University, 1982.

Peterson, D. R. *The Clinical Study of Social Behavior*. New York: Appleton, 1968.

Raush, H. L. Research, practice, and accountability. *American Psychologist*, 1974, *29*, 678–681.

Rosch, E., Mervis, C. B., Gray, W. D., Johnson, D. M., and Boyes-Braem, P. Basic objects in natural categories. *Cognitive Psychology*, 1976, *8*, 382–439.

Rosenhan, D. L., Underwood, B., and Moore, B. Affect moderates self-gratification and altruism. *Journal of Personality and Social Psychology*, 1974, *30*, 546–552.

Rotter, J. B. *Social Learning and Clinical Psychology*. Englewood Cliffs, NJ: Prentice-Hall, 1954.

Rotter, J. B., Chance, E., and Phares, E. J. (Eds.), *Applications of a Social Learning Theory of Personality*. New York: Holt, Rinehart and Winston, 1972.

Sarason, I. G. *Life stress, self-preoccupation, and social supports*. Presidential Address, Western Psychological Association, 1979.

Schwarz, J. C., and Pollack, P. R. Affect and delay of gratification. *Journal of Research In Personality*, 1977, *11*, 147–164.

Seeman, G., and Schwarz, J. O. Affective state and preference for immediate versus delayed reward. *Journal of Research in Personality*, 1974, *7*, 384–394.

Seligman, M. E. *Helplessness: On Depression, Development, and Death*. San Francisco: Freeman, 1975.

Shaw, B. F., and Dobson, K. S. Cognitive assessment of depression. In T. V. Merluzzi, C. R. Glass, and M. Genest (Eds.), *Cognitive Assessment*. New York: The Guilford Press, 1981.

Shure, M. B., and Spivack, G. *Problem Solving Techniques in Child Rearing*. San Francisco: Jossey-Bass, 1978.

Shweder, R. A. How relevant is an individual difference theory of personality? *Journal of Personality*, 1975, *43*, 455–484.

Shweder, R. A., and D'Andrade, R. G. Accurate reflection of systematic distortion? A reply to Block, Weiss, and Thorne. *Journal of Personality and Social Psychology*, 1979, *37*, 1075–1084.

Strong, E. K., Jr. *Vocational Interests 18 Years After College*. Minneapolis, MN: University of Minnesota Press, 1955.

Underwood, B., Froming, W. J., and Moore, B. S. Mood, attention, and altruism: A search for mediating variables. *Developmental Psychology*, 1977, *13*, 541–542.

Vernon, P. E. *Personality Assessment: A Critical Survey*. New York: Wiley, 1964.

Wallace, J. An abilities conception of personality: Some implications for personality measurement. *American Psychologist*, 1966, *21*, 132–138.

Wallach, M. A. Commentary: Active-analytical vs. passive-global cognitive functioning. In S. Messick and J. Ross (Eds.), *Measurement in Personality and Cognition*. New York: Wiley, 1962.

Wallach, M. A., and Leggett, M. I. Testing the hypothesis that a person will be consistent: Stylistic consistency versus situational specificity in size of children's drawings. *Journal of Personality*, 1972, *40*, 309–330.

Webb, N. Student interaction and learning in small groups. *Review of Educational Research*, 1982, *52*, 421–445.

Weigel, R. H., and Newman, S. L. Increasing attitude-behavior correspondence by broadening the scope of the behavioral measure. *Journal of Personality and Social Psychology*, 1976, *33*, 793–802.

White, R. W. Motivation reconsidered: The concept of competence. *Psychological Review*, 1959, *66*, 297–333.

Wolf, R. The measurement of environments. In A. Anastasi (Ed.), *Testing Problems in Perspective*. Washington, DC: American Council on Education, 1966.

Wright, J., and Mischel, W. The influence of affect on cognitive social learning person variables. *Journal of Personality and Social Psychology*, 1982, *43*, 901–914.

Yates, B. T., and Mischel, W. Young children's preferred attentional strategies for delaying gratification. *Journal of Personality and Social Psychology*, 1979, *37*, 286–300.

Ziegler, E., and Phillips, L. Psychiatric diagnosis and symptomatology. *Journal of Abnormal and Social Psychology*, 1961, *63*, 69–75.

Ziegler, E. and Phillips, L. Social competence and the process-reactive distinction in psychopathology. *Journal of Abnormal and Social Psychology*, 1962, *65*, 215–222.

Part IV

A RECONSIDERATION OF METHODS

Chapter 6

Self-Esteem Research

A Phenomenological Corrective

MORRIS ROSENBERG

The question of whether prejudice and discrimination have damaged the self-esteem of blacks has engaged theorists and researchers for over a generation (e.g., Clark and Clark, 1952; Lewin, 1948), and has served as the subject of literally hundreds of publications (for literature reviews, see Baldwin, 1979; Cross, 1978, 1985; Epps, 1981; Gordon, 1977; Miller, 1981, 1983; Porter and Washington, 1979; Wylie, 1979). One of the most tantalizing features of this literature has been the fact that persuasive theory has supported one conclusion whereas compelling methodology has supported the other. Prior to the sixties virtually all of the research on the subject was based on studies of dolls, pictures, or puppets (Gordon, 1977). In this body of research—of which the Clark and Clark study was the prototype and chief exemplar—young black children were usually presented with black and white dolls, pictures, or puppets and were asked such questions as which is the nice doll, which is the pretty doll, which doll would you like to play with, which doll looks like you, etc. Many black children, it turned out, showed a preference for the white doll or said the white doll looked like them, a finding widely interpreted as reflecting low self-esteem among black children. These findings were consequential for the fate of desegregation, for they were entered as evidence in the plaintiff's brief in *Brown vs. the Board of Education* and were used as support for the Supreme Court's conclusion that segregated education was damaging to the black child's self-esteem.

MORRIS ROSENBERG • Department of Sociology, University of Maryland, College Park, MD 20742.

To most writers at the time, the reasons for expecting blacks to have lower self-esteem appeared evident. In the literature of the fifties and sixties—some of which sounds rather anachronistic today—a number of reasons were advanced to account for the lower self-esteem of blacks.

The most obvious was the reality of race prejudice. From the earliest studies of Bogardus (1925) in the twenties, and continuing for decades (Bogardus, 1959), the data consistently showed blacks holding a low position in the ethnic status hierarchy. It appeared evident that if members of a group were derogated and disdained by the society as a whole, they would come to internalize the societal definition of their worth. The result would be both hatred of one's group and of one's self as a group member (Lewin, 1948).

Second, disprivilege feeds on itself, such that the primary disease of race prejudice comes to have secondary consequences that, independently of prejudice, damage self-esteem. Three of the consequences given the closest attention were poverty, family rupture, and poor academic performance. Although these are consequences of discrimination, they may have independent noxious consequences for self-esteem. There are good reasons to think that the economically unsuccessful would have lower self-esteem than the successful (Kohn, 1969; Lipset and Zetterberg, 1956; Rosenberg and Pearlin, 1978); that children from separated or never-married families would have lower self-esteem than those from intact families (Rainwater, 1966; Rosenberg and Simmons, 1972); and that children who perform poorly in school would have lower self-esteem than those who perform well (Brookover et al., 1964; Purkey, 1970; Wylie, 1979). Compared to whites, black children suffered in all three respects.

A third postulated threat to self-esteem lay in the derogatory stereotypes attached to low status groups (Katz and Braly, 1933; Laurence, 1970). If one sees oneself through the eyes of the prejudiced majority or because, as a member of society, one internalizes the general attitudes toward one's group (the generalized other) (Mead, 1934), it is plausible to expect one's self-esteem to be damaged.

Finally, some writers rooted black self-hatred in an aversion to dark skin color. Sociological research, for example, had revealed a preference for lighter skin color among blacks (Seeman, 1946), as expressed in a higher sociometric status for lighter blacks, the use of lighter-skinned models as standards of beauty in black publications, the widespread use of cosmetic devices to approximate the white model, and so on (Katz, 1976). Some psychoanalysts (Grier and Cobbs, 1968; Kardiner and Ovesey, 1951) tended to endow these findings with a deeper symbolic significance involving a learned association of black with evil and white with good.

Hence, in the literature of the forties and fifties, the assumption that blacks suffered damaged self-esteem was generally taken for granted. In the sixties, however, social scientists began to study self-esteem by means of the sample survey. In contrast to the findings from the doll studies, the survey findings indicated that black self-esteem was at least as high as white (Cross, 1985; Gordon, 1977; McDonald and Gynther, 1965; Schwartz and Stryker, 1971; Taylor and Walsh, 1979; Wylie, 1979).

The findings from the attitude surveys, being counterintuitive, caught researchers flat-footed. Nevertheless, they could not be dismissed because, in terms of scientific adequacy, the sample survey had several advantages over the doll studies. First, whereas the doll studies characteristically used samples of convenience, the attitude studies were more likely to use probability samples. Second, whereas the doll studies averred that black children had damaged self-esteem, they either implied that white children did not or that, if they did, the damage was less severe. The appropriate question was not whether black children's self-concepts were damaged—after all, whose isn't—but whether they were *more severely* damaged than whites'. Third, as Cross (1978, 1985) observed, the doll studies had failed to distinguish between personal identity, on the one hand, and reference group orientation, on the other. The implicit assumption of the doll research was that a black child who rejected his or her race was essentially rejecting the self; low racial self-esteem, it was taken for granted, inevitably produced low personal self-esteem. The sample survey, on the other hand, tended to examine personal self-esteem directly, making use of measures whose reliability and validity could be systematically assessed (Shavelson and Stuart, 1981; Wells and Marwell, 1976; Wylie, 1974). Finally, the sample survey permitted investigators to study a broader age range. Whereas the doll studies were necessarily limited to young children—mostly between 3–7 years of age—the sample survey could be used with much older populations (e.g., Crain and Weisman, 1972; Rosenberg, 1965).

In sum, whereas the general conclusion of the doll studies was that blacks had lower self-esteem, the conclusion from the attitude surveys was that they did not (Bachman, 1970; Cross, 1985; Gordon, 1977; Taylor, 1976). Because major policy decisions had apparently hinged in part on the facts of the case, these methodological issues were of more than academic interest.[1]

[1]An additional methodological issue relates to the historical period of study. Because the doll studies began in the forties, whereas the survey studies began in the sixties, the differing results yielded by the doll and the survey studies may not have rested on the differences in research methods but in changed self-attitudes stemming from the black pride movement. Gordon's (1977) review of the literature does not completely resolve this issue but it casts light on it. In what she calls the "early period" (1939–1953), the doll or puppet studies did tend to show a preference for the light-skinned doll; in the middle period (1954–1963), which overlapped the early survey studies, the doll studies continued and showed essentially the same results; and in the most recent time frame (1964–1973), most of the doll studies showed the same results as in the earlier period but several studies did *not* show a preference for the light-skin doll. These findings suggest that there has probably been some enhancement of racial pride in the more recent period, a view supported by Cross (1985). Because various doll studies in the sixties continued to show a preference for lighter skin at the same time

The aim of this chapter is to attempt to make sense of these findings and, in the process, to suggest how attitude research should be modified to advance the art of inquiry in desegregation research. In order to do so, it is necessary to adopt a phenomenological perspective. The central argument of this chapter is that the reason that the theorists had reached erroneous conclusions was that the issue had been conceptualized in terms of the framework of the objective social scientist rather than in terms of the phenomenal field—the subjective world— of the black child. In order to advance this argument, it is first necessary to consider the nature of the phenomenological approach.

1. THE PHENOMENOLOGICAL APPROACH

The phenomenological approach is concerned with the examination of the subjective worlds or perspectives of human actors (MacLeod, 1959; Psathas, 1973; Snygg and Combs, 1949). The importance of this approach has long been recognized in sociology. Max Weber (1947) recommended *Verstehen* as a fundamental research operation, Berger and Luckman (1966) spoke of the "social construction of reality," Schutz (1970) directed attention to "multiple realities," "meaning contexts," and "interpretive schemes" of the actor, Thomas and Thomas (1928) emphasized the "definition of the situation," etc. All shared a common concern—a concern with the phenomenal field, or psychological world, of the subject.

The phenomenological approach involves a shift from an external to an internal frame of reference. The task is to discover underlying meanings, to fathom the individual's subjective world. As expressed by Combs and Snygg:

> This approach seeks to understand the behavior of the individual from his *own* point of view. It attempts to observe people, not as they seem to outsiders, but as they ₋eem to themselves. People do not behave solely because of the external forces to which they are exposed. People behave in consequence of how things seem to them. (1959, p. 11)

What is encompassed by the phenomenal field? According to Combs and Snygg:

---

that surveys showed no self-esteem disadvantage among black subjects, the different results cannot be attributed exclusively to historical changes. The fact that, according to Gordon (1977), the results of the doll studies were much the same between the 1939–1953 and 1954–1963 period suggests that the shift from *de jure* to *de facto* segregation had little meaning for these young children.

For insightful discussions of other methodological flaws in research allegedly demonstrating lower self-esteem among blacks, see Banks (1976), Banks and Rompf (1976), and Stephan and Rosenfield (1979).

By the phenomenal field we mean the entire universe, including himself, as it is experienced by the individual at the instant of action. Unlike the objective physical field, the phenomenal field is not an abstraction or an artificial construction. It is simply the universe of naive experience in which each individual lives, the everyday situation of self and surroundings which each person takes to be reality. (1959, p. 20)

(For good reviews of psychological phenomenology, see Kuenzli, 1959, and Misiak and Sexton, 1973.)

2. VERSTEHEN: THE HERITAGE OF MAX WEBER

The rationale for the need for psychological phenomenology in social science was set forth most effectively by Max Weber. The central task of social science, according to Weber, is the discovery of intended meaning or "meaning-adequacy." He observed (1947, p. 100): "Statistical uniformities constitute . . . sociological generalizations only when they can be regarded as manifestations of the understandable subjective meaning of a course of action." It was Weber's view that one of the most distinctive features of social science—one that set it apart most radically from physical science—was precisely the concern with subjective meaning. The physical scientist has no need to fathom the intent of atoms when they bond to form a molecule. Their motives, definitions of the situation, purposes, and perceptions are irrelevant. Electrons do not repel one another because of learned racial animosity; oxygen and hydrogen do not bond because of flaming sexual passion. On the other hand, Napoleon's march on Moscow cannot be understood adequately by observing overt actions; such behavior requires a grasp of subjective meanings. It is thus not so much formal methodological approaches or scientific considerations that separate the social from the physical or natural sciences as the question of subjective meaning.

If the task of social science is the discovery of intended meaning, then the social scientist must seek to comprehend the respondent's viewpoint or psychological world. Although it is not possible to specify all that falls into the respondent's phenomenal field, we believe that it would certainly include his frame of reference, his taken-for-granted world, his scope of experience, his effective interpersonal environment, his system of motivation, his values, or, most generally, his "schemata" (Fiske and Linville, 1980; Markus, 1977).

Weber, we believe, pointed us in a correct general direction, but it is one that we have been hesitant to follow. If we are to understand the psychological impact of social structure or social context, we must understand how it structures and governs the individual's experience. We must see the world not as abstract social scientists, perceiving phenomena from our detached, Olympian vantage points, but as it is perceived and experienced by the participants in the situation. What may suffice for the statistician or economist does not necessarily suffice for the sociologist. The sociologist must also be an anthropologist and a psychologist. One must understand the subcultural context of experience and the processing of environmental data through phenomenal fields. Following in the Weberian tradition, one approach is to begin with a plausible, rational, sensible interpretation of the facts—an ideal type of explanation—in order thereby to highlight its difference from the world as perceived and experienced by the actor.

3. THE SOCIAL SCIENTIST AND THE INVOLVED ACTOR: CONTRASTING PERSPECTIVES

If an explanation is to be considered rational, in Weber's sense, it must rest on sound theoretical principles. At least three principles governing self-esteem formation would support the expectation that blacks would have lower self-esteem than whites: these are the principles of reflected appraisals, social comparison, and self-attribution. We will first describe these principles and indicate why, from the viewpoint of the social scientist, they would suggest that black children would have lower self-esteem than white children. We then consider these principles from the viewpoint of the child, and observe how they suggest a very different conclusion.

3.1. Social Science Principles

3.1.1. Reflected Appraisals

The self-concept is essentially a social product, arising out of the interactive process (Blumer, 1969; Mead, 1934). One essential feature of self-concept development is the process of seeing the self though the eyes of, and from the perspective of, others. Although Cooley's (1912) "looking glass" self was not intended to suggest that the individual sees himself or herself exactly as others see him or her—how could one do so, since others see the individual differently?—it did highlight the fact that others' attitudes toward a person importantly influence an individual's self-attitudes.

But if a group is subjected to massive social devaluation (Bogardus, 1925, 1959; Katz and Braly, 1933)—the fate of blacks in America throughout history—then these negative reflected appraisals would be expected to damage their self-esteem. As Pettigrew (1964) expressed it:

> For years, Negro Americans have had little else by which to judge themselves than the second class status assigned them in America. And along with this inferior treatment, their ears have been filled with the din of white racists egotistically insisting that Caucasians are innately superior to Negroes. Consequently, many Negroes, consciously or unconsciously, accept in part these assertions of their inferiority.

The principle of reflected appraisals thus suggests that a group massively derogated in the society will tend to derogate itself. And if one expression of this prejudice is school segregation, then segregation will exacerbate the self-esteem damage. Wertham (1952) vividly described the feelings of inferiority experienced by black children bussed past white schools to their own segregated and less adequate facilities.

3.1.2. Social Comparison

The social comparison perspective would also lead us to expect damaged self-esteem among blacks. Because of prejudice and discrimination, blacks have been less successful than whites in achieving the valued goals of society. Blacks, according to Pettigrew, accept the American emphasis on status and "success." But when they employ these standards for judging their own worth, their lowly positions and their relative lack of success lead to further self-disparagement. Overall, black adults still lag behind whites in terms of employment, income, and social class (Hefner, 1979; Hill, 1979). It is plausible to conclude that negative social comparisons in this central value realm will damage self-esteem.

The child's social comparisons are no more favorable. Insofar as the child is accorded the socioeconomic status of the adult, the poor or lower class black child will suffer by comparison with the higher status white. But other unfortunate but no less consequential comparisons are likely to afflict black children. The most important is school performance. Although the explanations vary, the consistently poorer performance of black children on standardized achievement tests is amply documented (Clark, 1965; Coleman et al., 1966; U.S. Commission on Civil Rights, 1967). In light of the importance of school performance for the academic self-concept (Brookover et al., 1964) and, to a lesser extent, global self-esteem (Purkey, 1970), the unfortunate social comparison consequences appear self-evident.

Black children are also more likely to be raised in single-parent households (Farley and Hermalin, 1971; Rainwater, 1966). Although American family norms are currently undergoing rather fundamental change, traditionally the intact nuclear family of father, mother, and children has been most generally approved by society. In this regard, negative social comparisons would again be expected to damage black self-esteem.

In sum, with regard to socioeconomic status, academic performance, and traditional family structure, social comparisons for blacks are unfavorable. It is plausible to expect such social comparisons to damage self-esteem.

3.1.3. Self-Attribution

Interest in how naive observers characteristically attribute motives, intentions, causes, dispositions, etc., to others on the basis of observation of their actions has grown rapidly in recent years, stimulating a large body of research and theory (Jones and Nisbett, 1972; Kelley, 1967). Although emerging from a different theoretical tradition, Bem (1967) nevertheless suggested that essentially the same process was reflected in self-perception. In Bem's view, rather than drawing conclusions about their states or dispositions by reference to inner processes, people draw conclusions about their own internal state by observing their own behavior and the associated circumstances under which it occurs. There is no need to subscribe fully to Bem's radical behaviorism; but it is undoubtedly true that people do draw conclusions about dispositional phenomena, including their own value and worth, by observing their own behavior and its outcomes. The child's self-judgment is influenced by seeing his or her test and report card marks, the adult's by noting his or her occupational success or failure, etc.

Insofar as the education, occupation, and income levels of black adults are lower than those of whites, and insofar as black children's school performance lags behind white, both social comparison theory and self-attribution theory support the prediction of damaged self-esteem among blacks.

3.2. The Child's-Eye View

From the viewpoint of the social scientist, these principles provide sound theoretical support for the expectation that black children would have lower self-esteem than white children. But now let us consider these three principles from the viewpoint of the child.

3.2.1. Reflected Appraisals

It is a sorry but familiar truth that negative attitudes toward blacks in American society have traditionally been strong, and social scientists have plausibly assumed that black children would suffer from such negative reflected appraisals. Although it is certainly true that the attitudes of others toward the individual will affect the individual's self-esteem, the question is—which others? Is it the attitudes of the society as a whole that primarily affect the child's feelings of worth or is it the people who directly enter the child's experience and who count most in the child's scale of values?

The empirical evidence is plain in showing that the more significant a person is in the eyes of the child, the more impact will that person's attitude (as inferred by the child) have on the child's self-esteem (Rosenberg, 1973). In other words, some others are more significant than other others. The relevance of this point is that the relationship between what the child believes the other person thinks of him or her and the child's own self-esteem depends on how much the child cares about and trusts the other's judgment. If the child cares about and trusts the other's opinion strongly, then the relationship is consistently more powerful than if the child does not (Rosenberg and Simmons, 1972). Our self-esteem is thus not simply affected by what others think of us but by who these others are.

Who, then, are the black child's significant others (Sullivan, 1947), the people who so importantly shape the child's self-concept? This answer is: mostly or exclusively other blacks. Consider those people who enter the child's role-set (Merton, 1968): the mother, father, brothers and sisters, other relatives, friends, classmates, and teachers. With the possible exception of teachers and, in desegregated settings, of classmates, the child's significant others are of the child's own race; whatever they might think of the child on other grounds, one would hardly expect them to be prejudiced against the child because the child is black.

Furthermore, the data show, not surprisingly, that actual reflected appraisals received from significant others by black children is at least as favorable as that received by white children. Asked what their mothers, fathers, teachers, and friends think of them, black children are just as likely as white to perceive these attitudes as favorable (Rosenberg and Simmons, 1972).

The level of prejudice in the society as a whole, then, is very different from the level of prejudice in the child's effective interpersonal environment. Younger black children, particularly those in segregated environments, are remarkably unaware of the level of prejudice that exists in the society as a whole. (This awareness increases as they grow older or enter desegregated settings.) (Rosenberg, 1979b). To the extent that full awareness is lacking, to that extent are the damaging self-esteem consequences minimized. Prejudice as it exists in the broader society is very different from prejudice as it is directly and immediately experienced by the actor.

3.2.2. Social Comparison

As noted earlier, black children compare unfavorably with white in terms of socioeconomic status; their academic achievement levels are markedly below those of whites; and they are less likely to match the American family ideal. Following Weber's rational ideal type, the social scientist may plausibly conclude that these unfavorable comparisons will damage self-esteem.

Although there is no doubt that people draw conclusions about their worth by comparing themselves to others, the question again is—which others? Do the slum children of Baltimore compare their socioeconomic status with the school pupils of Scarsdale or the Gold Coast? Do they compare their academic achievement with the national averages? Do they compare their family structures with those prevailing in rural Nebraska? The comparisons made by the detached and remote social scientist are often very different from those made by the child.

Consider academic achievement. Because black children's performance on standardized achievement tests is below that of white (e.g., Coleman et al.,

1966), and because academic success is important to both black and white children, Weber's rational social scientist would conclude that such unfavorable comparisons would tend to damage the black child's self-esteem, particularly his or her academic self-esteem.

And where such comparisons are in fact made, as in the desegregated environment, these damaging self-concept consequences are clearly evident (Coleman *et al.*, 1966; Rosenberg and Simmons, 1972). In general, however, black children, especially in segregated settings, are primarily comparing themselves with one another. It is this fact that makes it possible for black performance to lag perceptibly behind white at the same time that black children are at least as likely as white to consider themselves "good students in school," or, more generally, to have favorable academic self-concepts (Coleman *et al.*, 1966). From the social comparison perspective, it is no accident, as St. John (1975) demonstrated, that black children in segregated settings tend to have more positive academic self-concepts than those in desegregated settings.

Essentially the same principle applies to the ruptured family. Both black and white children from such families who attend white schools, where broken families are comparatively rare, have lower self-esteem than their classmates from intact families. But in predominantly black schools, where such family structures are less atypical, the self-esteem of children from broken and intact families does not differ (Rosenberg, 1975). Social comparison in this setting is not unfavorable.

Despite lower socioeconomic status, poorer academic performance, and higher rates of family rupture, then, the social comparison principle is still entirely consistent with high self-esteem among black children. Whereas the social scientist, however, compares the SES, marks, and family structures of black and white children in some broad population, the children compare their SES, marks, or family structures with others in their immediate environments. The conclusions that are drawn by the detached social scientific observer and the involved child about the child's self-esteem are entirely different.

3.2.3. Self-Attribution

Self-attribution, it will be recalled, suggests that people draw conclusions about themselves by observing the outcomes of their actions. Thus, the person whose efforts at home repairs constantly end in disaster concludes about himself, as he would conclude about anyone else on the basis of the same evidence, that he is mechanically inept. Black adults whose efforts at occupational and economic achievement are unsuccessful would thus be expected to draw corresponding conclusions about their own worth.

But research has made evident that the attribution of causes is complex. Asked to explain why someone acted in a certain way, people may explain the behavior in terms either of internal or of external causes (Duval and Wicklund, 1972; Jones and Nisbett, 1971). Explanations based on internal causes have implications for self-esteem that are radically different from those based on external causes.

McCarthy and Yancey (1971) suggested that one reason the lesser occupational and economical achievements of blacks have not damaged their self-esteem is because of what they call "system-blame interpretation." This explanation is certainly highly plausible. Blacks have in fact been subjected to the most appalling prejudice and discrimination over the years. Lesser achievement was obviously a reflection of economic barriers, not a reflection of lack of inner worth. Thus, a white who was an economic failure might develop low self-esteem, whereas a black with equally low achievement could attribute it to racism. Conversely, the successful black might be more self-congratulatory than the successful white because he had overcome the special disabilities of racism. The self-attribution principle could thus be supportive of black self-esteem despite lesser occupational and economic achievement.

It is unclear whether blacks do in fact use the system-blame interpretation (see Taylor and Walsh, 1979), but it is possible that external-locus-of-control attitudes have similar psychological consequences. Implicit in the external locus of control orientation is a system-blame interpretation, that is, the attitude that what happens to us in life is not under our control but is a consequence of external forces. The fact that blacks are more likely than whites to score high on external locus of control measures (Campbell et al., 1976; Gurin et al., 1969; Lao, 1970) may mean that they are less likely to interpret life outcomes as reflections of personal worth.

System blame, it should be stressed, does not necessarily represent a misreading of objective reality; on the contrary, it may be entirely accurate. Take the black child who encounters prejudice. Is this a consequence of the child's own inadequacy or the other's bigotry? Clearly the latter. If the problem lies "out there" rather than "in here," it is not necessarily damaging to self-esteem. Similarly, the black child who knows that she is poor, that her group has low prestige, that her family is stigmatized, will not necessarily interpret these facts as reflections of her own lesser worth. The reason is that race is an ascribed, not an achieved, status. Jacques and Chason (1977) showed that achievement does affect self-esteem but that ascription does not. The disprivileges experienced by the black child are not consequences of her own efforts and may therefore do little damage to her self-esteem.

In sum, the perspective of the objective social scientist will frequently differ from the perspective of the naive actor. If we are to understand human behavior, it is essential that we not only grasp the facts but also understand how the facts are internally experienced, processed, and interpreted. When dealing with children, this is not so easily accomplished.

4. SEGREGATION

Inadequate attention to children's phenomenal fields has also produced unexpected findings in desegregation research. The finding that school segregation is associated with higher rather than lower self-esteem (St. John, 1975) appears incredible. In terms of western values, segregation is an abomination. It symbolizes rejection, derogation, and an affirmation of a group's inferiority. This fact constituted a foundation for the Supreme Court's 1954 ruling. Then how is it possible that segregation should be associated with higher rather than lower self-esteem? Instead of viewing segregation from the Olympian perspective of the social scientist, let us focus on the *experience* of segregation and how it impinges on the child and the child's assessment of his or her worth.

1. Minority group members are more likely to experience race or ethnic prejudice when they are surrounded by members of the majority group (desegregation) than when surrounded by members of their own group (segregation) (Rosenberg, 1977). Although it is not the only way, probably the most important way in which prejudice will give rise to low self-esteem is through face-to-face contact. To damage his self-esteem, the black child must come face-to-face with white prejudice. One reason that the self-esteem of black children in segregated settings tends to be higher than in desegregated settings is that, in the segregated setting, the black child is comparatively insulated from the broad range of prejudice that exists elsewhere.

For example, in Baltimore our respondents were asked "Sometimes kids tease each other about things. I'd like you to tell me how often you have been teased, left out of things, or called names by other kids because of these things." A number of questions followed, including "How often have you been teased because you are colored or Negro?" The data show that those black children in predominantly white schools and neighborhoods were more likely to report such teasing than those in predominantly black contexts (Rosenberg and Simmons, 1972).

The same is true of religious prejudice. In a study conducted at a time when religious prejudice was more intense, Jewish children in predominantly gentile neighborhoods were much more likely than those in Jewish neighborhoods to report that they had been teased, left out of things, or called names because of their religion (Rosenberg, 1962). On the average, then, reflected appraisals will be more favorable in a segregated than in a desegregated environment.

2. In the segregated setting, children are less aware of the negative attitudes held toward their group; this truth is more clearly apparent in the desegregated setting. The Baltimore City study (Rosenberg and Simmons, 1972) showed that the larger the number of white children in the school, the more likely was the black child to believe that "most Americans" ranked blacks low in the racial-ethnic status hierarchy. The desegregated experience, then, is one

of enhanced awareness of the broader society's negative attitudes towards one's race.

3. The desegregated environment may be a dissonant cultural context, the segregated environment a consonant one. Every group develops shared perceptions, norms, and values that constitute essential elements of a culture. Such cultures may vary from thin and superficial, with a few shared norms, values and communication patterns, to an extensive and elaborate culture, with numerous and profound shared components. To the extent that an individual has internalized the elements of his or her own culture, he or she faces the problem of marginality in a dissonant context (Ramirez *et al.*, 1971; Rosenberg, 1962; Rovner, 1981). An interesting illustration is Pitts' (1978) finding that French-Canadians who had attended English-speaking schools ended up more occupationally successful than those who had attended French schools but that they had lower self-esteem. From the viewpoint of culture—values, ideals, implicit understandings—the individual may feel more comfortable, at ease with himself, adequate, and accepted in a consonant than in a dissonant context. The degree to which subcultural differences characterize blacks and whites in our urban environments is difficult to specify. Although we do not believe that such differences are great, to the extent that they do exist, a black child in a predominantly white school would be more subject to problems of marginality—of feeling strange, different, out of place, or somehow "wrong"—a circumstance clearly prejudicial to self-esteem.

4. Academic performance is the most public, visible, and direct evidence of achievement in the school context. In terms of self-concept implications, such performance will bear primarily on academic self-concept and secondarily on global self-esteem. Within the segregated environment, of course, black children compare themselves with others in their group, with corresponding self-esteem implications. In the desegregated environment, on the other hand, they tend to compare unfavorably with those around them. It is thus not surprising that Coleman *et al.* (1966) found that black children in desegregated schools showed better performance on standardized tests than those in segregated schools but that their academic self-concepts were lower.

5. There are other potentially or actually damaging self-esteem effects in desegregated settings. In segregated settings, the self-esteem of black children from separated or never-married families is just as high as that of children from intact families; but in the desegregated setting, it is substantially lower (Rosenberg, 1977). In addition, in desegregated settings black children are more likely to be poorer than those around them than in the segregated settings (Rosenberg and Simmons, 1972). In several important respects, social comparisons tend to be more unfavorable in desegregated than in segregated settings.

It should be stressed that self-esteem is only one of many outcomes of desegregation. Although desegregation does appear to damage global self-esteem modestly, and academic self-esteem more strongly (St. John, 1975), it is associated with positive consequences as well. For one thing, there is some evidence of improved academic performance by black children in white schools (Coleman *et al.*, 1966; Crain and Mahard, 1983; Rosenberg and Simmons, 1972) though the results are not always consistent. In addition, Crain (1970) suggested that the desegregated school may be an "opportunities context." Black adolescents in desegregated schools are apparently more successful than those in segregated schools in finding jobs after high school, a result explained by Crain in terms of a reference group network. White boys have better contacts for getting jobs and they pass their information on to a number of their black classmates. Crain and Weissman's (1972) study of Northern adults also showed that those who had attended desegregated schools ultimately fared better in terms of a number of criteria, such as steady jobs, stable families, home ownership, staying out of trouble with the law, etc. (see also Braddock *et al.*, 1984.) In fact, one of the few benefits that were *not* associated with desegregation was improved self-esteem. Writers supportive of desegregation have focused on precisely the wrong effect—enhanced self-esteem—to support their position.

These observations on segregation and desegregation highlight the hiatus between the world as intended and the world as experienced. Segregation, *de jure* or *de facto*, is usually a product of malice, of hostility, of ill-will. The experience of segregation, however, is in various ways protective of self-esteem. It is all too easy to draw conclusions about the effects of an institution by considering its purpose and origins instead of seeing it as it actually enters the individual's life experience.

5. PERSPECTIVAL DISCREPANCIES

That perspectival discrepancies are an inevitable feature of human experience is scarcely a novel idea. When Hamlet, expressing his feeling that Denmark is among the worst of prisons, is contradicted by Rosencrantz, who denies such a reaction, Hamlet replies: "Why, then, 'tis none to you; for there is nothing either good or bad, but thinking makes it so: to me it is a prison."

Long ago Karl Mannheim (1949) alerted us to the dangers of perspectival thinking. He noted that people observing the "same" reality from different perspectives essentially "saw" different things, and drew different conclusions from these observations. Mannheim rooted such differences in the individual's location in the social structure or group affiliations. Social classes, cultures, ethnic groups, generations, etc., saw social reality differently because of their social interests, common experiences, shared norms, etc. Given the inevitable bias of all social perception, however, it would appear impossible ever to arrive at social scientific truth. Only the detached scientific political scientist, according to Mannheim, could overcome the biasing effects of his position in society so as to see the social world real and whole.

Whether the social scientist is indeed able to grasp this truth is certainly open to question. But it is clearly the case that the social scientist's perspective is different from the social actor's. There are at least three reasons for the inevitability of perspectival discrepancies.

The first is the different "interests" of people. We use this term not in Mannheim's sense of political, social, or economic advantage but in the sense of being concerned, involved, or attentive to certain aspects of reality. Korzybski (1933) once described how different people might see, attend to, or focus on a cow. To the biologist, the cow is a complex anatomical and physiological structure; to the artist, a configuration of form, light, shadow, and color; to the physicist, a complex structure of atoms; to the farmer, an ego-extension; and so on. People thus do not simply "see" things; rather, they see them in terms that engage their interests; and insofar as these interests differ, their perceptions inevitably differ.

A second reason for perspectival discrepancies is the inevitability of different vantage points. Some recent findings from attribution research aptly illustrate this point. When individuals are asked to explain the causes of their own behavior, they tend to ascribe it to situations or external events; but when outsiders explain that individual's behavior, they are more apt to attribute it to the individual's dispositions (Jones and Nisbett, 1971). Why do the actor and the observer see things differently and hence make different causal attributions? Because, in general, people's attention tends to be directed outward. To the actor the situation is external; but to the observer the actor is external. It should be stressed that both may be correct; their perspectives, however, differ.

Third, perspectival discrepancies are inevitable because observed realities are never perceived as such but are always assimilated to preformulated schemas. A schema, according to Fiske and Linville (1980), "refers to cognitive structures of organized prior knowledge, abstracted from experience with specific instances; schemas guide the processing of new information and the retrieval of stored information." The classic study by Bartlett (1958) on memory is illustrative. Asked to repeat a story they had been told, members of a different culture consistently selected, ordered, rearranged, and transmuted the facts in a fashion consistent with the content of their culture. External facts are thus not perceived as such but are fitted into a preformulated framework.

Perspectival differences between the scientist and the naive actor thus inevitably differ because they begin with different schemata; external reality thus necessarily has a different meaning. An understanding of the "meaning" of objective facts thus requires knowledge of the actor's schema.

To say that the perspective of the scientist may differ from the perspective of the subject, however, does not tell us in what ways they differ and why they differ in those particular ways. It is this question to which we now turn.

6. *SCIENTIFIC AND NAIVE PERSPECTIVES*

The scientist is the product of a lengthy and intensive process of socialization intended to train him to approach and perceive social reality in a characteristic fashion. Such training is essential for the conduct of scientific research but it is apt to generate a viewpoint that is at variance with that of the naive actor. We will discuss four features of the scientific approach that may foster perspectival discrepancies.

First, the scientific attitude is one of detachment and objectivity. Second, the social scientific method is comparative; the meaning of facts inevitably entails implicit or explicit comparisons. Third, attitudinal researchers, interested in generalizing to broad populations, employ research techniques that depend on statistical principles. Finally, the social scientist operates on a high level of abstraction and, as an intellectual, is sensitive to the symbolic meanings of reality.

Although the black child in segregated and desegregated settings certainly shares some of these cognitive orientations or schemas, the child is not a social scientist. Hence, the child's perspective must inevitably differ from that of the scientist. Our understanding may therefore be enhanced by directing attention to certain of these perspectival discrepancies.

6.1. *Distal and Proximal Perspectives*

Social scientists are trained to bring a broad perspective to bear on the social reality they study. One might liken the social scientist to an orbiting astronaut who, at a glance, can encompass a grand panoramic view of continents and oceans, a view of staggering breadth. Psychological processes, in contrast, operate at ground level. The same reality looks very different when seen from these different vantage points.

Consider again the black's disadvantage described previously: greater poverty, lower academic achievement scores, higher rates of family rupture, the reality of prejudice and, by definition, minority group membership. From the distant view of the rational social scientist, the findings appear damaging to self-esteem.

But when one views these matters from the proximal perspective of the black child, especially the young child, matters appear differently. In the schools she attends and the neighborhood in which she lives, the black child is rarely a minority group member; on the contrary, almost everyone around her is of the same race. In these contexts, she is not conspicuously poor; she may be better off than some, less well off than others. Her school performance is not markedly below those around her; feelings of academic success or failure follow the usual distribution. The black child from a broken family is also not unusual in this environment (Rosenberg and Simmons, 1972). From the viewpoint of the broader society, then, black children suffer severe disadvantages; but in the worlds in which they live, and that represent the source of their most vivid, immediate, and impactful experiences, these disadvantages are not apt to be at the center of awareness.

The social scientist, examining the data on prejudice in the society as a whole, is apt to conclude that black children are exposed to massive negative reflected appraisals. But in the worlds in which most black children actually live, this broad level of prejudice is unlikely to enter directly. The black child is more apt to be concerned with, and aware of, the attitudes toward him of his mother, father, and other significant others than the attitudes of a remote and anonymous population (Rosenberg and Simmons, 1972).

6.2. Within- and Between-Group Perspectives

Although univariate analyses have a role to play in social science, particularly in descriptive studies, the sociological approach is fundamentally comparative. Survey researchers comparing samples of subjects in terms of such variables as age, education, race, gender, etc., characteristically explore the effects of these variables by observing differences among categories or across different positions on the continuum.

The point is that sociologists tend to make between-group comparisons whereas individuals tend to make within-group comparisons. Although there are exceptions, in general people tend to compare themselves to similar others (Festinger, 1954; Patchen, 1961; Pettigrew, 1967). Recall the classic level-of-expectation study of Chapman and Volkmann (1947). In this study, college students were told the average scores on a certain test achieved by WPA workers, college students, and college professors and were asked how well they expected to do on the test. It will surprise no one to learn that the college students' estimates hovered about the alleged college student mean. This unsurprising finding is less trivial than it appears. It suggests that people are more apt to make within-group than between-group comparisons.

In their study of young people in the southern community of Millfield, Baughman and Dahlstrom (1968) observed with some surprise that, although black children could see the many ways in which they were disprivileged compared to whites, they appeared to be unaffected by these gross discrepancies; the comparisons tended to be with one another.

That perspectives of the social scientist and actor differ is readily understandable. Fundamentally, the sociologist is interested in groups (i.e., collectives—groups, statuses, or social categories), and she can only understand group effects by making group comparisons. Even if she studies women, she makes implicit comparisons with men; if she studies blacks, she makes implicit comparisons with whites. The social scientist's professional interest thus centers on between-group comparisons.

The subject's focus, by contrast, is on the self. The self is the reference point, the phenomenal center, of all perceptions. In Lecky's (1945, pp. 152, 156) terms: "The individual sees the world from his own viewpoint, with himself as the center. . . . The most constant factor in the individual's experience . . . is himself and his interpretation of his own meaning." The individual tends to compare himself with those in the groups, statuses, or social categories that constitute his psychological world.

Another difference between the scientist's and actor's perspective relates to the meaning of group differences. The scientist may infer that if an individual who performs well in some respect has higher self-esteem than an individual who performs poorly, then a group that performs well (on the average) in this respect will tend to have higher self-esteem than a group that performs poorly. But an individual rarely bases his self-esteem on how well his group has done in comparison to another group but on how well he personally has done in comparison to relevant others. Take a black pupil who stands in the top 10% of her class. Will she have high self-regard because she does better than most of the people she knows or will she have low self-esteem because the average academic performance of her race is below the average performance of another race? Does the white in the bottom 10% of her class consider herself an excellent student because her race does better than another on standardized tests? Absurd as it seems, this is the implicit reasoning that underpins the conclusions of some writers.

The perspectives of the social scientist and the child are thus radically different—the scientist tending to focus on differences between groups, the child tending to compare himself or herself to those in the same general category. Is it any wonder that the scientist should draw erroneous conclusions about the child's self-esteem?

6.3. Discrepant Contextual Perspectives

The social scientist, concerned with understanding broad populations, characteristically uses the sample survey to accomplish his or her objectives in an economical and accurate manner. The essential feature of this method is that every member of the population has an equal chance of being selected, and that the selection is governed by chance. Given proper procedure, it becomes possible to depict with a high degree of accuracy the relationships between individual characteristics within specified populations.

The sample survey, however, treats each member of the sample as an isolated atom, unconnected with other members of the sample. The problem with this approach is that it tends to overlook the fact that lives are lived in defined contexts, and that sociodemographic variables may achieve different meanings within different contexts. For example, to ask about the effects of race or socioeconomic status or ethnicity is to attempt to understand what it is about the *experience* of being black or poor or Hispanic that affects attitudes and behavior. Race *per se* cannot affect attitudes. Only being defined and treated as a black or white in society can produce such an effect. But the nature and definition of such treatment depends in part on the social context in which it is embedded. It may be a very different experience to be a black in a white context than to be a black in a black context; to be rich in a rich context than to be rich in a poor context; to be Hispanic in a Hispanic context or an Anglo context, etc. Consequently, the survey researcher seeking to explore the effects of race, socioeconomic status, or ethnicity on self-esteem is apt to obtain an incomplete and probably distorted picture if the researcher overlooks the contexts in which these social identity elements are embedded.

Consider the following finding from the Baltimore study. Respondents in this sample were asked whether they knew any children whose families were poorer than theirs and any whose families were richer. Black children were less likely than white to say that they knew poorer children. This is understandable; having a low socioeconomic status, there is available only a small pool of potential socioeconomic inferiors. But the surprising point is that the black children are also less likely than the white to say that they know richer children, that is, those socioeconomically superior to themselves. It is the white children, who are on the average much richer, who are more likely to say that they experience socioeconomic disadvantages (Rosenberg and Simmons, 1972).

In order to understand this point, let us attempt to enter the psychological world of the child in order to see how socioeconomic comparisons are made. Consider the very poorest black children in the sample, that is, those in Class V (based on the Hollingshead measure). How do they compare socioeconomically with children in their schools? It turns out that nearly half are approximately average for their schools and most of the remainder are only one step below average. Only 1 black child in 20 is substantially below average for that child's school, that is, two levels below. Now consider the equally poor (Class V) white children. *All* of them are below average for their schools; four-fifths are one step below average and one-fifth are two steps below average. Comparatively speaking, then, the Class V white child is much worse off than the Class V black child. Similarly, Class IV black children also fare better than Class IV white children. For example, one-fourth of the Class IV black children are socioeconomically superior to the school mean whereas this is not true of any of the Class IV whites. When we turn to the high social class end of the scale, that is, Class I–II, black children are again better off. Black children from this level are much more likely than comparable whites to be socioeconomically superior to their fellows. Sixty-seven percent of the higher-class black children but only 16% of the higher-class whites were two or more Hollingshead steps above the school average. We thus encounter the anomaly that black children, who are much poorer, are able to make more favorable economic comparisons than white children, who objectively are much better off (Rosenberg and Simmons, 1972).

Furthermore, the black children draw the plausible inferences about their families' social status from their experience. The Baltimore data show that, at equivalent class positions, the black children are more likely than the white to say that they are "very proud" of their family's social position and to affirm that their parents have done "very well" in life; and the poorer the children, on the whole, the greater the black-white discrepancy. Although black children are much poorer than white, in the interpersonal worlds in which their day-to-day experiences take place, the socioeconomic comparisons are generally favorable.

I do not mean to suggest, of course, that sociologists invariably neglect contexts (see, for example, Campbell and Alexander, 1965; Lazarfeld *et al*, 1972; Meyer, 1970; Michael, 1966)—that is certainly far from true—but that sample survey methodology fails to focus attention on this issue. Many of the best contextual analyses are accidental by-products of multistaged sampling designs, with a particular stage—a school, a Census Tract, a Primary Sampling Unit—constituting a natural context. But even when social scientists do attend to contexts, perspectival discrepancies may occur because the scientist centers attention on one context whereas the actor is primarily concerned with another. One reason is that contexts are nested; there are contexts within contexts. One may thus draw erroneous conclusions by misunderstanding the perceived and experienced context of the actor. Let me illustrate the point with two examples.

Some years ago an attempt was made to assess the consequences of racial desegregation on black school performance. The results showed that black adolescents in desegregated schools showed little advantage over those in segregated schools; desegregation appeared to afford little academic benefit. A more careful analysis by McPartland (1969), however, showed that in these allegedly desegregated schools, most of the black pupils had been assigned to black classes. The desegregation was largely cosmetic; the smaller contexts of experience were actually mostly segregated. McPartland was able to demonstrate, in fact, that in those cases in which black pupils did attend desegregated classes, their academic performance was appreciably better. This finding persisted even in the face of certain statistical controls. Although the study is not foolproof, it demonstrates the importance of identifying correctly the effective interpersonal environment of the individual.

A second illustration appears in a study by Rogers *et al.* (1978) examining the question of whether, in a sample of underachieving children, achievement scores and self-esteem would be related. These authors studied a school of underachievers consisting of 17 classes with a total of 252 children. If one examined the entire sample, there was virtually no relationship between the child's IQ and self-esteem. But *within* the classroom, it was found, the higher the IQ, the higher the self-esteem, particularly academic self-esteem. Had the investigators limited their investigation to the study of the relationship between IQ and self-esteem in the school as a whole—a typical research procedure—they might have reached the reasonable but erroneous conclusion that intellectual competence had no bearing on self-worth among underachievers.

The particular relevance of contextual analysis lies in the fact that no person is ever exposed to the totality of a society; one is only exposed to that portion that enters one's experience. Furthermore, those features of that experienced context that will probably have the major impact are the ones most closely attended to by the actor. A context is thus a psychological world, a world as perceived and experienced from one's own point of view. It is important to study not only the objective nature of these contexts (a point frequently overlooked by psychological phenomenologists) but also the subjective interpretation of it. Both are essential in the quest for meaning adequacy.

6.4. Symbolic and Literal Perspectives

That there may be a vast gulf between what exists objectively and what is perceived subjectively is scarcely a novel observation. (A striking illustration of this point appears in the quality of life literature, e.g., Campbell, *et al.*, 1976.) But this means that the social scientist and the actor, looking at the same reality, may perceive different things. One example of such perspectival discrepancies is the tendency of one party to endow a fact with symbolic significance whereas the other interprets it literally.

Take the famous doll studies of Kenneth and Marie Clark (1952), conducted in the forties and replicated many times in the subsequent decades. As noted earlier, black children were shown a light doll and a dark doll and were asked which doll was the nice doll, the pretty doll, the doll with the nice skin color, the doll that looks like you, etc. In many cases, these black children showed a preference for the light doll and even said they looked like the light doll. Most investigators thereupon concluded that these children were rejecting their race and, by extension, themselves. It rarely occurred to anyone to consider whether showing preference for the light-skinned doll simply signified preference for light skin, and that saying that they looked like the light doll simply meant that they *did* look like the light doll.

Is there any indication that these children may have been responding literally to skin color rather than symbolically to race? The most interesting comes from the original Clark and Clark study itself. When asked: "Give me the doll who looks like you," Clark and Clark report that only 20% of the light (practically white) children, 73% of the medium (light brown to dark brown) children, and 81% of the dark (very brown to black) children identified themselves with the colored doll (Clark and Clark, 1952, p. 555). Plainly, then, children are responding to a substantial degree in terms of literal skin color rather than showing racial misidentification and disidentification. Furthermore, the fact that they found the light doll more desirable is entirely consistent with other research at the time (e.g., Seeman, 1946) showing that blacks considered lighter skin color more aesthetic or associated it with more desirable status characteristics. What researchers interpreted as racial preferences were, at least among many children, skin color preferences. To be sure, when asked which doll is colored or white, their racial identifications tended to be correct; but these questions were presented after, rather than before, the doll preferences. Indeed, as Clark and Clark note, if the doll studies had been initially defined in symbolic terms, their results would have been entirely different. They noted

> It was found necessary to present the preference requests first in the experimental situation because in a preliminary investigation it was clear that the children who had already identified themselves with the colored doll had a marked tendency to indicate a preference for this doll and this was not necessarily a genuine expression of actual preference, but a reflection of ego involvement. (1952, p. 552)

For the next quarter of a century, investigators continued to study the question of so-called racial preference, using light and dark dolls, pictures, or puppets, and generally emerged with the same results. It was not until 1968 that Greenwald and Oppenheim introduced two startling innovations into this research procedure that left one gasping at their ingenuity. The first was that instead of using two dolls, they used three—dark, medium, and white. The second was that they interviewed white children as well as black. Given these options, it turns out that more white than black children misidentified with their race, that is, more white children said they looked like the medium doll than black children said they looked like the white doll.

In sum, if a black child with light color skin says he looks more like a white doll than a dark doll, it may not be that he is disidentifying with his race and expressing racial self-hatred; it may simply be that he does look more like the white doll than the dark. Many children are thus responding literally to skin color. In her careful study of children's racial identifications, Alejandro-Wright (1980) found that, for the younger children, "the term black . . . is interpreted literally as the color black." It was not until the later ages—age 8–10—that the children classified blacks and whites in the social-biological terms employed by adults.

Perhaps nowhere has the orientation of symbolism held greater sway than with reference to racial segregation. That legal segregation of Jews in the European ghettos, blacks in the South, or other "pariah" groups (Weber, 1952) has been explicitly intended to mark the inferiority and unworthiness of the excluded group is beyond dispute. In its purpose and in its practice, segregation was intended to symbolize the social inferiority of the group discriminated against, desegregation to symbolize its equality. For most social scientists, it has been a short and easy step to conclude that children in segregated settings would feel inferior and have low self-esteem whereas those in integrated settings would feel equal and have a high level of self-respect.

The concrete world of experience, by contrast, is a very different matter. If someone attacks us with a racial epithet or laughs at our peculiar dress or speech mannerisms; if we answer the questions wrong when the teacher calls on us or we get the lowest mark on the test—these are things we know and experience and they affect us in a direct and immediate sense. Yet, these are the experiences that are more likely to afflict the black child in a desegregated setting. The concrete experience of segregated living—in contrast to its symbolic meaning—is very different. If a black child attends a black school day after day, week after week, year after year, this becomes the child's world of experience. It is within this setting that the child's feelings about self and others evolve. It seems extremely unlikely that the black child daily seeing black faces around her in class and neighborhood constantly feels personally inferior because this structural condition symbolizes the social inferiority of her race; nor, for that matter, if the faces are white, does she constantly feel personal pride and high self-esteem because of this symbol of social equality. The fact that black children in segregated schools appear to have higher self-esteem than those in desegregated schools (St. John, 1975) may surprise those who view social structures as symbolic affirmations of principles rather than as contexts of experience. From the perspective of the child's world, it is readily understandable.

Finally, one must consider the widespread and persistent view that an attitude toward one's race or ethnic group symbolizes attitudes toward oneself. Cross (1978, 1985) has persuasively argued that reference group orientation, on the one hand, and personal self-esteem, on the other, are radically different attitudes, and that their association should be investigated, not assumed. (See also Porter and Washington, 1979.) In fact, there is some evidence to indicate that not only are attitudes toward one's group and attitudes toward oneself not identical but they are scarcely even related (Rosenberg, 1979a). This does not mean that race is not important to the child—it is—but that many other features of the self are of equal or greater importance in determining the child's feelings of self-worth.

In sum, our intention in this discussion has been to direct attention to some of the dangers of perspectival discrepancies between the objective scientist and the naive actor. If social scientists were more alert to the perils of perspectival discrepancies and more attuned to the phenomenal fields of their subjects, the depth, richness, and meaningfulness of much attitude research would be enhanced.

7. DISCUSSION

As the philosophical doctrine of phenomenology, initially enunciated by Husserl, has entered psychology and sociology, it has assumed distinctly different shapes and forms. In psychology (e.g., Kuenzli, 1959; Snygg and Combs, 1949), scientists have advocated the use of rigorous methods to assess this internal world validly and to study it systematically. In sociology (e.g., Berger and Luckmann, 1966; Psathas, 1973; Schutz, 1970), the methodology has been primarily speculative and impressionistic. Let me explicitly state that the problem we confront is best solved by the approach of psychological phenomenology. It was this approach that was so influential in introducing the self-concept as a topic of research into the field of psychology in the first place (Raimy, 1948; Snygg and Combs, 1949) and that has continued to underpin self-concept research over the past 30 years (Wylie, 1974). To be sure, phenomenology does not represent the dominant thrust of contemporary psychology; but it is essential for sociologists to use this approach to enrich, deepen, and make more meaningful their systematic quantitative data.

Our emphasis on systematic quantitative research is, we believe, entirely consistent with Weber's position. Scientific data are essential but an understanding of their meaning is equally so. An adequate sociology obliges us to penetrate the psychological worlds of actors; we must make an effort to understand (in Weber's sense of *verstehen*) people's attitudes and behavior. The purpose of this effort, it should be stressed, is not to supplant quantitative systematic research, as some sociological phenomenologists would have us do, but to enrich and deepen their meaning.

In urging attention to phenomenal fields, we do not mean to imply that sociologists are currently uninterested in such phenomena. Obviously, they are. What is required, however, is more serious attention to the issue. All too often we find investigators who follow the presentation of their data with rather casual, off-the-top-of-the-head, commonsensical discussions that seem neither enlightening nor persuasive. The impression conveyed is that this feature of the work is not considered particularly interesting or important. We believe this is unfortunate. Social science remains the science of meaning; hence, bare or superficial meaning is inadequate social science.

Research investigators generally recognize that, during the exploratory phase of the investigation, careful phenomenological study is essential. In a well-conducted study, investigators will conduct open-ended or semistructured interviews to learn how a range of people think about the issues under consideration, i.e., what frameworks or schemata guide their interpretations of the issues. Such work makes it possible to ask more meaningful questions and to provide more meaningful response options in constructing the structured research instruments. Our suggestion in this paper, however, is that phenomenological research should also be conducted after, rather than simply before, systematic data collection and analysis. We might call such work "second-stage analysis." (For a good example, see Goodwin, 1982.) The aim of such analysis is to enliven, deepen, and enrich the meaning of the quantitative results, and is as appropriate for secondary data analysis (Hyman, 1972) as for primary data analysis. Insofar as it succeeds, it enables us to approach more closely Weber's goal of meaning adequacy.

One possible consequence of the approach suggested in this paper is to make social scientists more aware of their own biased perspectives. Such an outcome would improve our understanding not only of our research subjects but of ourselves as well. Although looking into ourselves to discover our biases may be bitter medicine, in the long run it will produce a healthier social science.

REFERENCES

Alejandro-Wright, M. The child's conception of racial classification: A socio-cognitive developmental model. In M. B. Spencer, G. K. Brookins, and W. R. Allen (Eds.), *Beginnings: The Social and Affective Development of Black Children*. Hillsdale, NJ: Lawrence Erlbaum Associates, 1985.

Bachman, J. G. *Youth in Transition, Volume II: The Impact of Family Background and Intelligence on Tenth-Grade Boys*. Ann Arbor, MI: Institute for Social Research, 1970.

Baldwin, J. A. Theory and research concerning the notion of black self-hatred: A review and interpretation. *Journal of Black Psychology*, 1979, *5*, 51–78.

Banks, W. C. White preference in blacks: A paradigm in search of a phenomenon. *Psychological Bulletin*, 1976, *83*, 1179–1186.

Banks, W. C., and Rompf, W. J. Evaluative bias and preference behavior in black and white children. *Child Development*, 1976, *44*, 776–783.

Bartlett, F. C. Social factors in recall. In E. E. Maccoby, T. M. Newcomb, and E. L. Hartley (Eds.), *Readings in Social Psychology* (3rd ed.). New York: Holt, Rinehart, and Winston, 1958.

Baughman, E., and Dahlstrom, W. G. *Negro and White Children: A Psychological Study in the Rural South*. New York: Academic Press, 1968.

Bem, D. J. Self-perception: An alternative interpretation of cognitive dissonance phenomena. *Psychological Review*, 1967, *74*, 183–200.

Berger, P. L., and Luckmann, T. *The Social Construction of Reality*. New York: Doubleday, 1966.

Blumer, H. *Symbolic Interactionism: Perspective and Method*. Englewood Cliffs, NJ: Prentice-Hall, 1969.

Bogardus, E. S. Measuring social distance. *Journal of Applied Psychology*, 1925, *9*, 299–308.

Bogardus, E. S. Race reactions by sexes. *Sociology and Social Research*, 1959, *43*, 439–441.

Braddock, J. H., Crain, R. L., and McPartland, J. M. A long-term view of school desegregation. *Phi-Delta Kappan*, 1984, *66*(4), 259–264.

Brookover, W. B., Thomas, S. and Paterson, A. Self-concept of ability and school achievement. *Sociology of Education*, 1964, *37*, 271–278.

Campbell, A., Converse, P. E., and Rogers, W. L. *The Quality of American Life*. New York: Russell Sage, 1976.

Campbell, E. Q., and Alexander, C. N. Structural effects and interpersonal relationships. *American Journal of Sociology*, 1965, *71*, 284–289.

Chapman, D. W., and Volkmann, J. A social determinant of the level of aspiration. In G. E. Swanson, T. M. Newcomb, and E. L. Hartley (Eds.), *Readings in Social Psychology* (revised ed.). New York: Holt, 1952.

Clark, K. B. *Dark Ghetto: Dilemmas of Social Power*. New York: Harper and Row, 1965.

Clark, K. B., and Clark, M. P. Racial identification and preference in negro children. G. E. Swanson, T. M. Newcomb, and E. L. Hartley (Eds.), *Readings in Social Psychology* (revised ed.). New York: Holt, 1952.

Coleman, J. S., Campbell, E. Q., Hobson, C. J., McPartland, J., Mood, A. M., Weinfeld, F. D., and York, R. L. *Equality of Educational Opportunity*. Washington, DC: U.S. Government Printing Office, 1966.

Combs, A. and Snygg, D. *Individual Behavior*. Rev. ed. New York: Harper, 1959.

Cooley, C. H. *Human Nature and the Social Order*. New York: Scribners, 1912.

Crain, R. School integration and occupational achievement of negroes. *American Journal of Sociology*, 1970, *75*, 593–606.

Crain, R. L., and Mahard, R. The effect of research methodology on desegregation-achievement studies: A meta-analysis. *American Journal of Sociology*, 1983, *88*, 839–854.

Crain, R. L., and Weisman, C. S. *Discrimination, Personality and Achievement: A Survey of Northern Blacks*. New York: Seminar Press, 1972.

Cross, W. E. Black families and black identity: A literature review. *Western Journal of Black Studies*, 1978, *2*, 111–124.

Cross, W. E., Jr. Black Identity: Rediscovering the distinction between personal identity and reference group orientation. In M. B. Spencer, G. K. Brookins, and W. R. Allen (Eds.) *Beginnings: The Social and Affective Development of Black Children*. Hillsdale, NJ: Lawrence Erlbaum Associates, 1985.

Duval, S., and Wicklund, R. A. *A Theory of Objective Self-Awareness*. New York: Academic Press, 1972.

Epps, E. Minority children: Desegregation, self-evaluation, and achievement orientation. In W. D. Hawley (Ed.), *Effective School Desegregation: Equity, Quality, and Feasibility*. Beverly Hills, CA: Sage, 1981.

Farley, R., and Hermalin, A. I. Family stability: A comparison of trends between blacks and whites. *American Sociological Review*, 1971, *36*, 1–17.

Festinger, L. A theory of social comparison processes. *Human Relations*, 1954, *7*, 117–140.

Fiske, S. T., and Linville, P. W. What does the schema concept buy us? *Personality and Social Psychology Bulletin*, 1980, *6*, 543–557.

Goodwin, L. *The social psychology of action in a natural setting: Predicting the economic independence of welfare fathers*. Paper presented at the American Sociological Association, Sept. 1982, San Francisco.

Gordon, V. V. *The Self-Concept of Black Americans*. Washington, DC: University Press of America, 1977.

Greenwald, H. J., and Oppenheim, D. B. Reported magnitude of self-misidentification among negro children: Artifact? *Journal of Personality and Social Psychology*, 1968, *8*, 49–52.

Grier, W. H., and Cobbs, P. M. *Black Rage*. New York: Basic Books, 1968.

Gurin, P., Gurin, G., Lao, R. C., and Beattie, M. Internal-external control in the motivational dynamics of negro youth. *Journal of Social Issues*, 1969, *25*, 29–53.

Hefner, J. A. The economics of the black family from four perspectives. In C. V. Willie (Ed.), *Caste And Class Controversy*. Bayside, NY: General Learning Press, 1979.

Hill, R. B. The illusion of black progress: A statement of the facts. In C. V. Willie (Ed.), *Caste and Class Controversy*. Bayside, NY: General Learning Press, 1979.

Hyman, H. H. *Secondary Analysis of Sample Surveys: Principles, Procedures and Potentialities*. New York: Wiley, 1972.

Jacques, J. M., and Chason, K. J. Self-esteem and low status groups: A changing scene. *Sociological Quarterly*, 1977, *18*, 339–412.

Jones, E. E., and Nisbett, R. E. *The Actor and the Observer: Divergent Perceptions of the Causes of Behavior*. New York: General Learning Press, 1971.

Kardiner, A., and Ovesey, L. *The Mark of Oppression*. New York: Norton, 1951.

Katz, D., and Braly, K. W. Racial stereotypes of 100 college students. *Journal of Abnormal and Social Psychology*, 1933, *28*, 280–290.

Katz, P. The acquisition of racial attitudes in children. In P. Katz, (Ed.), *Towards the Elimination of Racism*. New York. Pergamon Press, 1976.

Kelley, H. H. Attribution theory in social psychology. In D. Levine (Ed.), *Nebraska Symposium on Motivation*. Lincoln, NE: University of Nebraska Press, 1967.

Kohn, M. L. *Class and Conformity: A Study in Values*. Homewood, IL: Dorsey Press, 1969.

Korzybski, A. *Science and Sanity*. New York: International Non-Aristotelian Library, 1933.

Kuenzli, A. E. (Ed.). *The Phenomenological Problem*. New York: Harper, 1959.

Lao, R. C. Internal-external control and competent and innovative behavior among negro college students. *Journal of Personality and Social Psychology*, *14*, 262–270.

Laurence, J. E. White socialization: Black reality. *Psychiatry*, 1970, *33*, 174–194.

Lazarsfeld, P. F., Pasanella, A., and Rosenberg, M. (Eds.). *Continuities in the Language of Social Research*. New York: The Free Press, 1972.

Lecky, P. *Self-Consistency: A Theory of Personality*. New York: Island Press, 1945.

Lewin, K. *Resolving Social Conflicts*. New York: Harper and Row, 1948.

Lipset, S. M., and Zetterberg, H. A theory of social mobility. In R. Bendix and S. M. Lipset (Eds.), *Class, Status and Power* (2nd ed.). New York: The Free Press, 1956.

MacLeod, R. B. The phenomenological approach to social psychology. In A. E. Kuenzli (Ed.), *The Phenomenological Problem*. New York: Harper, 1959.

Mannheim, K. *Ideology and Utopia* (L. Wirth and E. Shils, Trans.). New York: Harcourt, Brace, 1949.

Markus, H. Self-schemata and processing information about the self. *Journal of Personality and Social Psychology*, 1977, *35*, 63–78.

McCarthy, J. D., and Yancey, W. L. Uncle Tom and Mr. Charlie: Metaphysical pathos in the study of racism and personal disorganization. *American Journal of Sociology*, 1971, *76*, 648–672.

McDonald, R. L., and Gynther, M. D. Relationship of self and ideal self-descriptions with sex, race, and class of southern adolescents. *Journal of Personality and Social Psychology*, 1965, *1*, 85–88.

McPartland, J. The relative influence of school and of classroom desegregation on the academic achievement of ninth-grade negro students. *Journal of Social Issues*, 1969, *25*, 93–102.

Mead, G. H. *Mind, Self and Society*. Chicago, IL: University of Chicago Press, 1934.

Merton, R. K. *Social Theory and Social Structure* (enlarged ed.). New York: The Free Press, 1968.

Meyer, J. W. High school effects on college intentions. *American Journal of Sociology*, 1970, *76*, 59–70.

Michael, J. A. On neighborhood context and college plans (II). *American Sociological Review*, 1966, *31*, 702–706.

Miller, N. Changing views about the effects of school desegregation. In M. Brewer, and Collins, B. E. (Eds.), *Scientific Inquiry in the Social Sciences*. San Francisco: Jossey-Bass, 1981.

Miller, N. Peer relations in desegregated schools. In J. L. Epstein and N. Karweit (Eds.) *Friends in School: Patterns of Selection and Influence in Secondary Schools*. New York: Academic Press, 1983.

Misiak, H., and Sexton, V. S. *Phenomenological, Existential and Humanistic Psychologies: A Historical Survey*. New York: Grune and Stratton, 1973.

Patchen, M. A conceptual framework and some empirical data regarding comparisons of social rewards. *Sociometry*, 1961, *24*, 135–156.

Pettigrew, T. F. *A Profile of the Negro American*. Princeton, NJ: Van Nostrand, 1964.

Pettigrew, T. F. Social evaluation theory: Convergences and applications. In D. Levine (Ed.), *Nebraska Symposium on Motivation*. Lincoln, NE: University of Nebraska Press, 1967.

Pitts, R. A. The effects of exclusively French language schooling on self-esteem in Quebec. *The Canadian Modern Language Review*, 1978, *34*, 373–380.

Porter, J., and Washington, R. Black identity and self-esteem: A review of studies of black self-concept, 1968–1978. *Annual Review of Sociology*, 1979, *5*, 53–74.

Psathas, G. (Ed.). *Phenomenological Sociology: Issues and Applications*. New York: Wiley, 1973.

Purkey, W. W. *Self-Concept and School Achievement*. Englewood Cliffs, NJ: Prentice-Hall, 1970.

Raimy, V. C. Self-reference in counseling interviews. *Journal of Consulting Psychology*, 1948, *12*, 153–163.

Rainwater, L. Crucible of identity: The negro lower-class family. *Daedalus*, 1966, *95*, 172–216.

Ramirez, M., Taylor, C., and Petersen, B. Mexican American cultural membership and adjustment to school. In N. N. Wagner and M. J. Haug (Eds.), *Chicanos: Social and Psychological Perspectives*. St. Louis, MO: C. V. Mosby, 1971.

Rogers, C., Smith, M. T. and Coleman, J. M. Social comparison in the classroom: The relationship between academic achievement and self-concept. *Journal of Educational Psychology*, 1978, *70*, 50–57.

Rosenberg, M. The dissonant religious context and emotional disturbance. *American Journal of Sociology*, 1962, *68*, 1–10.

Rosenberg, M. *Society and the Adolescent Self-Image*. Princeton, NJ: Princeton University Press, 1965.

Rosenberg, M. Which significant others? *American Behavioral Scientist*, 1973, *16*, 829–860.

Rosenberg, M. The dissonant context and the adolescent self-concept. In S. Dragastin and G. Elder (Eds.), *Adolescence in the Life Cycle: Psychological Change and Social Context*. Washington, DC: Hemisphere Publishing Company, 1975.

Rosenberg, M. Contextual dissonance effects: Nature and causes. *Psychiatry*, 1977, *40*, 205–217.

Rosenberg, M. Group rejection and self-rejection. *Research in Community and Mental Health*, 1979, *1*, 3–20.

Rosenberg, M. *Conceiving the Self*. New York: Basic Books, 1979b.

Rosenberg, M., and Pearlin, L. I. Social class and self-esteem among children and adults. *American Journal of Sociology*, 1978, *84*, 53–77.

Rosenberg, M., and Simmons, R. G. *Black and White Self-Esteem: The Urban School Child*. Washington, DC: American Sociological Association, 1972.

Rovner, R. A. Ethno-cultural identity and self-esteem: A reapplication of self-attitude formation theories. *Human Relations*, 1981, *34*, 427–434.

St. John, N. *School Desegregation: Outcomes for Children*. New York: Wiley, 1975.

Schutz, A. *On Phenomenology and Social Relations*. Chicago, IL: University of Chicago Press, 1970.

Schwartz, M., and Stryker, S. *Deviance, Selves and Others*. Washington, DC: American Sociological Association, 1971.

Seeman, M. Skin color values in three all-negro school classes. *American Sociological Review*, 1946, *11*, 315–321.

Shavelson, R. J., and Stuart, K. R. Application of causal modeling methods to the validation of self-concept interpretation of test scores. in M. D. Lynch, A. Norem-Hebeisen, and K. Gergen (Eds.), *Self-Concept: Advances in Theory and Research*. Cambridge, MA: Ballinger, 1981.

Snygg, D., and Combs, A. W. *Individual Behavior: A New Frame of Reference for Psychology*. New York: Harper, 1949.

Stephan, W. G., and Rosenfield, D. Black self-rejection: Another look. *Journal of Educational Psychology*, 1979, *71*, 708–716.

Sullivan, H. S. *Conceptions of Modern Psychiatry*. Washington, DC: The William Alanson White Psychiatric Foundation, 1947.

Taylor, M. C., and Walsh, E. J. Explanations of black self-esteem: Some empirical tests. *Social Psychology Quarterly*, 1979, *42*, 242–252.

Taylor, R. Psychosocial development among black children and youth: A reexamination. *American Journal of Orthopsychiatry*, 1976, *46*, 4–19.

Thomas, W. I., and Thomas, D. S. *The Child in America*. New York: Knopf, 1928.

U.S. Commission on Civil Rights. *Racial Isolation in the Public Schools* (Vol. 1). Washington, DC. U.S. Government Printing Office, 1967.

Weber, M. *The Theory of Social and Economic Organization* (A. M. Henderson and T. Parsons, Trans.). New York: Oxford University Press, 1947.

Weber, M. *Ancient Judaism* (H. H. Gerth and D. Martindale, Trans., Eds.). Glencoe, IL: The Free Press, 1952.

Wells, L, E., and Marwell, G. *Self-Esteem: Its Conceptualization and Measurement*. Beverly Hills, CA: Sage, 1976.

Wertham, F. Psychological effects of school segregation. *American Journal of Psychotherapy*, 1952, *6*, 94–103.

Wylie, R. *The Self-Concept* (revised ed., Vol. 1). *A Review of Methodological Considerations and Measuring Instruments*. Lincoln, NE: University of Nebraska Press, 1974.

Wylie, R. *The Self-Concept* (revised ed., Vol. 2). *Theory and Research on Selected Topics*. Lincoln, NE: University of Nebraska Press, 1979.

Chapter 7

Schools and Social Structure

An Interactionist Perspective

BENNETTA JULES-ROSETTE AND HUGH MEHAN

1. INTRODUCTION

There is a critical need to establish a bridge between the sociological literature on desegregation and several closely related areas, including cross-cultural education, interactional studies of schooling, and comparative educational stratification. This chapter discusses how desegregation is perceived and socially constructed in school settings. It also provides an overview of key theoretical implications of United States desegregation studies from an interactionist perspective and suggests the importance of both cross-cultural and individual-level variables for research on desegregation and educational stratification.

To this end, in our first two sections, we critically review some of the previous studies of school desegregation. We find that these studies do not address the social organization of desegregation in the everyday lives of educators and students. As a result, it is difficult to assess the social consequences of desegregation. In the third section of the chapter, we review selected ethnographic studies of schooling. These studies have examined everyday educational practices that have the unintended consequences of providing differential educational opportunities to students along class and ethnic lines. In a fourth section, we place the issue of United States desegregation in a broader cross-cultural perspective and conclude that United States policies and practices can be understood

BENNETTA JULES-ROSETTE AND HUGH MEHAN • Department of Sociology, University of California, San Diego, La Jolla, CA 92093.

as part of a more general process of educational stratification involving the exclusion of minority groups. In the two final sections, we analyze the policy implications of these lines of inquiry and outline suggestions for future research.

As a result of policy and funding contingencies, much of the literature on school desegregation in the United States frames the problem in a culturally and historically narrow manner. The 1954 *Brown* decision is treated as the touchstone for a series of dramas, conflicts, and evaluation studies centering around the processes and outcomes of United States desegregation. The studies may be divided into two major categories: (a) surveys of the attitudes toward and consequences of desegregation (e.g., Coleman *et al.*, 1975; Cramer, 1968; Drury, 1980) and (b) short-term social psychological case-studies bearing on the desegregation process (e.g., McDermott, 1976; Metz, 1978; Rist, 1979; St. John, 1975).[1]

Few conceptual linkages are explicitly made between policy studies and more detailed psychological and ethnographic research. Many of these studies have been limited to single schools and communities without longitudinal research. Even more salient is the tendency to define desegregation as an immediate, time-bound political issue in the United States rather than conceptualizing the research problem more broadly in terms of intercultural communication, educational stratification, and differential power relationships (see Ogbu, 1978, pp. 369–370).

2. REASSESSING SCHOOL DESEGREGATION FROM AN INTERACTIONIST PERSPECTIVE

Structurally, school desegregation has referred both to the elimination of racially separate or "dual" school systems and to the inclusion of minority students in previously uniracial schools. The legal process of desegregation has been studied in terms of attitudes toward projected and ongoing schemes for altering the racial/ethnic composition of schools. The problems of proportionate integration and token inclusion of minorities in previously segregated schools are related, though independent, topics of study. Among the positive potential outcomes of the desegregated school situation are (a) improved self-esteem of the participants, (b) reduced prejudice through intergroup contact, and (c) increased access of all participants to educational opportunities and career options. Some of the research on the topic has addressed these issues directly.

Survey data indicate that segregation is most pronounced in the largest school districts of major United States cities with populations of 100,000 or more. Coleman *et al.* (1975) concluded that segregation is proportionately higher

[1]Publications from the National Institute of Education (1976, 1977a, 1977b) should be consulted for a comprehensive overview of the case studies and policy-oriented research on desegregation.

in the elementary school grades than at the secondary level and that, on the average, white children have less school-structured contact with minority children than the minorities have with children of outgroups. Educational tracking appears to cross-cut desegregation efforts at the advanced stages of schooling.

Some of the correlational studies that have addressed the problem of ethnic imbalance in the classroom are methodologically flawed (see Drury, 1980; Lewis and St. John, 1974). These studies argue that academic and social contact with white students in itself improves the school performance of minority students (see Patchen et al., 1980). However, they leave two important topics unexamined: the influence of a minority presence on the total interracial setting and the social relationships among majority and minority students.[2]

Translated into interactional terms, these findings suggest that desegregation seldom leads to a balanced ethnic mix in school settings. Minority students may isolate themselves in the interracial classroom setting. Resegregation is also externally reinforced by the school's policies of tracking and academic stratification. Stigmas may be attached to the formation of friendship and network contacts outside of one's primary ethnic group (Patchen et al., 1976). In this way, the desegregated school setting mirrors and perpetuates existing structures of dominance and separation found within the society as a whole. It is important in this context to distinguish between legally mandated desegregation, assertive efforts toward school integration in academic and informal activities (Pettigrew, 1969; Pettigrew and Back, 1971), and multicultural education.

In a study of desegregation in two rural Georgia high schools, Bullock and Braxton (1973) found that black students were considerably more skeptical about the experience after they entered desegregated schools. Although initially fearful, white students regarded the desegregation efforts as successful; black students became even more keenly aware of racial imbalance, separation afterwards, and social stratification. This paradox in perception underlines the importance of studying interaction in desegregated environments.

Suggested foci of study include teacher–student interaction, student evaluation processes, labeling of students, and school referral practices. These experiences have a direct impact on students' processes of identity formation and expression in intercultural settings. The situational variables surrounding desegregation must be reexamined to locate the phenomenon of desegregation in the daily lives of educators and students and thereby to determine how its consequences may be most effectively assessed. Individual case studies are also essential to developing profiles of the "moral careers" (Goffman, 1963) and adjustment

---

[2]Patchen et al. (1980) and Lewis and St. John (1974) among others have suggested that contact with white students has positive academic and psychological effects on blacks. Seldom is the desegregation process regarded as a two-way exchange. The potential positive benefits of a minority presence in the classroom are neither acknowledged nor measured.

patterns of minority students in desegregated settings. We may ask how the individual student manages the adjustment to a desegregated school through the deliberate manipulation of aspects of the setting in daily interaction (Garfinkel, 1967). Avoidance and aggression, cited as responses to desegregation in a number of studies (e.g., Patchen *et al.*, 1977; St. John and Lewis, 1975), may be viewed as strategies for adapting to interracial settings under a variety of conditions.

In a summary of five studies of desegregated schools, Wax (1979) reported that contact among blacks and whites are different in academic and recreational arenas. Although blacks and whites were physically copresent in classrooms, there were barriers in social mixing for recreational activities, such as the school prom. Black students who affected white upper-class norms for clothing, hair-styles, speech patterns, and aspirations for future achievement were included in social activities by whites, whereas those who did not adopt such standards were overlooked and excluded from extracurricular activities.

There were also differences in resegregation in upper and lower academic tracks in three of the five desegregated schools. Although college-prep classes were biracial, lower-track classes were less so, thereby reinforcing a self-validating cycle of separation. Students in the lower track reported rarely participating in class or extracurricular activities because they found school unexciting. Their lack of involvement is followed by avoidance on the part of the school administration. In turn, this avoidance leads to the student's further withdrawal. Attempting to locate the cause of resegregation is difficult. Wax's study appears to miss two important points. First, interracial contact is not simply a matter of student selection or choice; it is structured by the sorting practices of the schools. Second, white students' cultural activities are not the only ones in an interracial school. Before concluding that blacks who are not participating in white activities are "withdrawn," we must consider their participation in alternative intracultural activities.

Hanna examined some aspects of interracial interaction in a "magnet" school in Texas with a court ordered 50/50 desegregation ratio (Hanna, 1982). She found that black and white students, although they ostensibly spoke the same language, did not share the same styles of social interaction and verbal and nonverbal communication. As a result, the perceived cultural gaps between black and white children widened in the desegregated situation. Initial fears and prejudices were encouraged, with children from both groups becoming increasingly defensive. Hanna documented these findings by demonstrating the dynamics of an aggressive social activity that she labeled "meddlin' ." Aggression was used as a dominance strategy triggered by new and ambiguously defined social settings, threats to self-esteem, and mutual feelings of uncertainty or inferiority. Black students used aggression to mark the social boundaries of groups and to compensate for insecurities in academic performance. White students reciprocated in these activities, thereby creating a situation in which formal classroom activities and informal recreational settings were separate for each group. Both black and white students were the targets of "meddlin' " behavior that originated in the classroom and extended beyond it into the community.

Furthermore, Hanna (1982, p. 339) contended that "meddlin' , " seemingly an innocent informal behavior among children in the desegregated setting. actually "contributes to segregation in desegregation." Through this process, black students are labeled as the instigators of aggression, and the potential for normal intergroup contact without conflict diminishes. She suggested that aggressive and negative stereotyping are the causal factors in a conflictful biracial situation from the child's point of view. The children in her sample do not react to problems of desegregation in a global or philosophical way. Instead, pupils of both races seek to pin the blame for difficulties on troublemakers and members of an outgroup. These troublemakers are stereotyped by teachers and students alike, with the result that desegregation reinforces negative preconceptions rather than destroying them. The roots of aggression, however, extend beyond the immediate setting to a larger cultural context. The styles of interaction and communication in the desegregated setting draw on the repertoire of interactive competencies and expectancies that the child brings to the new environment.

Underlying Hanna's approach is a model of cultural conflict that Ogbu (1978, and this volume) has criticized as incomplete. The cultural-conflict model analyzes problems of desegregation in terms of differences in interactional, linguistic, and cognitive styles. Ogbu has argued that such a model does not consider the institutional and economic bases for contrasting attitudes toward schooling that emerge in the desegregated situation. This criticism is pertinent to our review. Comparative data (Ogbu, 1978) indicate that severe discrepancies in academic performance and classroom adjustment occur wherever the minority population takes on caste-like characteristics that are reinforced by restricted occupational roles and limited social mobility. Although these barriers become apparent in classroom communication, their implications extend beyond the classroom to the social and economic structure of the society at large. Hence, Ogbu has contended that the job ceiling for United States blacks in the larger society directly influences their attitudes toward schooling on the whole as well as their work incentives and performance. Drawing on comparative data collected among West Indians in British schools and Buraku outcasts in Japan, Ogbu has concluded that problems in adjustment and performance result from limitations in the occupational and social possibilities of minority groups that face significant barriers in the larger society. Thus, whereas Hanna suggested that problems of communication stemming from the black child's aggressive reactions weaken the positive outcomes of desegregation, Ogbu has argued that classroom conflicts merely represent a microcosm of the society at large.[3]

---

[3]See Ogbu (1981). Here Ogbu argued that the academic performance of the black child is a reflection of disillusionment and lack of economic opportunity in the larger society. Although this hypothesis is illuminating, it does not account for a wide range of variation in classroom performance.

Similarly, in a sociometric study of a desegregated classroom setting, St. John (1975) found that the short-term effects of desegregation on the self-esteem of black students were, in some instances, negative. Barriers to forming friendship ties in the interracial setting have been traced in sociometric studies of the classroom (St. John and Lewis, 1975) and ethnographic research (Hanna, 1982; Metz, 1978; Wax, 1979). Leaving aside questions of measurement, one must ask what is taking place within the desegregated setting to create opportunities for increasing either cooperation or resegregation.

Schofield (1979) tested Allport's conditions for equal-status contact among seventh and eighth graders in a desegregated school. She found that intergroup contact increased among the seventh-grade students who spent the bulk of their time in a homogeneous school environment. In the eighth grade, however, students were separated into high and low tracks largely along racial lines. In Schofield's study, interracial peer contact declined as a result of academic tracking. Approximately 80% of the children in the accelerated program were white. They tended to remain together during lunchtime and recreational periods. The structuring of academic activities influenced the overall resegregation of students in both classroom and informal settings. Tracking generated a new means for assessing the student's academic and social status apart from background socioeconomic and cultural factors. Even within the same interracial school, the conditions of equal-status contact among students appear to be fragile indeed. Our discussion of the sorting practices in multicultural schools will return to this point.

Pettigrew and Back (1971, p. 92) emphasized the problems with some micro social-psychological studies in the mold of St. John's, Schofield's, and Patchen's research when they state that much of this work "has had more success in measuring such gross aspects as preference and amount of interaction than in teasing out the more intricate aspects of conduct." They suggested that a focus on desegregation rather than integration has generated a narrowness in both conception and method in the "status score" studies. If improved test performance on the part of the minority group members and their increased popularity in a biracial setting are the immediate measures of the success of desegregation, one can only conclude that many initial experiments have failed.

Despite significant areas of disagreement, the interactionist and institutional approaches can be reconciled by a model that takes into account the conditions of contact and cooperation between groups as seen in their own terms. The legacy of group failure and the potential for individual successes are played out at the situational level in classroom, testing, and referral settings in the desegregated school. These interactions are not merely reflections of a larger social structure, as some theorists have argued (Bourdieu and Passeron, 1977; Bowles and Gintes, 1976). They constitute the participants. Children in desegregated schools use a variety of techniques to cope with the setting. Rather than examining the desegregation situation in terms of "predictable" failures or ideal goals, we suggest that it may be approached in terms of the repertoire of knowledge, competencies, and strategies actually used by participants in the setting.[4]

From the point of view of this chapter, the debate over the long- and short-term benefits of desegregation is not an issue. Rather, a more subtle set of questions emerges when the dynamics of interaction in school are considered. First, does the mere copresence of white and black students in a single setting constitute desegregation? Second, how is desegregation perceived and played out in the school system, including the classroom setting? And third, what practices do students, teachers, and administrators use to manage, achieve, and report the desegregation process?

Figure 1 emphasizes that school events take place in a larger cultural and social environment. Socioeconomic status appears to influence peer contact in school, although studies are divided on the extent and direction of this influence. Occupational mobility clearly affects the child's academic motivation and career selection, as Ogbu has emphasized. In turn, the cultural capital that students bring to the school setting influences their performance and interpretations of the school environment. Even in the presence of these external influences, events in the school may be considered to retain an autonomy of their own within the larger social structure.

3. RESEARCH ON THE EFFECTS OF DESEGREGATION IN CLASSROOM AND SCHOOL SETTINGS

Studies of classroom interaction in both the United States and Great Britain emphasize the importance of establishing a relationship between the formal features of the learning situation and the range of interactions that take place between students and teachers (Bremme and Erickson, 1977; Bernstein, 1975; Cicourel et al., 1974; Gumperz and Herasmichuk, 1975; Mehan, 1978, 1979; Philips, 1972). Mehan (1979) demonstrated that there is a tacitly learned and hierarchically ordered structure of language use and interaction between students and teachers in the classroom. Inevitably, this ordering involves an evaluation of the sequence of instructional interaction by the teacher (see Goffman, 1981, and Mehan, 1978). These pedagogic exchanges take place in the context of student–teacher interactions and are colored by the mutual expectations of students and teachers. A student who has problems communicating in standard

---

[4]In a study of intergroup cooperation between two African churches, Jules-Rosette (1977) emphasized the necessity for mutually complementary skills in negotiating an interaction. Because church members have relatively similar expectations of each other, maintained through mutual stereotyping, they are able to cooperate effectively in a joint performance in spite of the occasionally negative or inaccurate connotation of their mutual stereotypes.

Figure 1. The school in social context.

English by virtue of language or dialectal differences is handicapped in routine interactions and can be subject to negative labeling. Bernstein (1964) and Labov and Robins (1969) have analyzed this situation in terms of the social consequences deriving from alternative speech codes.[5] This sociolinguistic approach raises the possibility that speech exchanges reinforce dominance and exclusion.

Variations in communicative competence emerge sharply in the desegregated classroom. Minority children who have difficulty mastering a standard

[5]Bernstein (1964) defined restricted codes as speech systems in which there are limited syntactic alternatives and few possibilities for verbal expansion. As a result of ethnicity and social-class factors, minority children are socialized in the use of restricted codes that handicap their ability to succeed in educational and occupational settings (Bernstein, 1972). In the interracial classroom, an interplay between restricted code use among minority pupils and the so-called elaborated code employed for instruction may be observed. In contrast to Bernstein, Labov (1972) argued that the assumption that verbal deprivation prevails among black students is a myth that does not take into account the expressive richness and syntactic complexity of the nonstandard dialects labeled by Bernstein as restricted codes. Labov argues for a closer analysis of the sociocultural context of the black child's language use and the ways in which verbal competence is assessed by teachers.

pedagogic format may be labeled by teachers and socially isolated from majority peers. Thus, it becomes necessary to examine the conditions under which the desegregated classroom may become internally stratified, with minority students both structurally and individually isolated in the new environment. On the more positive side, if such isolation does not occur, we must examine the conditions that promote success.

This situation is intensified in formal learning sessions in which intercultural conflicts surface. McDermott (1977) described two such settings. In the first case, a first-grade Hispanic student was prohibited from participating in a reading group because she was unable to compete effectively for a turn to read and demonstrate her skills. More than language was at issue. The student's entire interactional style effectively isolated her from instructional interaction and progress. In a second case, Oakland students speaking a black English vernacular were prevented by the teacher from reading aloud until they had mastered standard English. As a consequence, these students lagged behind their peers in demonstrable reading skills. They were both culturally and academically labeled (see Gumperz and Herasmichuk, 1975).

Labeling and stereotyping create mutual reactions. Students isolated from their peers in turn pursue the self-fulfilling activity of isolating themselves. Rubin (1972) suggested that this reaction is an artifact of the inferior quality of minority educational and classroom experiences in previously segregated settings. McDermott (1977, p. 209) also cogently summarized the results of this situation: "most minority groups that have relied on the public schools have paid the price; identity struggles replace learning tasks, and children often leave school knowing little more . . . than when they entered." Detailed analysis of interactional strategies in the classroom can contribute to desegregation research by attuning observers to the techniques that students and teachers employ to foster separation and stratification in an ethnically and culturally mixed environment. These techniques include "phantom performances," (Rist, 1973) in which the teacher presents material to an unresponsive and alienated audience, power plays by students and teachers, mutual stereotyping across racial/ethnic groups, teachers' sorting practices, and self-segregation within a desegregated environment. Findings concerning interracial avoidance in desegregated settings have been corroborated by experimental and ethnographic data (see Jacobson, 1977). It is difficult, however, to measure adequately these responses as reactions to desegregation on the interactional level without a cross-section of field data collected through intensive classroom observation.[6]

---

[6]Erickson (1975) and McDermott et al. (1978) have emphasized the importance of descriptive adequacy in interactionist studies of the classroom. Similar criteria may be applied to studies of the desegregated school environment. Until a comparative sampling of ethnographic and detailed observational materials is collected, it is difficult to assess exactly what desegregation means and how it works in a variety of settings.

Sociometric studies (e.g., St. John and Lewis, 1975) have demonstrated that group acceptance has a positive effect on academic performance in interracial classroom settings. Popularity in this case is measured by the formal ratings of peers and not by observation of classroom interaction. The influence of background factors, of changing situational expectancies, and of the evaluation of teachers is rarely examined or measured. One problem with both the literature on equal-status contact (e.g., Riordan, 1975) and the claims to disprove it (e.g., Patchen *et al.*, 1977) is a failure to investigate how status is perceived by the respective groups and to relate these categories to pupils' subjective perceptions of themselves in the school setting.

Along these lines, the impact of direct and mediated experiences outside of the classroom is seldom analyzed. Social psychologists working under controlled conditions (e.g., Mischel and Staub, 1965) have some difficulty disentangling the effects of generalized expectancies in interaction and situation-specific determinants of choice and behavior. Similar problems arise in using students' "folk" ratings of each other to determine group acceptance when private opinions and public interactional patterns are contradictory. The collection of data on preconceptions and stereotypes from children, as exemplified by Hanna's research, does not necessarily clarify the results. Children may blame outgroup members because it is accepted as "common knowledge" that the outsiders create troublesome situations. The larger question then becomes how this knowledge is generated and applied in the classroom setting.

The study of desegregation will not become adequate to its task until it turns to an in-depth study of how the participants in the desegregated setting respond to that setting. The desegregated school is supposed to be institutionally structured to prevent segregation. It is clear, however, that resegregation does occur. How does it occur? What do the participants in the desegregated setting do to create, maintain, and transform this resegregation?

4. SORTING PRACTICES IN DESEGREGATED AND MULTICULTURAL SCHOOLS

It has been noted that the process of resegregation may be initiated by the students in desegregated settings. We have also stated that these desegregated school settings, although institutionally structured in an attempt to avoid and prevent segregation, have recurrences of segregation. This suggests that the school structure is involved in the process of resegregation. Studies in multicultural schools that are not under legal desegregation mandates contain important insights on the processes of interracial interaction. These studies suggest that schools play an active role in structuring the intergroup contact and social lives of students. The fragility of the equal-status contact hypothesis has already been noted. Educational tracking appears to be a significant factor that reinforces the resegregation of minority students in multicultural and segregated schools. Therefore, it is useful to examine the sorting practices used in both desegregated and multicultural schools. We must ask how sorting practices work to promote resegregation and, alternatively, how they operate in successful integrated and magnet schools.

The tracking system for grouping students according to future occupations is one way in which the school plays an active role in structuring intergroup contact. Hollingshead (1949) found the social-class divisions of the community were reflected in school tracks. He also found that social-class divisions within the elementary school were recapitulated in the different courses of study offered in the high school. Adolescents from the upper social strata dominated the college preparatory track. The general curriculum drew the majority of its students from Hollingshead's third and fourth social classes, whereas the commercial courses primarily received students from the lowest socioeconomic classes. Hollinsghead showed that it was accepted practice to sort students into educational programs based on their social-class backgrounds rather than individual effort or performance. The cream did not rise naturally to the top of this school. It was driven there by the sorting practices of the school.

Rosenbaum (1976) placed in sharper focus the sorting practices that affect the academic careers of students. The stated policy of the junior and senior high school that Rosenbaum studied seemed to minimize divisions in the school, maximize options, and maintain free choice. The only division in the junior high school was a single elective, and the divisions in the senior high school permitted opportunities across a considerable array of tracks. Free choice was emphasized in each division, and none of the divisions was said to close off the possibility of track change. Although Rosenbaum found that the school policy was ambivalent, he said that the image projected by the school was one of a "contest" mobility system. In such a system, students would be free to compete for courses and subsequent career opportunities. When Rosenbaum examined school records that depicted track changes over time, he found very little mobility. Most students stayed in their initial track. The changes that did occur fit into a pattern of downward mobility. Of those students who did move up, very few moved beyond the adjacent track. Fewer than 3% of the students progressed from the noncollege to the college tracks. In contrast, 21% of the college students changed to a noncollege track the following year. Downward track mobility was, therefore, seven times as great as upward track mobility. This pattern is also particularly noteworthy in the case of minority students in the desegregated environment.

The guidance counseling system for grouping students according to ability and interest plays a major role in sorting students (Cicourel and Kitsuse, 1963; Erickson, 1975; Rosenbaum, 1976). Cicourel and Kitsuse (1963) interviewed high school counselors to determine how they decided to tell black and white students of different socioeconomic backgrounds whether they should apply to college and, consequently, anticipate a professional or nonprofessional occupation. They found that black students who had average to high academic records were systematically steered away from college careers, whereas white students of high socioeconomic rank who had mediocre and low academic records were encouraged to attend college.

Similarly, Erickson and Shultz (1982) analyzed more than 80 counseling interviews between junior college counselors and their students. The authors provide a description of some of the interactional practices that structure stages in students' careers. They demonstrated how aspects of social identity not related to the school setting are introduced into the decisions that occur at school. Their analysis of the degree of synchrony between counselor and student during interviews reveals that the counselor and student together actively construct educational options for students.

The importance of school sorting procedures is even more poignantly reflected in Mercer's (1974) study of students placed in special "mentally retarded" classrooms. California public schools at the time of Mercer's study utilized committees composed of psychologists, nurses, teachers, and administrators to evaluate recommendations about students made by teachers, parents, or principals. Students were referred to these committees for a number of reasons, including discipline for misconduct and treatment of poor or outstanding academic performance. The ultimate decision that these committees made was crucial for the social identity of the student. The committee could recommend several educational alternatives: (a) return the student to the regular classroom, maintaining the identity "normal student"; (b) switch the student to some other classroom; or (c) demote or place the student in a "special" education classroom that bestowed the identity of "special student."

Decisions about the special placements are informed by IQ test results. The cutoff point on the IQ test for mental retardation in service at the time of Mercer's study was 80. A student scoring above that point to about 100 IQ points, was defined by the test as normal, albeit "slow." A student scoring below that point was defined by the test as "mentally retarded." Although this system seems objective, Mercer found that placement into the mentally retarded category was not automatic. Some 1,234 students were referred to the various psychological service committees in the schools in her study, and 865 wer given the IQ test. Of the 865, 134 scored below 80. However, only 64% of those students who scored less than 80 were recommended for placement in mentally retarded (MR) classrooms. Of the students placed in MR classrooms, 75% were Mexican-American and 22% were black. These figures are disproportionate given the distribution of boys and girls in the overall school population.

These results could be used to reinforce the view that the prior background of students, whether genetically (Jensen, 1969) or socioeconomically established

(Bereiter and Engleman, 1972; Coleman *et al.*, 1966), causes differences in school achievement. This classification was not, however, merely the result of poor, minority, and male students failing the IQ tests more often than their counterparts. Mercer found that students who had similar scores on an objective test were treated differentially by school personnel. The disproportionate number of poor, minority, and male students in the MR category suggests that mental retardation is not an inherent characteristic or quality of these individuals but a label affixed to the student by the institutional practices of the school.

Rist (1970) reported similar conclusions regarding labeling. He observed the progress of a group of children in an all-black St. Louis school from the first day of school through the school year, and continued to visit the classroom until the end of the second grade. Within the first few days of school, high performers were seated near the front, the middle group near the middle of the class, and the lowest group in the back. The distribution of students seemed to be based on characteristics associated with social class and from cultural background, that is, neatness, style of dress, and skin color. Children from one-parent households with an unemployed worker were more likely to be assigned to the low group. Rist also observed differences in treatment of the three groups. Those designated as "slow learners" were taught less frequently and subjected to more control-oriented behavior. Placement into the three groups took on a caste-like character. Once students were sorted into the groups, it was difficult to escape (see Eder, 1981).

Mehan *et al.* (1986) studied the special education referral system in a midsize California suburban school district. That school district, like other school districts that operated under the "Education for All Handicapped Students Act," established special education programs to serve the needs of students who meet its criteria. These programs included special classrooms, learning disabilities (LD) classrooms, and in-class remedial assistance. The special education referral process is an important aspect of this program. The Act directs school districts to establish a systematic procedure to assess and place students in the learning environments that best meet their special educational needs. In the school district they studied, the referral process was composed of a series of actions, including school-site committees, psychological assessment, parent conferences, and district-level committee meetings. The purpose of this process was to meet the needs of the handicapped student by developing an "individualized educational plan" (IEP).

The Act indicates that 12% of the school-aged population will be served by special education programs. The compulsory thrust of this law provides an incentive to search for, identify, and place students into special education programs, to meet mandated quotas. The legal requirement to search for special students is buttressed by financial incentives. School districts are provided funds from state and federal sources for each student in regular classrooms and a greater amount of money for students in special education programs. They receive more money for students in LD classrooms, and still more funding for students in "whole day" programs on a sliding scale.

The number of students already assigned to special education programs eliminated other options from consideration, whereas programs that were "open" and had not reached the legally mandated quota remained subject to consideration. Vagaries in the school calendar influenced the consideration of placement options. The district operated on a "year round" schedule. Instead of conducting classes from September until June, and designating the summer months as vacation, a staggered schedule of classes and vacations was maintained. Because of this segregated schedule, regular and special education teachers who were to cooperate in the education of certain students often found themselves on incompatible track schedules. This incompatibility of schedules eliminated certain placement options from consideration.

These legal, fiscal, and practical constraints have an influence on educational placement, IEPs, and students' identities. Educational placements are not decided, and IEPs are not solely written, on the basis of students' educational needs. These actions are taken based on an interlocking of these issues and such factors as space and money available. It means that students' identities are constructed by the institutional practices of the school. Thus, the designation "handicapped student" is as much a product of the school calendar, the demographic characteristics of the school population, and other features of the social organization of the school as it is a response to some inherent characteristics of the student.

These studies of the multicultural schools' sorting practices are important because they explore the schools' contribution to students' access to an academic curriculum that influences later life options. Yet, these studies leave many questions unanswered. For example, how are students placed in one track rather than another, for example, the college-prep track versus a general or commercial track? The "contest mobility system" assumed to operate in United States schools would suggest that students have considerable influence over track placement. Students would move to different levels by choice, constrained only by ability and effort. The structural considerations involved in tracking in the multicultural environment are, however, more complex. Institutional decisions and sorting practices result in the internal stratification of students in the multicultural school along racial, ethnic, and socioeconomic lines. It is our hypothesis that these sorting practices may assume even more importance in the desegregated setting, where racial and cultural factors directly influence educational policies and decision-making (see also Longshore and Prager, 1985). Coalitions formed across subgroups of students when more than one minority group is present in the multicultural setting are influenced by the structure of school sorting practices.

We may also infer that the intergroup contact among students in desegregated settings cannot be treated as a matter of free choice in an isolated environment.

5. MINORITY EDUCATION IN CROSS-CULTURAL SETTINGS

The previous section has emphasized the variety of social functions that schooling in desegregated and multicultural settings serves beyond educational instruction. Although desegregation has a specific legal definition in United States schools, the social organization of multicultural schooling may productively be examined in a comparative perspective as a larger phenomenon. Placing United States desegregation in a broader perspective is the topic of this section. Cross-cultural studies focus attention on more universal patterns of stratification common to several societies.

Comparative data on the Zambian school system and the treatment of West Indians and other minorities in the British school system (Ogbu, 1978) suggest that employment discrimination, impoverishment, and rapid but uneven techno-economic development are worldwide factors that influence the increasing isolation of minority groups in modern educational systems. An overview of the social conditions and economic strategies that appear to hold constant across these cases would broaden the theoretical scope and methodological effectiveness of United States desegregation research. Ultimately, such a task requires an important conceptual shift in desegregation research toward an analysis of the impact of educational stratification on the social and political inclusion of marginal groups on a global scale.

In his study of West Indians in Britain, Ogbu (1978) noted patterns of tracking and internal segregation similar to those already cited for United States cases. According to a 1973 parliamentary report cited by Ogbu, 70% of the 5,500 immigrant students placed in special schools for the educationally handicapped were West Indians. Although the percentage of West Indian students in classes and schools for the retarded was low (only 7%) nationwide, these children constituted 60% to 70% of the students placed in schools for the educationally subnormal in certain sections of London. The use of a creole dialect with differential exposure to standard English was cited as a major reason for the poor performance of West Indian pupils on standardized tests.

Two policies were introduced to handle these problems of acculturation and educational lag: a quota system requiring the dispersal of immigrant children in excess of 33% of the school population prior to 1965, and remedial education programs for immigrants first instituted in 1965. Prior to 1962, a *laissez-faire* attitude was taken toward the integration of West Indian students into normal schools. With the legal restriction of immigration in the 1960s, remedial education programs became a major solution to the difficulties encountered in mixed schools. Ogbu (1978) proposed that the ceiling on West Indian employment in Britain has operated as a negative incentive with respect to school performance. Educational policy has mirrored the problems of a pluralizing urban society. The result has been resegregation through educational policy in a context where formal racial and ethnic barriers were not previously enforced. It is important to note that differences in language mastery were critical to the labeling and tracking of West Indian students into British remedial programs.

In many developing countries, language and ethnicity are also the locus of major educational and policy decisions. Education is viewed not only as a resource for job training but also as a vehicle for the creation of national identity and political integration. For instance, in Zambia where English is the official language, children are exposed to at least one of seven nationally recognized African dialects in the primary school setting (Kashoki, 1977).[7] As a result of the high geographic mobility and urban-rural migration rates after Zambian independence, the vernacular language of instruction is not necessarily the child's mother tongue. Furthermore, the diverse language of northern and southern Zambia are not mutually intelligible. In such a situation, the phenomena of diglossia and triglossia develop. The child is called upon to use English in classes related to mathematics, science, and technology and an official vernacular language in other instructional settings. In still other settings with friends, the child may use a third shared language. Serpell (1976) noted that even at the university level with a minimum of 8 years of formal instruction in English, Zambian students chose to converse with close friends in a language other than English. Public learning and private discourse appear to occur in separate cultural domains. This finding mirrors the separation of academic and social activities that was found among blacks and whites in desegregated schools. Sociolinguistic research has demonstrated that code switching operates as a bridge between these public and private domains (Gumperz and Hernandez, 1971).

Multilingual instructional policies in Zambia serve much the same purpose as school desegregation mandates in the United States. Differences of ethnicity and status in a pluralizing society are believed to be minimized when more than one language is offered. In fact, however, those students who speak English at home are socialized to succeed in a formal educational setting where that language

[7]Kashoki (1977) tested over 600 school children on their comprehension of seven Zambian vernacular languages. His aim was to discover the extent of between-language communication possible based on knowledge of one's own mother tongue. He found little comprehension of the Lozi and Tonga languages among those who were not native speakers. This finding suggests that lessons and conversations conducted in these languages would virtually exclude other students and could result in a linguistically stratified classroom if these languages were to be officially adopted.

is dominant. One the other hand, a student who speaks neither the accepted vernacular lingua franca nor English at home is at a distinct disadvantage. Serpell (1976) compared the latter situation to that of the black American working-class student with sporadic exposure to the use of standard English outside of the classroom.

Cognitive studies of test performance in West Africa (Cole *et al.*, 1971; Price-Williams, 1962) and Zambia (Deregowski and Serpell, 1971) demonstrate that exposure to European languages introduces patterns of conceptual ordering and recall that are not explicit in some African languages. For example, Greenfield's experiments among Senegalese and French students (Greenfield *et al.*, 1966) found that certain superordinate categories denoting color and shape were absent from the Wolof language. Therefore, monolingual Wolof-speaking children asked to sort objects in terms of color and shape had more difficulty than French students and bilingual Wolof students. Clearly, these results are, in part, artifacts of the sorting test. However, they are also predictors of the future performance of children who have not mastered French in a Western-oriented educational system. In this context, language is linked to ethnicity and social class and operates as a touchstone for formal school performance.[8]

Both the West Indian and African examples emphasize the interplay of language and ethnicity in the classroom. The vernacular language used to establish the student's personal identity is a hindrance in the public domain of academic performance. Disparities in language use and performance are invoked in the school structure to isolate students in terms of manifest abilities and ethnicity. In the British case, the weight of subtle linguistic differences is coupled with racial and regional origins to track students into special classes and separate schools. Success in the Zambian case is predicated on the student's mastery of English and ability to use and switch to alternative language codes in the appropriate contexts. The vernacular language is used to introduce the child to schooling and to support the political structure of a multicultural society. The vernacular alone, however, is increasingly less useful at the higher rungs of educational attainment where English use and the mastery of diglossia or even triglossia become essential. These cross-cultural studies emphasize the importance of examining how multicultural settings, including desegregated schools, either promote or discourage the bicultural and bilingual adaptations of minority students. Available social psychological data on intergroup contact in United States desegregated settings barely touch on this problem.

---

[8]Cole *et al.* (1971) showed that nonliterate Kpelle subjects demonstrate significantly different classificatory and recall abilities than literate school children trained in English. A larger array of conceptual categories and a greater ability to recall objects in these categories were demonstrated by the literate, English-speaking subjects.

6. POLICY IMPLICATIONS OF THE INTERACTIONAL DATA ON SCHOOL DESEGREGATION

Ten years ago, in reviewing the sociological literature on desegregation, Pettigrew and Back (1971, p. 120) proposed "that a great upsurge of research activity directed at desegregation will be forthcoming in the 1970s." Indeed, although such studies have been abundant, their impact is still subject to question. The studies of status scoring (see Yarrow, 1958) begin in the late 1950s and research on attitude change have become increasingly sophisticated and elegant in terms of modeling procedures and methodology. In fact, large segments of the technical social psychological literature on desegregation are not opaque enough to be inaccessible to most legal experts, school administrators, and teachers. Policy technocrats and social scientists are needed to decode what participants see taking place in their own classrooms.

Although it may be possible to measure more effectively academic and task performance, the influence of peer contact, and the internal dynamics of power coalitions, surprisingly little attention has been devoted to the experience of desegregation and the child's description of the desegregated setting. Given the time factor, longitudinal studies of desegregation processes are still relatively rare (see Crain, 1968, and Pettigrew and Back, 1971).[9] Multicultural schools that have evolved in the 1970s as a result of desegregation rulings and the increased occupational and geographic mobility of minorities are also important settings for testing assumptions about interaction across racial and ethnic groups.

A major problem with microanalytic studies in social psychology is a tendency to treat the school and the classroom as ideal laboratories for studying interaction and academic performance. The school, however, is an environment shaped by policy decisions, community reactions, and cultural preconceptions that lie beyond its walls. The conditions of cooperation and conflict generated within the school often do not meet the minimum requirements for intergroup cooperation anywhere. In such settings, alienation, apathy, and mutual distrust may develop as socially acceptable strategies for handling desegregation (Riordan, 1976). More often, however, the subgroups involved in the desegregated settings subtly separate themselves and are structurally separated by tracking, performance measures, and cultural history. The irony of multicultural programs honoring each subgroup's activities within the school is to be found in the

---

[9]Pettigrew and Back (1971) emphasized that large-scale longitudinal studies of desegregation have been rare due to limited funding and heated public controversy over the issue of desegregation. Instead, small-scale case studies and low-budget reports on single communities have emerged, without an effort to draw comparative conclusions that extend across several time periods. The focus on measuring peer contact in single school settings without introducing comparative data or studying the impact of policy changes suggests major shortcomings in much of the research on school desegregation.

knowledge that these groups do not share an equal social and economic status outside of the school.

Researchers who have focused on various forms of face-to-face interaction in schools have been somewhat successful in demonstrating that schools are not simply passive vehicles through which students move on their way to predetermined positions in the social order. The exuberance of this position, however, can have unfortunate, albeit unintended, consequences for future research. Microethnographic studies have included statements like: "classroom events are assembled in the interaction among participants," "educational test results emerge in the interaction between tester and student," and "students' identities are interactionally constructed." Although they call into question a static view of schools as social institutions, such statements leave room for the conclusion that social structures are entirely interactional productions. Discussions of the culture of the classroom and the acquisition of cultural knowledge and communicative competence associated with it can lead to the inaccurate interpretation that school is autonomous from the society in which it functions.

In reviewing desegregation laws on the macro level, Elmore (1980) distinguished between two forms of policy implementation: the regulatory approach, in which control is exercised from the top (i.e., from the Federal government), and the programmatic view, in which control is exercised locally.[10] The former entails hierarchical control over policy; the latter involves delegated local control over policy. Desegregation laws in the United States have been prime examples of hierarchically controlled policies. Projected changes in policies toward desegregation at the federal level also raise serious questions for the prospects of sociological research. Over a decade ago, Pettigrew and Back (1971, pp. 105–106) isolated three factors that continue to dilute the potential impact of sociological studies of desegregation. (a) the funds for work in this "controversial" area; (b) an atmosphere of resistance to racial change by stern segregationists, and (c) a sociological bias in race relations toward studying the static and segregation-maintaining elements, rather than the dynamic, desegregation-impelling features.

Social scientists are still faced with the same challenges to the scope and relevance of their work. These problems are compounded in the 1980s by the thrust of the "new Federalism" away from civil rights initiatives and large-scale social research. Prevailing policy in the 1980s seems to be aimed at removing the Federal government's jurisdiction in local affairs. The current trend has broad implications for desegregation efforts and the influence of desegregation research at the local level. On the one hand, it provides local agencies with greater freedom

---

[10]Elmore (1980) distinguished between federal- and local-level initiatives in desegregation policy. The shift in control to the local level requires further comparative studies of the relationship between schools and political forces in the larger community.

and flexibility in deciding how to achieve goals of racial balance and equality of education. On the other hand, the call for greater autonomy can become an excuse for inaction.

7. PROSPECTS FOR FUTURE INVESTIGATION

Educational research reflects the either/or dichotomy long established in Western scientific thinking. We have tacitly retained this way of thinking in our brief review of studies that point to the active role that school plays in the lives of students. In so doing, we may allude to a number of apparently mutually exclusive categories: "schools do make a difference," "schools don't make a difference;" "schools are active," "schools are passive;" "research inside schools," and "research outside of schools."

These dualisms are a consequence of the more general distinction between macro and micro studies in sociology (see Knorr-Cetina and Cicourel, 1981). In the former, social structure is treated as a stable entity, and desegregation is viewed as the product of legal mandates. In the latter, insofar as it is said to exist, the school's structure evidenced in sorting practices are treated as a construction that emerges in interaction. Neither of these approaches, however, accepts the existence or the inclusion of the opposite in the foundation of its analytic design.

Davis and Moore (1945) and Parsons (1959) have established a clear relationship between school and society. In so doing, they uncritically accept the autonomy of each and the meaning of the connection between the two. Coleman *et al.* (1966), Jencks *et al.* (1972), and Rubin (1972) have acknowledged a relationship between school and society while criticizing the noticeable fact of inequality in schooling for minority groups. They view this connection as part of a unidirectional causal argument that social-class background prefigures experiences both in and out of school. Although these theories acknowledge a school-and-society relationship, none of them explicitly expresses the substantive manner in which institutionalized forms of inequality are reflected in the interaction across racial and cultural groups. We must do more than appeal to factors such as the class-background characteristics of students, group stereotypes, and the structure of class relationships in society, when making claims about the consequences of schooling for students' careers.

As a first step in collapsing the structure–interaction dualism, we must show how institutional arrangements operate and are worked out in the day-to-day activities of educators in the arena of schooling. A second step in collapsing the structure–interaction dualism involves insuring that close scrutiny of school and classroom subunits does not result in treating them as autonomous configurations in research. Classrooms and other subunits of the school are influenced by the bureaucratic organization of the school and the society of which they are a part. Administrative policy concerning curriculum content, textbook choices, teaching methods, and testing practices established by school boards and state departments of education impinge on educational practice in the classroom. The demands of the economy for a technically trained, literate, and compliant labor force make the school responsive to external forces. Furthermore, parents, having been to school themselves, voice opinions about how their children should be educated.

It is this relationship between schooling and society that must become a clearer focus of research on desegregated settings. If there is a correspondence between the organization of society and the organization of schools (Bernstein, 1981), social scientists need to study interactional mechanisms by which the structures of class and intercultural relations in society are reflected in educator–pupil relations. Schooling is the acquisition and transmission of specific cultural practices and information. Consequently, how the specific institutions of schooling, including the workings of the curriculum, are organized to transmit this "cultural capital" across generations should become a topic of inquiry.

To be more specific, it seems to us that it should be possible to conduct comparative studies of schooling in relationship to their communities and the policies that we have outlined. To do so, we would start with participants' definitions of the educational situation in desegregated schools. We would ask educators and policymakers at federal, state, and local levels to identify different types of schools and districts, for example, those that are "effectively integrated," "recently desegregated," "starting to desegregate," and "racially isolated." With these members' definitions in hand, we would assign teams of researchers to such schools to examine their educational practices. The goal would be to discover what makes some schools effective and others not. Although this investigation would have an observational base, we would certainly not recommend limiting observations to classroom practices. The allocation of funds and personnel and the interplay between local, district, county, state, and federal levels would be essential aspects in the analysis. Here the goal would be to locate and highlight schools that have accomplished integration successfully. Thus, the structural arrangements and interactional patterns of schools that promote desegregation or perhaps resegregation can be identified as guides for future action.

We suggest that projected work on desegregation become more sensitive to the fact that social structure and school structure do not exist in a simple technical relationship but are linked by practical operations performed by individuals and groups with specific interests. When we realize that social structure is both a product and a process of human activity, three questions arise. Whose human activity? For what purpose? What spirit defines, shapes, and controls the conditions of human activity? It is our recommendation that a significant portion of the future research on desegregation be aimed at uncovering the structures of inequality that appear in the larger society and are perpetuated and reproduced by sorting practices and interactional decisions in the desegregated school setting.

REFERENCES

Bereiter, K., and Engleman, S. *Teaching the Disadvantaged Child in the Preschool.* Englewood Cliffs, NJ: Prentice Hall, 1972.
Bernstein, B. Elaborated and restricted codes: Their social origins and some consequences. *American Anthropologist*, 1964, *66* (Special Issue), 55–69.
Bernstein, B. Social class, language, and socialization. In P. Giglioli (Ed.), *Language and Social Context*. Harmondsworth: Penguin Books, 1972.
Bernstein, B. Class and pedagogies: Visible and invisible. *Educational Studies*, 1975, *1*, 23–41.
Bernstein, B. Codes, modalities and the process of cultural reproduction. *Language in Society*, 1981, *10*, 327–363.
Bourdieu, P., and Passeron, J. *Reproduction in Education, Society, and Culture*. Beverly Hills, CA: Sage Publications, 1977.
Bowles, S., and Gintis, H. *Schooling in Capitalist America*. New York: Basic Books, 1976.
Bremme, D., and Erickson, F. Relations among verbal and nonverbal classroom behaviors. *Theory and Practice*, 1977, *16*, 153–161.
Bullock, C., and Braxton, M. The coming of school desegregation: Before and after study of student perceptions. *Social Science Quarterly*, 1973, *54*, 132–138.
Cicourel, A., Jennings, K., Jennings, S., Leiler, K., Mackay, R., Mehan, H., and Roth, D. *Language Use and School Performance*. New York: Academic Press, 1974.
Cicourel, A., and Kitsuse, J. *Educational Decision Makers*. Indianapolis, IN: Bobbs-Merrill, 1963.
Cole, M., Gay, J., Glick, J., and Sharp, D. *The Cultural Context of Learning and Thinking: An Experimental Anthropology*. New York: Basic Books, 1971.
Coleman, J., Campbell, E., Hobson, C., McPartland, J., Mood, A., Weinfield, F., and York, R. *Equality of Educational Opportunity*. Washington, DC: U.S. Government Printing Office, 1966.
Coleman, J., Kelly, S., and Moore, J. *Trends in School Desegregation, 1968–1973*. Washington, DC: The Urban Institute, 1975.
Crain, R. *The Politics of School Desegregation*. Chicago, IL: Aldine, 1968.
Cramer, M. Factors related to willingness to experience desegregation among students in segregated schools. *Social Science Quarterly*, 1968, *49*, 684–696.
Davis, K., and Moore, W. Some principles of stratification. *American Sociological Review*, 1945, *10*, 242–249.
Deregowski, J., and Serpell, R. Performance on a sorting task: A cross-cultural experiment. *International Journal of Psychology*, 1971, *6*, 273–281.
Drury, D. Black self-esteem and desegregated schools. *Sociology of Education*, 1980, *53*, 88–103.
Eder, D. Difference in communicative styles across ability groups. In L. Wilkinson (Ed.), *Communicating in the Classroom*. New York: Academic Press, 1981.
Elmore, R. *Complexity and Control*. Washington, DC: U.S. Department of Education, National Institute of Education, 1980.
Erickson, F. Gatekeeping and the melting pot. *Harvard Educational Review*, 1975, *45*, 44–70.
Erickson, F. and Shultz, S. *The Counselor as Gatekeeper*. New York: Academic Press, 1982.
Garfinkel, H. *Studies in Ethnomethodology*. Englewood Cliffs, NJ: Prentice-Hall, 1967.
Goffman, E. *Stigma*. Englewood Cliffs, NJ: Prentice-Hall, 1963.
Goffman, E. *Forms of Talk*. Philadelphia, PA: University of Pennsylvania Press, 1981.
Greenfield, P., Reich, L., and Olver, R. On culture and equivalence: II. In J. Bruner, R. Olver, and P. M. Greenfield (Eds.), *Studies in Cognitive Growth*. New York: Wiley, 1966.

Gumperz, J. with Hernandez, E. Bilingualism, Bidialectalism, and Classroom Interaction. In J. Gumperz *Language in Social Groups*. Stanford, CA: Stanford University Press, 1971.

Gumperz, J., and Herasmichuk, E. The conversational analysis of meaning: A study of classroom interaction. In M. Sanchez and B. Blout (Eds.), *Sociocultural Dimensions of Language Use*. New York: Academic Press, 1975.

Hanna, J. Public social policy and the children's world: Implications of ethnographic research for desegregated schooling. In G. Spindler (Ed.), *Doing the Ethnography of Schooling: Educational Anthropology in Action*. New York: Holt, Rinehart, and Winston, 1982.

Hollingshead, A. *Elmstown's Youth*. New York: Wiley, 1949.

Jacobson, C. Separation, integrationism, and avoidance among black, white, and Latin adolescents. *Social Forces*, 1977, *55*, 1011–1027.

Jencks, C., Smith, M., Adand, H., Bane, M., Cohen, D., Gintis, H., Heyns, B., and Michelson, S. *Inequality: A Reassessment of the Effect of Family and Schooling in America*. New York: Basic Books, 1972.

Jensen, A. How much can we boost IQ and scholastic achievement? *Harvard Educational Review*, 1969, *39*, 1–123.

Jules-Rosette, B. Grass-roots ecumenism: Religious and social cooperation in two African churches. *African Social Research*, 1977, *23*, 185–216.

Kashoki, M. Between-language communication in Zambia, *Lingua*, 1977, *41*, 145–168.

Knorr-Cetina, K., and Cicourel, A. *Advances in Social Theory and Methodology*. London: Routledge, Kegan, Paul, 1981.

Labov, W. The logic of nonstandard English. In P. Giglioli (Ed.), *Language and Social Context*. Harmondsworth: Penguin Books, 1972.

Labov, W., and Robins, C. A note on the relation of reading failure to peer-group status in urban ghettos. *Florida FL Reporter*, 1969, *7*, 54–57.

Lewis, R., and St. John, N. Contribution of cross-racial friendship to minority group achievement in desegregated classrooms. *Sociometry*, 1974, *37*, 79–91.

Longshore, D., & Prager, J. The impact of school desegregation: A situational analysis. In R. Turner (Ed.), *Annual Review of Sociology* (Vol. 11). Palo Alto, CA: Annual Reviews, 1985.

McDermott, R. *Kids Make Sense*. Unpublished doctoral dissertation, Sanford University, 1976.

McDermott, R. Social relations as contexts for learning in school. *Harvard Educational Review*, 1977, *47*, 198–213.

McDermott, R., Gospodinoff, K., and Aron, J. Criteria for an ethnographically adequate description of concerted activities and their contexts. *Semiotica*, 1978, *24*, 245–275.

Mehan, H. Structuring school structure. *Harvard Educational Review*, 1978, *48*, 32–64.

Mehan, H. *Learning Lessons*. Cambridge, MA: Harvard University Press, 1979.

Mehan, H., Hertweek, A., and Meihls, J. *Handicapping the Handicapped*. Stanford: Stanford University Press, 1986.

Mercer, J. *Labeling the Mentally Retarded*. Berkeley, CA: University of California Press, 1974.

Metz, M. *Classrooms and Corridors: The Crisis of Authority in Desegregated Secondary Schools*. Berkeley, CA: University of California Press, 1978.

Mischel, W., and Staub, E. Effects of expectancy on working and waiting for larger rewards. *Journal of Personality and Social Psychology*, 1965, *2*, 625–633.

National Institute of Education. *The Desegregation Literature: A Critical Appraisal*. Washington, DC: U.S. Department of Health, Education and Welfare, 1976.

National Institute of Education. *School Desegregation: A Report of State and Federal Administrative Activity*. Washington, DC: U.S. Department of Health, Education, and Welfare, 1977a.

National Institute of Education. *School Desegregation in Metropolitan Areas*. Washington, DC: U.S. Department of Health, Education, and Welfare, 1977b.

Ogbu, J. *Minority Education and Caste: The American System in Cross-Cultural Perspective*. New York: Academic Press, 1978.

Ogbu, J. *Cultural-ecological context of classroom interaction.* Paper presented at the Annual Meetings of the American Educational Research Association, April, 1981, Los Angeles, California.

Parsons, T. The school as a social system. *Harvard Educational Review*, 1959, *29*, 297–318.

Patchen, M., Hoffman, G., and Davidson, J. Interracial perceptions among high school students. *Sociometry*, 1976, *39*, 341–354.

Patchen, M., Davidson, J., Hoffman, G., and Brown, W. Determinants of interracial behavior and opinion change. *Sociology of Education*, 1977, *50*, 55–75.

Patchen, M., Hoffman, G., and Brown, W. Academic performance of black high school students under different conditions of contact with white peers. *Sociology of Education*, 1980, *53*, 33–51.

Pettigrew, T. The negro and education: Problems and proposals. In I. Katz and P. Gurin (Eds.), *Race and the Social Sciences.* New York: Basic Books, 1969.

Pettigrew, T. with Back, K. Sociology in the desegregation process: Its use and disuse. In T. Pettigrew (Ed.), *Racially Separate or Together?* New York: McGraw-Hill Books, 1971.

Philips, S. Participant structures and communicative competence: Warm Spring children in community and classroom. In C. Cazden, D. Hymes, and V. John (Eds.), *Functions of Language in the Classroom.* New York: Columbia University Press, 1972.

Price-Williams, D. Abstract and concrete modes of classification in a primitive society. *British Journal of Educational Psychology*, 1962, *32*, 50–61.

Riordan, R. *The conditions and effects of equal-status contact: A critical review.* Paper presented at the Annual Meetings of the American Sociological Association, September,1975.

Riordan, R. Introduction. In *Education, Participation, and Power: Essays in Theory and Practice.* Cambridge, MA: Harvard Educational Review, Reprint Series No. 10, 1976.

Rist, R. Student social class and teacher expectations: The self-fulfilling prophecy in ghetto education. *Harvard Educational Review*, 1970, *40*(3), 411–451.

Rist, R. *The Urban School: A Factory for Failure.* Cambridge, MA: M.I.T. Press, 1973.

Rist, R. (Ed.), *Desegregated Schools: Appraisals of an Experiment.* New York: Academic Press, 1979.

Rosenbaum, J. *Making Inequality.* New York: Wiley, 1976.

Rubin, L. *Busing and Backlash.* Berkeley, CA: University of California Press, 1972.

St. John, N. *School Desegregation: Outcomes for Children.* New York: Wiley, 1975.

St. John, N., and Lewis, R. Race and social structure in the elementary classroom. *Sociology of Education*, 1975, *48*, 346–368.

Schofield, J. The impact of positively structured contact on intergroup behavior: Does it last under adverse conditions? *Social Psychology Quarterly*, 1979, *42*(3), 280–284.

Schofield, J. W. *Black and White in School.* New York: Praeger, 1982.

Serpell, R. *Culture's Influence on Behavior.* London: Metheren, 1976.

Wax, M. (Ed.). *Within These Schools* (Project Report, NIE-G-789-0046). Washington, DC: National Institute of Education, 1979.

Yarrow, M. (Ed.). Interpersonal dynamics in a desegregation process. *Journal of Social Issues*, 1958, *38*, 3–63.

The Research Agenda

New Directions for Desegregation Studies

J. MILTON YINGER

In studying the chapters in this book and discussing them, I have kept several questions in mind. I believe the reader of this volume who has intellectual and policy interests ought to find answers (sometimes indirect) or clearly stated, researchable propositions, related to the following questions.

What do we know reasonably well, from the "obvious" to the counterintuitive, about school desegregation? What remains especially problematic?

Which factors encourage, which ones discourage, the use of what we know in specific contexts and under two different conditions: (a) when nearly everyone agrees on the goals to be sought, and (b) when there are competing and conflicting goals? The former are technical and resource questions; the latter are social problems. Although they are often linked, failure to distinguish them can lead to poor understanding of desegregation settings and to poor choice of policies.

Going further into the policy domain, what do we know about ways to encourage the use for humane purposes of what is known, under conditions (a) and (b)?

A question not much discussed, but which, just by the asking, may help us keep our topic in perspective, relates to the widest context: Why did desegregation begin? It has touched every part of society, not just the schools, as a result of long-run secular changes. Ralph McGill once remarked that desegregation began with the boll weevil—a wonderful way of noting that changes

J. MILTON YINGER • Department of Sociology and Anthropology, Oberlin College, Oberlin, OH 44074.

affecting the cotton economy and Southern agriculture generally were trans-
forming racial relations. These changes were closely related to demographic
trends, to the size and location of minority populations, and to the growth of a
stable urban working class and a middle class among minority groups. One could
add many other factors: World War II, the collapse of empires, the appearance
of activist groups and leaders—these are among the forces that indirectly or
directly shaped the context within which desegregation was set in motion.

In advancing the art of inquiry in school desegregation research, few will
disagree, I believe, with the emphasis in these papers on the need for ethnographic
and quantitative survey studies. They are not only complementary, they can be
highly interactive. Ethnographic studies are best designed to uncover the critical
variables and the structures of interaction in which they occur, whereas survey
research can examine the significance of those variables in a wide range of
carefully sampled populations. Only by reciprocally setting the strengths of some
studies against the weaknesses of others can we move toward definitive findings.

Nor is there likely to be much disagreement, at least in principle, on the
need for both micro and macro perspectives. The limits of these terms are not
self-evident, because what is macro in one context—for example, the school
system of a community when one is focusing on individual students—is micro
in another context—for example, the study of the impact of federal policy or
demographic trends on particular school systems. The task, whatever the appropriate boundary in a given study, is to see their interdependence. The influence
of neither can be identified without reference to the other, for we are dealing
with "simultaneous equations," each containing unknowns. The equations can
be solved, to continue with this figure of speech, only together (J. M. Yinger,
1965). In an important application of the micro-macro unit, Mischel, Rosenberg,
and others speak of the need to study the interaction of personal tendencies and
situations, the *field* context of desegregation. We can visualize the field, in its
simplest terms, by use of Figure 1.

The likelihood of a given action, Figure 1 suggests, depends not on the
strength of individual inclination alone nor on situational opportunities and costs
alone, but on the conjunction of a certain set of inclinations, positive or negative,
with a set of opportunities or costs. Desegregation will not proceed if individuals
ready for it in terms of most of their attitudes and skills interact in a school
setting poorly designed to promote it. Oppositely, if school districts are desegregated, but little attention is paid to individual attitudes and skills or to interpersonal encounters within the desegregated setting, the outcomes are likely to
be disappointing. Neither theory nor policy can avoid the truth of the old adage:
No chain is stronger than its weakest link.

The need to study individual tendencies and situational influences as interacting parts of a single field is emphasized in the extensive literature that examines
the relationship of attitudes to behavior. (For recent reviews and commentaries

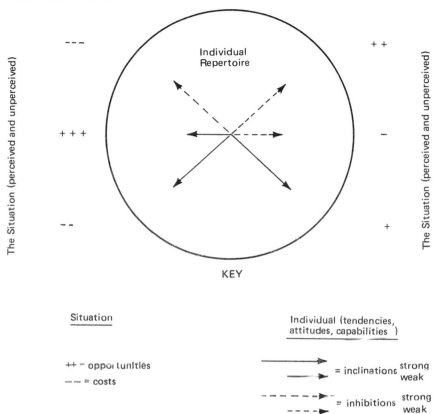

Figure 1. The field context of desegregation

see Eagly and Himmelfarb, 1978; Fishbein and Ajzen, 1975; Hill, 1981; Schuman and Johnson, 1977; and the papers by Schuman, Fishbein, Maynes, and Kelman in Yinger and Cutler, 1978.) It is well established that attitudes toward school and housing desegregation have become much more tolerant in the United States in the last quarter century (Smith, 1981), but it is equally well established that resistance to desegregation has sometimes been strong. Does this simply reflect the fact that those who have remained intolerant are resisting? Or is there a difference between generalized attitudes and those that are activated in particular contexts? Indeed, is it sometimes true that behavioral changes, sometimes under compulsion, are followed by attitudinal change that helps to reestablish some consistency (Jacobson, 1978)? These questions can be answered only in a field-theoretical context.

It is vital that we learn the lesson emphasized by Mischel that children's "traits" do not determine their behavior. Feelings of helplessness, for example, are expressed in particular situations, some of which may confirm and strengthen the feeling, others of which may furnish different interpretations and activate different tendencies. The need to combine individual tendencies and the situations within which they are expressed into a single unit of analysis has been recognized for several decades in psychology and sociology (Coutu, 1949; Levin, 1935; and, applied directly to intergroup relations, Simpson and Yinger, 1953), but attention to it keeps fading. Mischel brings it into the foreground. Such a pattern as "delay of gratification" he notes, is not simply an individual trait. It can be expressed in different ways and with different intensities as contexts vary.

1. THE ROOTS OF SEGREGATION

To understand school desegregation, we must understand school segregation—the forces that created and the forces that sustain it. These range from the institutional structures of power to demographic trends, to the legal and customary processes of school decision making, to parental ambitions and attitudes, to the tendencies of students and teachers. Such factors as these are highly interactive; they can be understood only as part of a field of forces.

Several authors have emphasized different factors in the system of segregation, even while discussing desegregation. Ogbu's distinction between immigrant and subordinate groups rests on his argument (Ogbu, 1978) that schools and families have collaborated to socialize black children to the expectation of failure or little social mobility. In so doing, they simply reflect, and seek to adapt to, an occupational system that needs a corps of unskilled—and nearly powerless—workers. We need to ask whether public policies with respect to the education of the children of undocumented workers and of refugees have the same effects. Historical, demographic, and attitudinal influences have left the door open for immigrant groups, but not for the subordinate groups. Gutman has developed a similar theme, although he speaks of more impersonal forces. Relatively recent patterns of migration reflecting economic changes, not the drag of history, have been, in effect, a new Enclosure Movement. "Peasants" have been driven off the land at a time when the lower rungs of the skill ladder in the urban occupational system have been cut away. Gutman observed (1977, pp. 468–469) that "neither the economy nor those who dominate the political decision-making process have as a priority the creation of useful work for those driven in such great numbers from the land." The distinction Suttles makes between insiders and outsiders in our national myths is similar to the immigrant–subordinate contrast drawn by Ogbu. Some new groups are incorporated into insider status by the historical reconstruction of the national myth.

These are valuable concepts, if we take them, not as statements of hard reality, but as analytic contrasts. If we treat *immigrant* and *subordinate* or *insider* and *outsider* as points on a scale, we are led to ask: What conditions affect placement on the scale? What conditions cause or permit changes? And, from the perspective of an interest in school desegregation, what structural and symbolic barriers are identified by study of these concepts? How does placement in one or another of these categories influence preparation for, and attitudes toward, desegregation? How does the great diversity in subordinate or outsider groups— in class, occupation, family experience, and individual tendency—qualify the impact of the labor market and the prevailing national myths?

The temptation is strong to explain segregation, with its accompanying disadvantages, as a result of either the structures of power or the prejudices and other attitudes of individuals. Even together these are inadequate. To some degree segregation is the unintended and unwanted consequence of action that may temporarily seem to serve an individual purpose but that, in the long run, injures individual purposes and collective interests—the long-observed "tragedy of the Commons" or, in more current terms, the problem of the critical mass.

> In some schools, the white pupils are being withdrawn because there are too few white pupils; as they leave, white pupils become fewer so that even those who didn't mind yesterday's ratio will leave at today's ratio, leaving behind still fewer, who may leave tomorrow. (Schelling, 1978, pp. 93–94)

In his chapter, Granovetter skillfully illustrates this tipping process to emphasize that a high level of segregation may occur even though few persons, at first, wanted it. To explain this result by reference to individual motives is often wrong. It is the interplay of attitudes and the ways they are activated by the initial distribution that is crucial. Each parent, pressing hard for the best school for his or her own child, may take actions that alongside other parents' actions collectively have the opposite result from the one sought.

In *Fatal Remedies*, Sieber discusses a disheartreningly long list of such unanticipated negative consequences. We know little about how to anticipate the unanticipated. It is easy to agree with Sieber's recommendation that "the same measures be taken to assess the negative outcomes of social interventions as are increasingly taken to assess the second- or third-order consequences of new technologies" (1981, p. 216). But anticipation is not enough. We need research on how to prevent these self-defeating actions. It is a good start to remember, with Cooley, that most of the harm in the world is done with the elbows, not the fists (he was not anticipating current basketball styles), that we bump and injure without intending to. Knowledge alone will not be persuasive; it must be accompanied by ability and willingness to take a long view, which in turn requires confidence in the system. We need research on what might be called "*stopper variables*"—new factors that are introduced into a system to prevent tipping from continuing to its "logical" conclusion of resegregation or desegregation without integration. These stoppers might include different patterns of reward that change parental and student priorities—superior curricula, payments to stay in school, credits toward college expenses, for example. The tipping process is "inevitable" only if no new elements are added to the system within which it has begun.

Stoppers that prevent or inhibit segregative actions are needed as well as those that facilitate integrative actions. Thus, policies indicating that there are no longer all-white communities to which prejudiced persons can escape—based, for example, on scattered subsidized housing—could help to block the tipping process (J. Yinger, 1980).

2. SHARED AND COMPETING GOALS OF DESEGREGATION

We need, in my judgment, much more research on the goals of desegregation for various groups and study of the extent to which they are shared. There is probably substantial agreement on the goals of better school performance, improved self-esteem, continuance in school, and reduced prejudice. The desirability of more interracial and interethnic contact, however, or full equality in post-school access to jobs and other opportunities, may be less well agreed on. On the societal level, better use of human resources, reduced conflict and alienation, and greater justice are probably widely accepted as aims of desegregation, however diversely they may be defined. Whether desegregation should be within a basically pluralistic or a universalistic frame, however, is a subject of controversy.

Thus, we are confronted not simply with technical problems (how to do it), but also with social, moral, and political problems (whether to do it, to what degree, as well as how—for methods affect outcomes). If research is based on a limited technical definition, it will be inadequate. The social, moral, and political disagreements are seldom absolute; they are often due to different hierarchies and timetables. This opens opportunities for accommodation, but it does not transform them into simple questions of method.

Perhaps the most important disagreement involves the degree to which school desegregation should permit, perhaps even encourage, distinctive group identities or, on the other hand, should be color-blind and culture-blind (whose color? whose culture?) in an effort to maximize individual opportunities and societal gains. We are in need of research that helps us to understand which cultural differences, if any, can be allowed or even emphasized without a school being caught in the dilemma of pluralism versus performance.

2.1. Bilingualism and Desegregation

The most significant point at which the dilemma is revealed involves bilingualism and the associated biculturalism. Through the centuries, language supremacy and the "purity" of the dominant language have been focal points of struggle over power and over national or ethnic-group identity in many lands—in Germany, Turkey, Canada, India, and Malaysia, for example. The patterns of stratification are often clearly revealed, and reinforced, by variations in language and dialect. It is against this background that we should think about bilingualism in American schools.

Three policies, not usually clearly articulated, compete in the public arena.

1. Resist the growth of bilingual training in the schools. This is a one-language country, to everyone's advantage.

2. Recognize as a temporary fact that for some students, English is not the native language. Bilingual policy should be to create a bridge over into English.

3. Accept bilingualism as a fact of life in the United States and as an advantage to the country. Pluralism in language as in other cultural qualities is desirable. In areas where many persons are non-English speakers, other languages should be given some kind of official standing.

One could describe a number of variations on these three themes, but the brief comments may indicate the range. Since the Bilingual Education Act of 1968, indeed on a state and local basis for several years before then, official policy has approximated Statement 2. Agreement on goals, however, has not increased. Indeed, it may have decreased, as bilingual education has become a major civil rights issue among some groups even while resistance to it has also grown, as in Texas, Florida, and New Jersey (Burke, 1981). Part of the resistance is fiscal (several language groups may make claims), part is opposition to the separatism (pluralism to its supporters) that is involved, and part is based on educational grounds.

The educational and socioeconomic implications of bilingualism vary among societies, classes, age-groups, and groups of different sizes. In South Africa, a repressive regime supports education in tribal languages for those outside the major cities "to make sure that cultural pluralism and social stratification coincide" (Harrington, 1978, p. 2). In the United States, although Latino immigrants are switching to English at a rate similar to earlier groups (most speak English predominantly by the third generation), some native Spanish speakers "may be electing to bypass the process of acculturation and assimilation that turned previous immigrant groups into English-speaking Americans" (Nunis, 1981, p. 29), presumably to try to make sure that cultural pluralism and social stratification do *not* coincide.

In my view, the need for bilingual education is unquestionable. But it should be education that opens up opportunities rather than closing them. Those who speak a "non-state" language require training in the language of their intimacy and the language of their functional polity, as Joshua Fishman puts it. (Needless to say, those who speak the "state language" natively would also profit, and society would profit, if they learned a second language.)

In discussing bilingualism, it is important to remember that it is one thing to teach "English as a Second Language" (there are numerous ESL programs) by providing supplementary training in English. It is something else to teach bilingualism, on the premise that maintaining and improving competence in the first language is a goal complementary to the goal of mastering English.

Our interest here is on the effects of various language programs on desegregation and the various consequences that flow from desegregation. Or, to put the issue negatively: To what degree do language differences and different competencies in English stand as barriers to desegregation both among and within schools? We need more research of several kinds, some of it dealing with the individuals involved, some with group relations. Do bilingual programs set groups apart, emphasizing their differences, or do they furnish greater opportunities for communication and interaction? How do various kinds of bilingual programs affect the school performance, self-concepts, job opportunities, and life chances generally for persons from different classes and communities with different lingual mixes (Jules-Rosette and Mehan, this volume; Lopez, 1976)? Referring to students whose first language is Spanish, Cafferty emphasized that

it must be determined whether Hispanic students master both the English and the Spanish language in bilingual programs; whether bilingual programs increase the students' achievement in other subjects; and what percentage of such students graduate from high school and continue on to college, in contrast to those Hispanic students not in a bilingual program. (Cafferty, 1982, p. 126)

A question not often asked deals with the sources of the perpetuation of language differences. How much are those differences cultural products, and how much are they better described as conflict-produced barriers, counter-languages, the symbolic expressions of separating countercultures (Adams, 1977; Halliday, 1976; Labov, 1972; J. M. Yinger, 1982, pp. 161–165)? In personal conversation, Ogbu has noted that two groups of second generation Mexican-Americans may not speak standard English for different reasons. For one, since English is not the first language,they rely on Spanish in many contexts. For the other, Spanish is a conflict language, a way of indicating their disdain for a society that they reject, as they believe it has rejected them.

This second question leads readily to a third that refers to dialects rather than languages. In many ways, dialectical differences are less easily dealt with than lingual differences. Nonstandard dialects are more often clear signs of socioeconomic differences; fewer people grant them authenticity as languages. With desegregation of schools, however, they have become a fact to be dealt with. Early students (e.g., Bernstein, 1964) stressed, however sympathetically, the limiting influence of what they saw as restricted dialects on cognition. Language deprivation equals cognitive deprivation. Bernstein's critics (e.g., Labov, 1972) believe that he missed the richness of nonstandard dialects, with their own syntax, grammar, and vocabulary. These critics sometimes failed to note that dialects adapted to restricted settings may not be good media if one wants to move freely in wider circles. Nor did they note that to some degree these were antilanguages, in Halliday's sense, designed to oppose the larger society while communicating with one's group. We greatly need research that shows the conditions under which differences of language and dialect stand as barriers to the internal desegregation of schools and the kind of school policy that can overcome those barriers. It seems possible to deal with language differences in such a way that they even become, in the process of reduction, integrative.

3. EFFECTS OF SCHOOL DESEGREGATION

Of the numerous effects or possible effects of desegregation, four have been given most attention, in this volume and elsewhere: effects on the self-esteem of students from minority groups, on achievement, on the extent and friendliness of new contacts, and on the racial and ethnic make-up of the communities involved. I will comment briefly on each one.

3.1. Sources and Effects of Levels of Self-Esteem

Rosenberg's rich study of the theories and methods that have been applied to the sources of self-esteem raises a number of important issues (see also Rosenberg, 1979; Rosenberg and Simmons, 1972). Although early studies of black self-esteem referred more to prejudice and discrimination than to the degree of segregation, they seemed to confirm what was held to be a fairly self-evident fact: the burdens of minority status and its personal consequences lowered self-esteem. Methodological weaknesses, however, raised doubts. The samples used in the doll studies, for example, were small and nonrandom; seldom was there a white comparison group; the children were required to select from few options; self-esteem was not clearly distinguished from group esteem.

By the late 1960s, self-esteem was being measured by survey methods based on probability samples of both blacks and whites. Respondents came from a broader age range. And self-esteem, not group esteem, was clearly the focus of attention. The results of the numerous studies by Rosenberg and those he has discussed sharply challenge and to a large degree contradict the earlier studies. Black self-esteem is not lower and is sometimes higher than white self-esteem. When the question of segregation is introduced as a variable, it has usually proved to increase, not decrease, black self-esteem. (See, e.g., Drury, 1980; Goering, 1972; Heiss and Owens, 1972; Katz, 1976, Chap. 4; McCarthy and Yancey, 1971a; Taylor and Walsh, 1979. For general reviews and commentaries and some confirmation of earlier findings, see Adam, 1978; Asher and Allen, 1969; Porter, 1971; Porter and Washington, 1979; Williams and Morland, 1976.)

What is the significance of this body of literature and of Rosenberg's interpretation for school desegregation research? Although recent survey methods have many advantages, we must be aware that the verbal behavior they measure may not correspond with other behaviors that express levels of self-esteem. We must ask to what degree it may have been a shift of generation, rather than a shift of methods, that produced such a sharp reversal in the findings. Many events, typified by the direct training of the Reverend Jesse Jackson, taught black children in the 1970s to say, "I am *somebody*." It is also essential, in any comparison, that we take account of age and sex distributions, socioeconomic status, regions, race of the testers, and effects of the measuring instrument.

The most significant part of Rosenberg's chapter, in my judgment, both for its insights and for its problems, is the emphasis on the phenomenological approach: To understand the roots of self-esteem, we must see the world from the child's point of view. Rosenberg explicitly rejects any tendency to define this as the only point of view of significance for behavior. We ought perhaps to emphasize, however, that for some scholars, the subjective world *is* the only real world, thus reversing Marx, who tended to dismiss the subjective world as "false consciousness" unless it corresponded to his picture of objective reality. In my view, we are wise to emphasize the interactions between the inner and outer worlds.

Looking out at the world from the child's perspective, we must ask, Rosenberg notes, how much does a child care about a given appraisal, and how much confidence does he place in it? In segregated settings, Rosenberg believes, reflected appraisals and social comparisons are more positive than in desegregated settings. Attribution of blame to oneself is deflected by "system blame," made easier by knowledge of discrimination. At least one can infer this tendency from studies that show that blacks score higher on measures of perception of the external locus of control. Taylor and Walsh (1979), however, found system blame to be correlated with low self-esteem, not a way of avoiding it.

Further research along the lines suggested by Rosenberg's analysis is needed to examine a number of issues. Segregation does not mean lack of contact. It is often associated with menial, degrading contact. Symbolic contact through the mass media may be extensive. Adults significant in the child's life may have contact with the dominant group that affects the signals they send. We need to find ways to measure the extent to which verbal self-esteem corresponds with deeper feelings and with behavior.

We need further study of the conditions under which children in segregated settings are more likely to be exposed to sources of race pride. This seems more likely to be true of younger than older children. What happens when they have contact with the larger world only to discover that their heroes have been drawn from a narrow circle? Is the selection of heroes in a segregated community likely even to reinforce the system of discrimination? Arthur Ashe, Harry Edwards, and other blacks are saying: Don't be seduced by the glamor of athletics and the entertainment world; only a few make it in that world; we need a wider variety of accomplishments. We need also to ask: What happens to white students who are likely to be blocked by segregation from the opportunity to learn of the full range of black achievements?

In their chapters, Rosenberg and Granovetter (see also Hunt, 1977) note the positive effects of desegregated schools: higher academic achievement, the opening of more postschool opportunities, more stable families, less crime. If lower self-esteem, as presently measured, is a negative outcome, we need to ask whether there are ways to reduce this deflationary effect. Perhaps it is produced, not by desegregation *per se*, but by some of the processes—labeling, tracking, internal resegregation, and the like—that are sometimes the accompaniment of desegregation. Knowledge that self-esteem can be lowered under some conditions is a new variable that can lead to counseling, discussion, and other activities that can prevent it from happening.

A similar experience affects some white students who attend academically selective colleges. Ninety percent of them are likely to have been in the top 10% or 20% of their high school classes; but two-thirds of them are in the bottom two-thirds of their college classes. This "desegregation" is a shocking experience for some and a blow to their self-esteem. Yet most of them stay, they find new grounds for self-esteem, they borrow from the prestige of the college, they employ a larger comparison group, and most of them believe they have made the right choice. If this analogy is of any value it may lead us to be alert to the long-run as well as the short-run effects of desegregation on self-esteem.

In his discussion of "discrepant contextual perspectives," Rosenberg makes the important observation from his Baltimore study that black children are less likely than white children to know others who are either poorer or richer than they.[1] Blacks are more likely to say they are proud of their family's position and to think their parents have done well. In this discussion, there is some tendency, however, to slip over into what one might call "radical phenomenology." "If a black child attends a black school day after day, week after week, year after year," Rosenberg observes, this is his world "as experienced." Would it not be better to say that the child thinks it is his world of experience—a thought that can distort his view of the actual array of forces governing his life? That he is not aware of them does not mean that those forces are not part of his world of experience.

There is a fascinating parallel between the shifts in self-esteem studies so well reviewed by Rosenberg and two other significant areas of research in racial and cultural relations—slavery and language use. I can only hint at that parallel here. Discrimination and inequality, said Clark and Clark and many other researchers in the 1940s and 1950s, had a crushing impact on self-esteem. Slavery, said Elkins and in a somewhat different way Stampp, had a crushing

---

[1]This may not be a common situation, however. Segregation often throws blacks of different classes together residentially.

impact on personality development, leading to a childlike "Sambo." Isolation and deprivation, said Bernstein, created restrictive language codes. All of these scholars describe in sympathetic—but also mournful—tones the destructive power of segregation and discrimination.

All three positions have now been challenged, the parallel changes suggesting a new moral and political climate as well as continuing research. Interpretations are now more "up-beat," emphasizing the creativity and powers of resistance among the disadvantaged. Taking a child's eye view, Rosenberg and a host of other researchers now say, we see that a segregated environment contains numerous resources and processes that enhance self-esteem. Slavery created a harsh and demanding context in which self-enhancing community and subcultural supports were created by the slaves, say Genovese, Fogel and Engerman, and especially Gutman. Labov and many other contemporary linguists declare that Bernstein missed the "expressive richness and syntactic complexity of the non-standard dialects," as Jules-Rosette and Mehan put it.

How can we account for this shift in emphasis on the effects of segregation and discrimination. Is it the result of new and better evidence? Of a new paradigm that produces different questions and perceptions? Of shifting ideologies that demand that we express not only opposition to discrimination and sympathy for the unjustly treated, but also appreciation of their creative powers?

In my judgment we know a lot more now than we did 25 years ago with respect to those questions. The speed with which the received wisdom shifted, however, gives me pause and causes me to wonder what tomorrow's scholars will think of today's knowledge. It is imperative if we are to advance the art of inquiry that we be aware of these rapid changes—in some cases nearly reversals—in our explanations. That awareness may lead us, in terms of the immediate topic, to more powerful explanations of self-esteem and of the effects of deseg-regation on it. We may find that the swing of the pendulum was caused not simply by better research designs and evidence. New problems are being addressed, new questions asked. When changes of interpretation occur we are less likely, looking at them in this way, to say that "discrediting this tradition is, we believe, necessary" (McCarthy and Yancey, 1971b, p. 591). The task is to build on the tradition. We can also share Adam's concern that the newer studies of self-esteem may deflect attention from study of the negative impact of discrimination without, however, assuming that such deflection is inevitable or that the evidence and argument of those studies should simply be set aside. He argued that

> self-esteem has become a psychological abstraction which allows the effects of a racist social structure simply to fade away. . . . The fundamental problem raised by the early writers, of the production and reproduction of social order, has been side-stepped and ultimately obscured by the redefinition of the self-esteem concept over time. (Adam, pp. 49, 51)

Certainly Rosenberg and the other who have found evidence of positive self-esteem even in the face of discrimination would disagree with Adam's statement. To find that individuals have ways of coping with prejudice and discrimination is scarcely to deny their negative impact.

The value of the enormous body of research on self-concept and self-esteem for improving studies of school desegregation will be sharply reduced unless we can avoid these swings of the pendulum. Pettigrew has wisely suggested a framework within which the diverse, but not necessarily contradictory findings, can be drawn together.

> (1) Oppression and subjugation do in fact have "negative" personal consequences for minority individuals that are mediated by behavioral responses shaped through coping with oppression. (2) There are also some "positive" personal consequences for minority individuals as well as negative personal consequences for majority individuals. (3) Many of the "negative" consequences for minority group members are reflected in personality traits that in a range of situations can act to maintain, rather than challenge, the repressive social system. (4) Not all minority group members will be so affected nor are most traits of most minority members so shaped, since a sharp disjunction between the "real," personal self and the racial self is generally possible. (5) Thus, proud, strong minorities are possible despite "marks of oppression." And this strength becomes increasingly evident as the minority itself effectively challenges the repressive societal system. (Pettigrew, 1978, p. 60)

3.2. Desegregation and Academic Achievement

Findings regarding the effects of the desegregation of schools on academic achievement vary widely. Although to Weinberg (1975) the preponderance of the evidence indicates beneficial results, Bradley and Bradley (1977) see little gain. An important research task is to try to discover whether the differences in the findings reflect better and poorer methods of research or whether they indicate study of different sets of facts and different conditions, or, most likely, both of these things.

Because this topic is discussed in nearly every chapter, I will simply list some of the variables that are deemed important in this volume and elsewhere, limiting comment to a few of them. The list is quite long and could be made longer, for we are dealing with a complex situation. By facing the complexity we may reduce the tendency to retreat into oversimplifications. (We should note also that many of these variables affect not only academic achievement but the probability that a school will remain multiracial.)

1. The effects of various ratios of different races, ethnic groups, and classes (Granovetter, Blalock). On one hand, the "solo" literature (e.g., Kanter, 1977; Taylor, 1981) indicates that a group with small representation is likely to be isolated and stereotyped. We do not know the ratios or absolute numbers required

before these effects are reduced, although 20% or 30% is sometimes suggested (Epps, 1975; Willie, 1976). This proportion, however, begins to lead to the opposite problem—reactions stemming from the feeling that the other group is too large. Recent public opinion polls indicate that three-quarters of white parents say they would not object to having the children attend schools in which half of the pupils were black, but there is some evidence that withdrawals increase when the ratio reaches 30%. This may be because schools with such ratios suffer various disadvantages—poor financial support, location, a class mix deemed undesirable by the parents—and not because of the majority–minority ratio itself. Or it may be that the one-quarter of parents who say they would object to sending their children to schools in which half of the pupils were black begin to withdraw them when the ratio reaches 30%, creating a higher ratio for those remaining, and thus stimulating additional withdrawals—the Schelling effect.

2. Influence of age at which children enter desegregated schools.

3. Strength of an academic emphasis in the national school culture (Suttles). If it is weak, students are more likely to sort themselves into partially conflicting "subcultures," with boundaries that correspond quite closely with racial and ethnic boundaries (Harrington, 1975).

4. Preschool preparation. The evidence is not yet decisive, but it now seems likely, contrary to earlier judgments, that children who enter school with some preschool educational experience are, indeed, off to a "head start." Insofar as such experiences are less available to students from minority backgrounds, their academic achievements will be comparatively weaker.

5. School control methods: discipline versus "institutionalization of ignorance" (Blalock, this volume; Grant, 1981; Metz, 1978). Either a clear pattern of authority and discipline or a more open, "progressive" style can work among students trained to matching expectations. A mixture, however, as Blalock suggests, weakens both. One wonders how much this might be modified if a teacher laid his or her cards on the table, talked about the dilemma, and self-consciously sought to create a blend. There is evidence that firm discipline accompanied by respect, love, and parental involvement significantly increases the level of academic achievement (Grant, 1981; Henry, 1980).

6. Sorting processes, by tracking, counseling, labeling (Jules-Rosette and Mehan, Granovetter). There is now substantial evidence not only of official and planned tracking of pupils but also of unplanned and unintended steering and labeling. The effects are often to reinforce differences in academic achievement and to increase segregation (Alexander et al., 1978; Erickson, 1975; McDermott, 1977; Rist, 1970; Rosenbaum, 1976).

7. Degree of teacher and staff desegregation and special training on problems likely to be faced in desegregated schools. Such training, which is not widely used, interacts with the values and attitudes that teachers and administrators bring into the school situation (Lacy and Middleton, 1981; Summers and

Wolfe, 1977). It is often emphasized that teachers are role models. They may not be in desegregated schools—indeed, may seem to be opponents—if they are not encouraged and helped to see the nature of the new teaching situation.

8. Goals of those who are dominant in society—the postschool opportunities they furnish, or deny, members of various groups (Ogbu).

9. Presence or absence of generational continuity in attitudes and values (Suttles). With calculated exaggeration, Margaret Mead once remarked that for the first time in history, people no longer have (cultural) ancestors, just as they have no descendants. There is wide variation in the degree to which this is true, variation that is reflected in differences of academic achievement.

10. Cultural "fairness" in the curriculum and throughout the school. Few would disagree that cultural fairness is not adequately served by holding an Ethnic Fair or celebrating "X week." But there is much less agreement on what it does entail in nonacademic and academic programs. We also need more research on the consequences of emphasis on cultural fairness on the pluralism–universalism dilemma. Under what conditions do programs based on the value of cultural fairness accentuate boundaries and reinforce sorting processes that work in the opposite direction from those intended?

This partial list of the variables that affect academic achievement in desegregated schools perhaps suggests the complexity of the research task (see also Pettigrew, 1975, pp. 234–239). If we also recognize the various meanings attached to the term *academic achievement*, the reasons for controversy are even more apparent. At least three distinctions need to be drawn.

First, does academic achievement mean attained level or extent of improvement over the entering level? Both measures are important, but in my judgment the extent of improvement (or loss) is the more significant.

Second, does it mean acquisition of certain skills or, in addition to that, a set of values favorable to intellectual growth generally? If a society in which rapid changes of occupational and other patterns demand flexibility, the learning of specific skills must be complemented by attitudes favorable to continuing education and retraining. Studies of desegregation have taught us little about its effects on such attitudes. Our measures of attainment are designed almost entirely to show levels of information and skill. In my judgment, the acquisition of attitudes and values favorable to continuing development is equally important. Those attitudes and values can be part of the culture of a school. Is that culture promoted by desegregation? Does desegregation bring some students into schools, from which they formerly were excluded, within which that culture is strong.

Third, is the sheer fact of remaining in school and getting a diploma or degree the main achievement, or is the level of competence the chief measure? Considering how poorly academic record predicts later success, except in a few occupations, and yet how much can be predicted by knowledge that a person has a diploma or degree, without knowledge of class rank, we need much more study of the effect of completing a course of study in segregated compared with desegregated schools.

3.3. Desegregation and Contact

Another topic of great interest and importance is the effect of desegregation on interracial and interethnic contact, and then the effect of various levels of contact on academic achievement, job placement, and other actions and tendencies—of teachers as well as students (Robinson and Preston, 1976). Many of the variables affecting academic achievement also affect the extent and varieties of contact. Ratios, age, and sorting processes ought particularly to be noted in this regard.

In studying contact, we need to be aware of the barriers and gateways brought into the school as well as the opportunities for contact furnished or blocked by the school. As Blalock well emphasizes, we are greatly in need of analysis of the intrinsic costs and rewards of contact (those applying to persons experiencing the contact) and of the extrinsic costs and rewards (coming from persons not directly in the contact situation), under various sets of conditions. It should not require emphasis, but seems often to be forgotten, that if contact seems to some participants mainly to entail costs, with little perceived opportunity for gains—judged against their past experience and the interpretations of their groups—contact will be resisted or used as an opportunity to try to improve their competitive situation.

Granovetter's work is filled with valuable concepts and research leads on this topic. The range of contacts is scarcely measured by sociometric tests that, for example, identify only dyadic ties with three best friends in a fixed choice procedure. "Weak ties" are important not only in themselves, but also because they link persons who move in different circles, thus furnishing direct and indirect group contacts.

Neglect of study of weak ties should not be overcome by failing to study strong ties. Granovetter suggests that emphasis on the latter is associated with an assimilationist model. He observes that blacks with strong ties to whites may so weaken their ties to other blacks that networks are not enlarged. I wonder if weak ties are not of significance precisely because there are some strong ties, and that without the latter, weak ties are experienced as tokens. Whether or not this guess is true, much more extensive research is needed on the full range of contacts and the conditions under which they occur. In a recent chapter, Granovetter (1983) noted that, although weak ties "provide access to information and resources beyond those available" to one's closest associates, those with whom one has strong ties are more strongly motivated to help and more readily available. What needs study, I believe, are the results of various combinations of weak and strong ties. Under what conditions is a strong racial or ethnic organization in a high school, for example, a separating barrier that prevents weak ties with others? (One thinks here of the concept of the "ethnic mobility trap" in Wiley, 1967.) And under what conditions is such an organization a source of self-confidence and of leadership able to promote the cultivation of weak ties?

Without imaginative teaching methods, classroom contact among persons of widely different levels of preparations can reinforce stereotypes. Large amounts of cooperative team learning and small amounts of tracking (e.g., no student put into a "homogeneous" classroom for more than one subject) can help to prevent that reinforcement. Unhappily, school policies more often reflect the opposite choice (Schofield, 1979). As we have noted, various sorting procedures can effectively segregate racial and ethnic groups within the walls of a "desegregated" school.

Outside the classroom, extracurricular activities, playgrounds (Silverman and Shaw, 1973), and summer programs (Heyns, 1978; Yinger et al., 1977) affect, or have the possibility of affecting, interracial and interethnic contact. Suttles and Granovetter suggest the need for much more intensive study of ethnic subcultures, both in and outside of schools. In the early 1960s, studies by Clark (1962) and Coleman (1961) were valuable maps of the internal "thematic" structure in schools. Students differ significantly in the strength of their attachments to "academic," "fun," or "delinquent" subcultures. We need now to know more about the way in which these thematic subcultures interact with or cut across ethnic subcultures, not only because they influence the amount and kinds of contact, but also because they affect levels of achievement (Harrington, 1975). Where thematic subcultures are not allowed to become dominant, Suttles observes, students do not " 'burn their bridges' to school before they attempt to enter the job market."

3.4. Community Effects of School Desegregation

No topic has received more intensive public and research attention than the effect of school desegregation, particularly if brought about by court order, on the communities involved. We are confronted with the puzzling fact that public attitudes have become steadily more liberal regarding integrated housing and schools at the same time resistance to particular plans and policies has often been severe. The tendencies engaged when one is asked how one would respond to a given level of integration are often different from those activated when a specific plan is being discussed or carried out.

One can desegregate schools either by changing the racial and ethnic household mix in communities or by changing the mix of children in schools, or by a combination of the two. The two processes, in fact, are inevitably linked. Less attention has been paid to the prior integration of communities, however, except perhaps by urban economists. Far more than "white flight" is producing quasi-segregated communities along with the suburbanization of most of the wh'te middle-class. Clotfelter (1979, p. 366) cited three major factors:

> relatively innocent market forces, including rising incomes and changes in production and transportation technology; public policies providing subsidies to transportation and middle-income housing; and outright discrimination against blacks, causing them to be concentrated in central cities and under-represented in suburbs relative to their economic status.

These and other factors operate in an environment where the Schelling tipping process can readily be set in motion because there are some with strong opposition to integration and others who are opposed if the minority exceeds some critical proportion—30% being a figure often given. The result can be more extreme segregation than almost anyone wants.

If I can suggest a metaphorical parallel to McGill's "desegregation began with the boll weevil," I would say that the segregation of metropolitan areas "began" when home buyers were allowed to deduct interest payments from taxable income and when a combination of auto, steel, rubber, oil, and cement interests, linking to America's love affair with the automobile and assisted by public subsidy, ringed our cities with highways. Of course households have always sorted themselves by income. Government-induced suburbanization, however, facilitated the growth of separate—and segregated—school districts.

Obviously, one would sound no more sane in suggesting that the way to increase integration is to change drastically these factors in the ecology of America's metropolitan communities than if one recommended a full-scale attack on the boll weevil as the wisest course. There are actions, however, that can be taken, and some have been taken, to counter the process of metropolitan segregation. Insofar as they are successful, school desegregation will be one of the results.

Open housing laws by themselves are useful but incomplete, because they run into housebuyers' prejudices (and the Schelling effect), sellers' prejudices (not unaccompanied by their economic interests), sales conditions with monopolistic elements, and wide income differences between whites and blacks— conditions that furnish incentives to brokers to discriminate.

> Only a theory that involves discrimination can explain why blacks are concentrated in a central ghetto, why blacks pay more for comparable housing than whites in the same submarkets, why prices of equivalent housing are higher in the ghetto than in the white interior, and why blacks consume less housing and are much less likely to be home owners than whites with the same characteristics.(J. Yinger, 1979, p. 459)

New and imaginative action is required to break up this pattern. In addition to strengthening open housing laws, desegregation bonuses could be awarded to communities and individuals. The profit from segregation could be reduced by an increased flow of information in the housing market. Present multiple listing services are incomplete, often excluding minority brokers or limiting their access (J. Yinger, 1979).

Changes in these structural factors will retard the resegregation of our communities and thus of our schools. Those changes are likely to be slow, however, so that the problem needs to be approached from the other end as well—to direct efforts to desegregate schools. Under many circumstances, this helps to desegregate communities, setting a beneficent cycle in motion, as illustrated by the declining need for busing in Riverside, California (United States Commission on Civil Rights, *Civil Rights Update*, December, 1980; see also Finger, 1976; Loewen, 1979; Rossell, 1978; Taeuber, 1979). What do we know about efforts to desegregate schools through direct action, about their intended and their unintended effects? We are concerned here only with their effects on communities, particularly with the effects of integrating schools on the desegregating of the communities involved or their further segregation. Much of the vast literature on this topic (see, e.g., Coleman *et al.*, 1975; Farley, 1976; Pettigrew and Green, 1976; Sly and Pol, 1978; Wilson, 1979) is discussed in various chapters of this volume. Although disagreements are numerous in that literature, at a minimum one can say that school desegregation brought about by individual household mobility, for example, the suburbanization of black families (Long and DeAre, 1981), or occurring in relatively small school districts, for example, Little Rock (see *The New York Times*, Sept. 13, 1981, p. 15), or in school districts where minority enrollment is not more than one-third of the total, is likely to contribute to, rather than reverse, community desegregation. This may occur only after a year or two of influence in the opposite direction (Farley *et al.*, 1980).

On the other hand, where changes are piecemeal, where school desegregation occurs only on the borders of ghetto areas, and where administrative policy is vacillating, school desegregation is likely to be associated with resegregation of the communities involved. This is not to say that school desegregation caused resegregation in the form of white flight. It may simply be that the items mentioned are correlated with the diminishing appeal of the largest central cities, that diminishing appeal being the cause of suburbanization for any family with such an option, as Orfield (1978) put it.

I have come to the conclusion that to continue to try to determine the proportion of the resegregation of city schools and of the cities themselves due to white flight from desegregation, particularly when produced by busing, is a nearly useless exercise. (I cannot resist adding, however, that in my judgment, major long-run structural changes in our metropolitan areas and the economy are the root causes. Where those causes are operating most strongly, in Detroit, for example, school desegregation can have a multiplier effect.) However that may be, we do know that resegregation has occurred in many cities. If school desegregation is desirable, even mandatory, as I believe it is, then we need to ask: How can the causes of that resegregation be dealt with? The problem must be approached from both ends: desegregating communities in order to desegregate schools, and desegregating schools in order to desegregate communities. That is a controversial statement. Some will say there is no legal or judicial mandate to desegregate communities. That is the position taken by the Supreme Court in *Milliken v. Bradley* (1974). If schools can be desegregated only by maintaining or bringing about integrated communities, however, and if school integration is mandated, then the 1974 Supreme Court decision in the Detroit case cannot stand. That is the position taken by Justice Douglas in joining the minority of four on the Court.

> When we rule against the metropolitan area remedy we take a step that will likely put the problems of blacks and our society back to the period that antedated the "separate but equal" regime of *Plessy v. Ferguson*. (United States Reports, 1974, p. 759; see also Henderson and von Euler, 1979; Orfield, 1978).

We need to know much more about the legal, attitudinal, and structural (often impersonal) forces standing in the way of metropolitan-area remedies, starting both from the school and the community end. In my view, no research related to the study of school desegregation can be of greater importance.

4. CONCLUSION

Several points that have not been given much direct attention in this series of chapters ought perhaps to be noted. Our questions, research strategies, and judgments would be influenced, I think for the better, if we recognized explicitly that we are dealing with a two- or three-generational problem. (I take this to be a sound empirical judgment, albeit not easily documented, and in no sense the expression of a desire or a counsel to go slow. There is some risk of a self-fulfilling prophecy being bound up in the statement, so I hope that some, at least, do not share the judgment.) Insofar as it is true, assessment of the impact of desegregation should refer to trend lines, not to goals obtained in a year or two. Research can be based on the study of settings where change is rapid and extensive compared with settings where it is slow, accompanied by study of the degree to which these various settings are becoming more common.

We need to be as alert as possible to unintended effects, not only the one most commonly studied—resegregation—but those that may occur in particular communities, schools, and individuals. Does desegregation increase parental involvement? Does it stimulate greater awareness of the growing language issue in the United States? Does it have spillover effects on other aspects of community life, for example, home prices, school taxes? Does it lead, among some, to a loss of the sense of "my school," with accompanying alienation, when one's ethnic group can no longer be seen as the only or main group? And how do these unintended effects feed back into the desegregation process, strengthening or deflecting it?

Research on the effects of media attention and interpretation, both before and after school desegregation, is in short supply. It is a truism that conflict gets the best press. Reports of events then feed back into the ongoing reality of events, partly shaping them.

To what degree do the changes that school desegregation brings about involve not only gains for all, but some transfer of advantages, that is, zero-sum gains? There is little doubt that many of the opponents of desegregation believe that what others might gain, they and those with whom they identify are likely to lose. In examining the issues of equity of dominance, we need to study the possibility, indeed the probability in my judgment, that educational and occupational opportunities are to some degree zero-sum. "Society as a whole" is likely to benefit, but some individuals pay a price. And—to show the toughness of the stratification system—it is mainly the least well-off of the dominant group who pay the price and best-off of the subordinate groups who profit from the changes. Until we learn how to spread the cost of dominance-reduction to include the best-off of the dominant group and spread the gains to include the least well-off of the subordinate groups, we will have satisfied only poorly the requirements of justice, as I understand them. The research question, purified from these politico-moral judgments, is, Which forms of school desegregation are or could be progressive (in an income-tax sense), which ones proportional, which ones regressive?

There is now substantial evidence that academic competence and even intelligence, as measured by standard tests, are strongly influenced by activities—or the lack of activities—during the summer months (Heyns, 1978). Because differences in academic competence are among the factors influencing attitudes toward, and the success of, desegregation, we need more intensive study of the differences among children in the nature of their summer experiences. We need more study of the kinds of summer experiences that link strongly to the programs of the academic year. Without such linkage, without follow-through, the effects of summer enrichment are likely to fade quite rapidly. In *Middle Start*, my colleagues and I found that there were three ingredients to a successful summer program: A decisive new, stretching and stereotype-breaking experience; a sponsor to show that new possibilities were available and to explain each step, because each step was into foreign territory; and a circle of supporting other, complementing the instrumental guidance of the sponsor with emotional support. Whether or not these ingredients are essential in all instances, we can be sure, I think, that wide differences in the way summers are spent compound other difficulties faced in the process of desegregation.

The art of desegregation research will be further enhanced by more extensive comparative study. We can learn from, and contribute to, the understanding of school situations, perhaps especially in Europe and Canada, but also in Latin America, Japan, Malaysia, New Zealand, Australia, and elsewhere.

Finally, we need to keep continuously in mind the several levels, from the most macro to the most micro, and their interdependence if we are to advance our understanding of the complicated process of desegregation. It might be useful to note these levels.

Levels of analysis	Variables to consider
Society as a whole	Demography Major technical and economic changes Housing policies
Relationships among school districts	All of the above, plus— Laws bearing on desegregation Court decisions Media attention
Relationships within school districts	All of the above, plus— School board policies, with regard, e.g., to school locations, busing, teacher selection and training Ratios of different groups Sorting processes
Relationships within a school	All of the above, plus— Methods of discipline Peer groups, youth cultures Language variation Processes affecting weak ties Teaching methods Effects on self-esteem
Relationships within a class-room or other specific activity	All of the above, plus— Age of the students Range of socioeconomic status Criteria for participating in the activity
The Individual	All of the above, plus— Racial or ethnic group Socioeconomic status Attitudes concerning desegregation Levels of competence Ambition, distinguishing plans (aspirations) from motivation (expenditure of effort)

We are dealing with a very complicated part of nature. The several levels of analysis and the illustrative variables listed here surely give us pause. Nothing is to be gained, however, from the belief that by studying one or two levels and a few variables we can advance the art of inquiry in school desegregation research.

ACKNOWLEDGMENTS

I have profited greatly from the close reading of an earlier draft of this chapter by Julian Samora, George E. Simpson, John Yinger, and Jeffrey Prager, as well as from discussions with authors of the other chapters in this volume and other participants in two preparatory conferences.

REFERENCES

Adam, B. D. Inferiorization and "self-esteem". *Social Psychology*, 1978, *41*, 47–53.
Adams, R. M. *Bad Mouth: Fugitive Papers on the Dark Side*. Berkeley, CA: University of California Press, 1977.
Alexander, K. L., M. Cook, and E. L. McDill. Curriculum tracking and educational stratification: Some further evidence. *American Sociological Review*, 1978, *43*, 47–66.
Asher, S. R., and V. L. Allen. Racial preference and social comparison processes. *Journal of Social Issues*, 1969, *25*, 157–166.
Bernstein, B. Elaborated and restricted codes: Their social origins and some consequences. *American Anthropologist*, 1964, *66* (Special Issue), 55–69.
Bradley, L. A., and Bradley, G. W. The academic achievement of black students in desegregated schools. *Review of Educational Research*, 1977, *47*, 399–449.
Burke, F. G. Bilingualism/biculturalism in American education: An adventure in wonderland. *Annals of the American Academy of Political and Social Sciences*, 1981, *454*, 164–177.
Cafferty, P. The language question: The dilemma of bilingual education for Hispanics in America. In L. Liebman (Ed.), *Ethnic Relations in America*. Englewood Cliffs, NJ: Prentice-Hall, 1982.
Clark, B. *Educating the Expert Society*. San Francisco: Chandler, 1962.
Clotfelter, C. School desegregation as urban public policy. In P. Mieszkowski and M. Straszheim (Eds.), *Current Issues in Urban Economics*. Baltimore, MD: Johns Hopkins University Press, 1979.
Coleman, J. *The Adolescent Society*. New York: Free Press, 1961.
Coleman, J., Kelly, S., and Moore, J. A. *Trends in School Desegregation, 1968–1973*. Washington, DC: The Urban Institute, 1975.
Coutu, W. *Emergent Human Nature: A Symbolic Field Interpretation*. New York: Knopf, 1949.
Drury, D. W. Black self-esteem and desegregated schools. *Sociology of Education*, 1980, *53*, 88–103.
Eagly, A. H., and Himmelfarb, S. Attitudes and opinions. *Annual Review of Psychology* (Vol. 29). Palo Alto, CA: Annual Reviews, 1978.
Epps, E. Impact of school desegregation on aspiration, self-concepts, and other aspects of personality. *Law and Contemporary Problems*, 1975, *39*, 300–313.
Erickson, F. Gatekeeping and the melting pot. *Harvard Educational Review*, 1975, *45*, 44–70.
Farley, R. Is Coleman right? *Social Policy*, 1976, *6*, 1–10.

Farley, R., Richards, T., and Wurdock, C. School desegregation and white flight: An investigation of competing models and their discrepant findings. *Sociology of Education,* 1980, *53,* 123–129.

Finger, J. A., Jr. Why busing plans work. *School Review,* 1976, *84,* 364–372.

Fishbein, M., and Ajzen, I. *Beliefs, Attitudes, Intentions, and Behavior: An Introduction to Theory and Research.* Reading, MA: Addison-Wesley, 1975.

Goering, J. M. Changing perceptions and evaluations of physical characteristics among blacks: 1950–1970. *Phylon,* 1972, *33,* 231–241.

Granovetter, M. The strength of weak ties: A network theory revisited. In Randall Collins (Ed.), *Sociological Theory.* San Francisco: Jossey-Bass, 1983.

Grant, G. The character of education and the education of character. *Daedalus,* 1981, 110, 135–149.

Gutman, H. G. *The Black Family in Slavery and Freedom: 1750–1925.* New York: Vintage Books, 1977.

Halliday, M. A. K. Anti-languages. *American Anthropologist,* 1976, *78,* 570–584.

Harrington, C. C. Bilingual education, social stratification, and cultural pluralism. *Equal Opportunity Review,* 1978, Summer, 1–4.

Harrington, C. C. A psychological anthropologist's view of ethnicity and schooling. *IRCD Bulletin,* 1975, *10,* 1–9.

Heiss, J., and Owens, S. Self-evaluations of blacks and whites. *American Journal of Sociology,* 1972, *78,* 360–370.

Henderson, R. D., and von Euler, M. What research and experience teach us about desegregating large northern cities. *Clearinghouse for Civil Rights Research,* 1979, *7,* 2–14.

Henry, D. Love and discipline spawn education in midst of despair. *New York Times,* November 16, 1980, p. 14.

Heyns, B. *Summer Learning and the Effects of Schooling.* New York: Academic Press, 1978.

Hill, R. J. Attitudes and behavior. In M. Rosenberg and R. Turner (Eds.), *Social Psychology: Sociological Perspectives.* New York: Basic Books, 1981.

Hunt, J. G. Assimilation or marginality? Some school integration effects reconsidered. *Social Forces,* 1977, *56,* 604–610.

Jacobson, C. K. Desegregation rulings and public attitude changes: White resistance or resignation? *American Journal of Sociology,* 1978, *84,* 698–705.

Kanter, R. M. Some effects of proportions on group life: Skewed sex ratios and responses to token women. *American Journal of Sociology,* 1977, *82,* 965–990.

Katz, P. A. (Ed.). *Towards the Elimination of Racism.* New York: Pergamon Press, 1976.

Labov, W. *Language in the Inner City: Studies in the Black English Vernacular.* Philadelphia, PA: University of Pennsylvania Press, 1972.

Lacy, W. B., and Middleton, E. Are educators really prejudiced? A cross-occupational comparison. *Sociological Focus,* 1981, *14,* 87–95.

Levin, K. *A Dynamic Theory of Personality.* New York: McGraw-Hill, 1935.

Loewen, J. W. Desegregating schools can help desegregate neighborhoods. *Clearinghouse for Civil Rights Research,* 1979, *7,* 14–18.

Long, L., and DeAre, D. The suburbanization of blacks. *American Demographics,* 1981, *3,* 16–21, 44.

Lopez, D. E. The social consequences of chicano home/school bilingualism. *Social Problems,* 1976, *24,* 234–246.

McCarthy, J.D. and Yancey, W. L. Uncle Tom and Mr. Charlie: Metaphysical pathos in the study of racism and personal disorganization. *American Journal of Sociology,* 1971a, *76,* 648–672.

McCarthy, J. D. and Yancey, W. L. Reply to Washington. *American Journal of Sociology,* 1971b, *77,* 590–591.

McDermott, R. P. Social relations as contexts for learning in school. *Harvard Educational Review*, 1977, *47*, 198–213.

Metz, M. H. *Classrooms and Corridors: The Crisis of Authority in Desegregated schools*. Berkeley, CA: University of California Press, 1978.

Nunis, D. B., Jr. American identities. *Society*, 1981, *19*, 29–30.

Ogbu, J. *Minority education and caste*. New York: Academic Press, 1978.

Orfield, G. *Must we bus*. Washington, DC: Brookings Institution, 1978.

Pettigrew, T. F. (Ed.). *Racial Discrimination in the United States*. New York: Harper and Row, 1975.

Pettigrew, T. F. Placing Adam's argument in a broader perspective: Comment on the Adam paper. *Social Psychology*, 1978, *41*, 58–61.

Pettigrew, T. F., and Green, R. L. School desegregation in large cities: A critique of the Coleman white flight thesis. *Harvard Educational Review*, 1976, *46*, 1–53.

Porter, J. R. *Black Child, White Child: The Development of Racial Attitudes*. Cambridge, MA: Harvard University Press, 1971.

Porter, J.R., and Washington, R. E. Black identity and self-esteem: A review of studies of black self-concept, 1968–1978. *Annual Review of Sociology*, 1979, *5*, 53–74.

Rist, R. C. Student social class and teacher expectations: The self-fulfilling prophecy in ghetto education. *Harvard Educational Review*, 1970, *40*, 411–451.

Robinson, J. W., Jr., and Preston, J. D. Equal-status contact and modification of racial prejudice: A reexamination of the contact hypothesis. *Social Forces*, 1976, *54*, 911–924.

Rosenbaum, J. *Making Inequality*. New York: Wiley, 1976.

Rosenberg, M. *Conceiving the Self*. New York: Basic Books, 1979.

Rosenberg, M., and Simmons, R. G. *Black and White Self-Esteem: The Urban School Child*. Washington, DC: American Sociological Association, 1972.

Rossell, C. *Assessing the Unintended Impacts of Public Policy*. Washington, DC: National Institute of Education, 1978.

Schelling, T. D. *Micromotives and Macrobehavior*. New York: Norton, 1978.

Schofield, J. W. The impact of positively structured contact on intergroup behavior: Does it last under adverse conditions? *Social Psychology Quarterly*, 1979, *42*, 280–284.

Schuman, H., and Johnson, M. P. Attitudes and behavior. In A. Inkeles, J. S. Coleman, and N. J. Smelser (Eds.), *Annual Review of Sociology* (Vol. 2). Palo Alto, CA: Annual Reviews, 1976.

Sieber, S. D. *Fatal Remedies: The Ironies of Social Intervention*. New York: Plenum Press, 1981.

Silverman, I., and Shaw, M. E. Effects of sudden mass school desegregation on interracial interaction and attitudes in one southern city. *Journal of Social Issues*, 1973, *29*, 132–144.

Simpson, G. E., and Yinger, J. M. *Racial and Cultural Minorities* (5th ed.). New York: Plenum Press, 1985.

Sly, D. F., and Pol, L. G. The demographic context of school segregation and desegregation. *Social Forces*, 1978, *56*, 1072–1086.

Smith, A. W. Tolerance of school desegregation, 1954–1977. *Social Forces*, 1981, *59*, 1256–1274.

Summers, A. A., and Wolfe, B. L. Do schools make a difference? *American Economic Review*, 1977, *67*, 639–652.

Taeuber, K. E. Housing, schools, and incremental segregative effects. *Annals of the American Academy of Political and Social Sciences*, 1979, *441*, 157–167.

Taylor, M. C., and Walsh, E. J. Explanations of black self-esteem: Some empirical tests. *Social Psychology Quarterly*, 1979, *42*, 242–253.

Taylor, S. E. A categorization approach to stereotyping. In D. L. Hamilton (Ed.), *Cognitive Processes in Stereotyping and Intergroup Behavior*. Hillsdale, NJ: Erlbaum, 1981.

United States Commission on Civil Rights, *Civil Rights Update*, Dec. 1980.

United States Reports. Milliken v. Bradley, 1974, *418*, 717–815.

Weinberg, M. The relationship between school desegregation and academic achievement. *Law and Contemporary Problems*, 1975, *39*, 241–270.

Wiley, N. The ethnic mobility trap and stratification theory. *Social Problems,* 1967, *15*, 147–159.

Williams, J. E., and Morland, J. K. *Race, Color and the Young Child*. Chapel Hill, NC: University of North Carolina Press, 1976.

Willie, C. Racial balance or quality education. *School Review*, 1976, *84*, 313–325.

Wilson, F. D. Patterns of White avoidance. *Annals of the American Academy of Political and Social Sciences*, 1979, *441*, 132–141.

Yinger, J. Prejudice and discrimination in the urban housing market. In P. Mieszkowski and M. Straszheim (Eds.), *Current Issues in Urban Economics*. Baltimore, MD: Johns Hopkins University Press, 1979.

Yinger, J. *On the possibilities of achieving racial integration through subsidized housing*. Unpublished manuscript.

Yinger, J. M. *Toward a Field Theory of Behavior*. New York: McGraw-Hill, 1965.

Yinger, J. M. *Countercultures: The Promise and Peril of a World Turned Upside Down*. New York: Free Press, 1982.

Yinger, J. M., and Cutler, S. J. (Eds.). *Major Social Issues: A Multidisciplinary View*. New York: Free Press, 1978.

Yinger, J. M., Ikeda, K., Laycock, F., and Cutler, S. J. *Middle-Start: An Experiment in the Educational Enrichment of Young Adolescents*. London: Cambridge University Press, 1977.

Author Index

255

Subject Index